Gravissimum Educationis

Gravissimum Educationis

Golden Opportunities in
American Catholic Education
50 Years after Vatican II

Edited by
Gerald M. Cattaro and Charles J. Russo

ROWMAN & LITTLEFIELD
Lanham • Boulder • New York • London

Published by Rowman & Littlefield
A wholly owned subsidiary of The Rowman & Littlefield Publishing Group, Inc.
4501 Forbes Boulevard, Suite 200, Lanham, Maryland 20706
www.rowman.com

Unit A, Whitacre Mews, 26-34 Stannary Street, London SE11 4AB

British Library Cataloguing in Publication Information Available

Library of Congress Cataloging-in-Publication Data Available

ISBN 978-1-4758-1097-4 (cloth : alk. paper) — ISBN 978-1-4758-1098-1 (pbk. : alk. paper) — ISBN 978-1-4758-1099-8 (electronic)

∞ ™ The paper used in this publication meets the minimum requirements of American National Standard for Information Sciences Permanence of Paper for Printed Library Materials, ANSI/NISO Z39.48-1992.

Printed in the United States of America

Contents

Acknowledgments

Beautiful indeed and of great importance is the vocation of all those who aid parents in fulfilling their duties and who, as representatives of the human community, undertake the task of education in schools. This vocation demands special qualities of mind and heart, very careful preparation, and continuing readiness to renew and to adapt. (GE5)

As with any book, there are many people to be thanked. Four sets of people, in particular, were very helpful in helping to put this book together. First, many thanks to Tom Koerner, vice president and editorial director at Rowman & Littlefield Education, who has been supportive of this project from its inception. Thanks also to Ms. Carlie Wall, associate editor, and Ms. Lynn Zelem, production editor.

Second, it almost goes without saying that we are grateful to the authors for their valuable contributions to this book.

Third, we would like to thank Charlie's assistant, Ms. Elizabeth Pearn at the University of Dayton, for her efforts in copyediting and helping to prepare the final manuscript for publication.

Fourth, I, Jerry, would like to offer my deepest appreciation to thank Dr. Edward Fale for his support with this book.

Fifth, but certainly not least, I, Charlie, would like to express my deepest appreciation for my wife, Debbie, for her ongoing love and support, without which none of this work would have been completed.

Introduction

Gerald M. Cattaro and Charles J. Russo

On October 28, 1965, acting on behalf of the Council Fathers, Pope Paul VI promulgated the only document on education produced by the Ecumenical Council known as Vatican II. This document, *Gravissimum Educationis*—literally, "the importance of education"—addresses how extremely important Catholic education, in particular, is in modern life.

The 50th anniversary of the release of *Gravissimum Educationis* is a cause for celebration and reflection for American Catholic schools in the 21st century. The time span of the Council was a significant, pivotal period in the history of the United States and the world. In the United States, external events such as Vietnam, Woodstock, women's liberation, secularism, pluralism, and many other -isms impacted the Catholic Church and its schools as institutions.

At the same time, internal changes in the Catholic Church had a profound impact. These changes ranged from the decline in vocations to the religious life, to collegiality, to governance, to the advancement of the Catholic laity, to the education of the laity. The shift from immigrant to respectability with the election of John Kennedy had an impact on Catholic education. Further, Catholic education reached its peak in terms of student registrations even as *Gravissimum Educationis* was released and has been in a steady decline since that time. Serious concerns continue to emerge over the continuing viability of American Roman Catholic elementary and secondary schools in light of demographic shifts and the move toward charter schools in many locations, particularly cities where they have long been a presence.

The goal of this book, then, is to review development of American Catholic schools since the publication of *Gravissimum Educationis*. The book also serves to reflect on changes that have transpired in what was the most eventful period since the establishment of American Catholic schools as a major force in the United States in the wake of the Third Plenary Council of Baltimore of 1884. The Baltimore Council, a gathering of American Catholic bishops, forever changed the shape of non-public education in the United States in its decree that all parishes in the United States were to construct Catholic schools for the education of children.

This volume is also designed to benefit Catholic educators at all levels from primary to higher education. The chapters in this book, prepared by leading experts on various aspects of Catholic (or other forms of non-public) education in the United States, provide a history about the recent development of Catholic schools.

The book thus provides the context of change and the current state of Catholic schools in the United States and in some sense the global perspective. The scope of the book goes beyond the professional educator in Catholic schools as it also addresses the stakeholders of Catholic education such as parents who are consumers, pastors, religious educators, and donors.

Insofar as the Vatican will commemorate the 50th anniversary of *Gravissimum Educationis* with a seminar in October 2015, we hope that this volume will not only enhance the celebration but also add to the international scope of the research on Catholic education.

OVERVIEW

Following this brief introduction, the chapters in this volume offer an array of perspectives on the impact that *Gravissimum Educationis* has had over the past 50 years. Lead editor Gerald M. Cattaro, Fordham University, provides an overview of the historical development and context giving rise to *GE* in chapter 1. Charles J. Russo, University of Dayton, examines the legal status of American Catholic schools, the largest non-public school system in the nation in chapter 2.

In chapter 3, Sr. John Mary Fleming, O. P., executive director for Secretariat of Catholic Education, at the United States Conference of Catholic Bishops, offers an overview of key Church documents on education from Vatican to the present. Sr. Dale McDonald, P.B.V.M., director of Public Policy and Educational Research for the National Catholic Education Association (NCEA), examines demographic shifts impacting American Catholic education over the past 50 years in chapter 4.

Chapter 5, School Governance, by Regina Haney, Ed.D., executive director of the Department of Boards and Councils at the NCEA, and Karen Ristau, a former president of the NCEA, examine how leadership has changed in Catholic schools over the past 50 years. Chapter 6, by Shane Martin, dean of the School of Education, and Jordan Gadd, at Loyola Marymount University, examines Catholic schools and the option for the poor.

Shifting gears, chapter 7, by Rev. Michael J. Garanzini, S.J., president of Loyola University Chicago, looks at the status of Catholic higher education in the United States. Chapter 8, by Bruce Cooper and Ming Zhu, examines a necessary corollary to the status of American Catholic education by offering an ecumenical perspective on faith-based schools. Chapter 9, by John Convey, former provost and now a faculty member at the Catholic University of America, examines how Catholic schools have impacted the common good in the United States.

A final brief chapter, or epilogue, by Charles J. Russo and Gerald M. Cattaro, reflects on the future of American Catholic education while offering suggestions for leaders who are dedicated to keeping the great "Gift to the Nation" of American Catholic education alive and well.

The first book of its kind, this volume consists of a collection of essays designed to enhance a common understanding of the impact on *Gravissimum Educationis* (*GE*) and American Catholic education. Of course, no single book can ever hope to cover the myriad of topics on the expansive topic of Catholic education. Even so, we hope that these informative, thought-provoking, well-written, and researched chapters, authored by leading academics and/or practitioners in the field, can serve as up-to-date and ready sources of information to help keep educational leaders, academics, and students abreast of the many changes in the ever-growing area of Catholic education.

Chapter One

Catholic Schools

Purpose, Presence, and Prophecy

Gerald M. Cattaro

"School can and must be a catalyst, it must be a place of encounter."
—Pope Francis

In one of his first public audiences as Vicar of Rome, on June 7, 2013, Pope Francis described education as a key mission of the Catholic Church when he met with over 9,000 students from schools entrusted to the Jesuits of the Italian province in Italy and Albania (Francis, 2013, *L'Osservatore Romano Weekly Edition* in English, 2013, p. 5). This gathering demonstrated Francis's clear appreciation for the importance of Catholic education and brought to light the now-familiar declaration of his pontificate, encountering, a process where one is open to newness and dialogue.

While meeting with students, Francis also gave voice to his notion of encounter. For Francis, encounters allow Catholics to navigate and renew their efforts to explore the newness of Vatican II and, in particular, *Gravissimum Educationis* (*GE*), the Declaration on Christian Education, in framing a new theory or philosophy of Catholic education.

By his expression of awareness and priority, Pope Francis highlighted his commitment to and appreciation of Catholic schools. More specifically, he reminded all that the mission of Catholic schools is unequivocally shared with the mission of the Church. Accordingly, Francis cemented the singular bond Catholic schools have to the overall mission of the Church. In his words, Francis recognized the unambiguous role of Catholic schools in the achievement of the Church's mission by reinforcing his understanding of the Second Vatican Council in its approach to Catholic education.

As a former Catholic schoolteacher, the Pope has the ability to internalize the importance and unique character of Catholic schools in his ministry. In fact, Pope Francis further exemplified his commitment to Catholic schools in his first apostolic exhortation, *Evangelii Gaudium* (*EG*; "The Joy of the Gospel"; 2013).

In *EG*, the Pope proclaimed that Catholic schools "always strive to join their work of education with the explicit proclamation of the Gospel, are a most valuable resource for the evangelization of culture" (para. 134). In this way the Pope again highlighted the mission of Catholic schools as central to that of the Church.

The premise that Catholic education is central to the Church's mission is consistent with the thinking of the Council Fathers of Vatican II. This is particularly evident in Pope Paul VI's proclamation of *GE* on October 28, 1965. As Catholics commemorate the 50th anniversary of *GE*, the present offers a compelling motive to reflect on the efforts of the many who toil in the vineyard of Catholic schools in the 21st century. It is also a time to pay tribute to those many educators who went before them on what is sometimes seen as a protracted journey.

The reflections in this volume come at a time when American Catholic education faces a moment of truth as to which direction it will take. Issues that were not prominent in the United States in 1965 have surfaced in the aftermath of Vatican II, particularly enrollment, Catholic identity, outside threats, isomorphism, secularism, and relativism.

The focus of this introductory chapter, then, considers the context of the Vatican Council's Declaration on Christian Education, *GE*, particularly as it correlates to the development of American Catholic schools. This contextualization places groups, religion, education, and mission in the historical, political, social, and economic context within which Catholic schools find themselves while providing the theoretical framework for the transitions they are undergoing (Geertz, 1971). This approach devotes attention to the interpretation of the meanings of social actions and the conditions which lead to their implementation.

Consequently, this chapter reviews the process and development of *GE* within the framework of the events in the world and the United States. The chapter also explores the contexts of the Second Vatican Council ideologically and theologically because these were pivotal factors in the development of the Council documents. Further, the chapter highlights the importance of the historical development of Catholic schools as they established a presence in the American educational marketplace. Finally, this chapter suggests prophecy as the lens enabling Catholic schools to look to the future.

AMERICAN CATHOLIC EDUCATION

In 1965, the year *GE* was released, the number of Catholic elementary schools in the United States was at its all-time high of 10,667, with a population of over 4,431,000 students (Center for Applied Research in the Apostolate [CARA], 2015). This was a period when every Catholic pastor and bishop strived toward the ideal of having a Catholic school in every parish, as mandated by the 1884 Third Plenary Council of Baltimore, a goal that was never fully achieved. The Council also obligated Catholics to send their children to these schools unless their Bishops granted them permission to do otherwise (Buetow, 1970).

Fifty years after *GE*, the 5,399 Catholic elementary schools remaining in the United States are about half of the number that existed in 1965. Also, the 1,392,000 students are about one-third of the total in 1965 (CARA, 2015). This drastic drop signifies the challenge of maintaining parish schools as their numbers continue to diminish.

In a related development, parishes, which were so prominent in the establishment of the American Catholic school system, may no longer play a major role. If anything, growing numbers of schools may no longer be considered Catholic as they morph into educational institutions operating under a variety of governance structures such as being led by school boards, private ownership, or are merged into regional schools.

Since the promulgation of *GE*, there has also been a dramatic drop in religious sisters and brothers to staff the schools. In 1965 there were 181,421 religious sisters; today there are 49,883 (Berrelleza, Gautier, & Gray, 2014, p. 1), 91% of whom are over the age of 60. Only 1% are under 40 (Berrelleza et al., 2014, p. 2). Catholic identity is highlighted by the absence of these canonical persons.

The issue of identity is also exceedingly troublesome. If one were to view a film on Netflix or retrieve a YouTube clip of a film such as *The Bells of St. Mary's*, it would reveal a Catholic school tradition that is alien to most who were born after the Second Vatican Council. Such films present a different world, where all knew their places and stations in Catholic life. It was a time when father blessed, sister or brother taught, parents paid, and students obeyed.

The transition—or rather, transformation—to the post-Conciliar time, when the "Kumbaya" generation developed, where father played the guitar, where sisters and brothers walked out of the classroom, where parents formed parent associations, and where students questioned their faith is under way. O'Gorman (1987) puts it all in perspective in his description of a class photo in the late 1940s, in which the Father was in his cassock and the Sister in her wimple. Today the picture would look very different: Father might be missing, and as to Sister, who or what is that? The color and genders of the students would be different, and the lay principal would be present, with perhaps the board president.

The identity of a Catholic institution, which was taken for granted, now becomes a source of importance, as the baby was perceived to have been thrown out with the bathwater. In an address to the Catholic Education European Council in October 2014, Bishop Claude Duguns of Angoulême, France (also a member of the *Académie française*), described the present generation of Catholic school officials as caught in the midst of what he called the transition breaks of the baby boomer generation. He spoke of school officials trying to sustain institutional identity as inheritors of a strong, visible Catholic identity they inherited from the priests, brothers, and sisters who created the schools.

The generation of the religious who took the reforms of the Second Vatican Council seriously bore witness to the 1965 Decree on the Renewal of Religious Life, proclaimed *Perfectae Caritatis* on the same day as *GE*. Yet many religious teachers returned to their foundations, in what sociologist Gerald Arbuckle (1997) would call refounding, namely to the grace of their foundations.

The sharp declines in the ranks of the religious occurred shortly after the Council's call for *aggiornamento*, or bringing up to date, a move which confronted leadership in religious orders with the task of determining what updating meant for their particular institutes. The Council also led a clarion call for a renewal through a return to the sources. For many, looking back to their initial foundation and charisms suggested ways to read the "signs of the times" to facilitate renewal of their institutes.

Some communities of religious women responded to these divisions by breaking from their institutes in order to establish new groups while others sought dispensations from their vows altogether (Berrelleza et al., 2014). Moreover, many religious women went back to the "streets," such that the apostolate of education was no longer to schools but to the imprisoned, immigrants, adults, and unwed mothers—in other words, to their refounded roots.

Finances continue to be worrisome as Catholic schools continue to acclimate to new realities. It may shock some to realize that the average tuition in the Catholic schools from pre-Council days was minimal, if anything. Today, the average per-pupil cost in Catholic schools is well over $10,000 (McDonald & Shultz, 2014, p. 18). Parish schools that were able to function at low cost due to the minimal stipends offered religious sisters and brothers were based on false economies. Today, school officials have to work closely with union officials in many instances and so must offer competing salaries to retain quality staff. In addition, school officials and parishes must provide for health insurance, pension funds, and the like.

On a related matter, classrooms in Catholic schools must now be "smart" and are therefore costly as they are hooked up to Internet accessibility. Further, interactive whiteboards, laptops, and room configurations add to the cost of operations. The upkeep of the infrastructure of many Catholic school buildings is costly because they are typically large structures left from the golden days. Exacerbating matters, many of these buildings are in large city neighborhoods once home to Catholic populations. However, now they contain gentrified populations, many of whom are not Catholic and who do not support parishes.

In the suburbs, Catholic schools followed moving populations and may face environmental issues such as asbestos. Limited funding from federal, state, and local governments, including public school boards, help to defray some, but not all, of the mounting costs for transportation, textbooks, testing, special education, nursing, and health technology. These costs contribute to the bleak financial picture confronting Catholic schools. Moreover, contractors who a generation ago might have worked for the education of their children or for the "good sisters" now charge market prices, further deepening financial worries for Catholic schools.

Charter schools represent an outside threat, as they offer free educations of choice to new immigrant minority groups and inner-city students, some under the guise of faith-based education. Charters grew in student population from 448,343 in 2000–2001 to over 2,057,599 a decade later (National Center for Educational Statistics, [NCES], 2013a). During this period, the percentage of students attending charter schools increased. This is undoubtedly at the expense of Catholic schools, as over 55% of the students enrolled in charter schools are from urban areas (NCES, 2013b). In one year alone, between 2010–2011 and 2011–2012, the number of students enrolled in charter schools increased from 1,787,091 to 2,057,599 (NCES, 2013a).

Institutional isomorphic relativism (Lynch, 2006) is also an outside threat to Catholic schools as they mimic public programs to attract students. In some instances, public school standards, such as accreditation, registration, licensing approval, teacher/principal certification, length of school year/days, curriculum, recordkeeping/reports, health and safety requirements, and special education, are forced on Catholic schools. These standards become costly.

These difficulties, present 50 years after the promulgation of *GE*, are challenging to both the very nature and existence of American Catholic schools. Therefore, the anniversary of *GE*, the only Council document on the importance of education—let alone Catholic education—provides a golden opportunity for scrutiny as to the purpose and presence of Catholic schools in America. Fittingly, it is a time to take stock of the evolution in the development of American Catholicism on the fiftieth anniversary of *GE*.

PROCESS

Vatican II

"An event of enormous importance is taking place: the Church is awakening within souls," as Catholic priest and academic Romano Guardini once said (Ratzinger, 2002, p. 5). In order to understand *GE*; one must have knowledge of the Second Vatican Council, its tone, its spiritual dimension, and the predisposition of the Council Fathers. Vatican II was an ecclesial, theological, and ecumenical congress that began over 50 years ago. It covered the span of three years, from October 11, 1962, to December 8, 1965.

There were 2,800 bishops present at Vatican II, 489 from South America, 404 from North America, 374 from Asia, 84 from Central America, and 75 from Oceania (Morrison, 2002, para. 13). Representing a truly global perspective, the Council Fathers produced 16 documents, two dogmatic and pastoral constitutions, nine decrees, and three declarations seeking to define the nature, scope, and mission of the Church. The time span of the Council was a significant, pivotal period in the social history of the United States and, one might say, the world.

An array of external factors impacted the Church and transformed American society. Key among these events were the Vietnam War, which also divided a nation; the social revolution of Woodstock, which divided a generation; the cultural changes engendered by the women's liberation movement, which challenged a male-dominated society; the upheaval of a racial divide, which raised awareness about the American justice system; the emergence of militant secularism in a nation that prided itself on being "one Nation under God;" the war on poverty, which recognized the cultural and wealth divide; and the introduction of relativism and the growth of pluralism.

In tandem, internal milieus, such as the uncertainty of Catholic identity, the loss of vocations, and a de-emphasis on education, occurred within the Church's structure because of the Council and its documents. The upshot was that the time was ripe for the educational and social change ushered in by the Vatican Council in the United States (and beyond).

Studying the 16 documents of the Second Vatican Council individually, without considering them part of an integral corpus, is one of the key mistakes of understanding the meaning behind its constitutions, decrees, and declarations (O'Mally, 2010). The four largest and most important documents are constitutions; the shorter works dealing with more particular issues are either decrees or declarations. All of these documents are listed in Appendix A and identified as to the category they belong to.

GE is a declaration. However, O' Mally (2013) cautions that one should not get caught up in the hierarchical approach to the Council documents. Put another way, while there is a certain level of weightiness in these classifications, it is important to review the documents chronologically to grasp their interdependence. Therefore, most documents cannot be fully understood without the consideration of the Dogmatic Constitution on the Church because it set the tone for collegiality established by those attending the Council.

O'Mally (2013) specifies that the document on the bishops, for instance, could not have been introduced into the Council until the one on the Church was fundamentally in place. This sequencing was important because of the crucial importance of the doctrine of collegiality debated in *Lumen Gentium* ("Light of the Nations"), The Dogmatic Constitution on the Church in the Modern World, promulgated on November 21, 1964.

The Vatican II documents paraphrased, borrowed from, and adapted from one another as the Council developed to form a coherent and integral whole that must be studied in this way. Perhaps the most significant connections refer to the two main Constitutions, *Lumen Gentium* and *Gaudium et Spes* ("Joy and Hope"), The Pastoral Constitution on the Church in the Modern World, released on December 7, 1965.

As a reflection of its significance, *GE* often refers to *Lumen Gentium*, while *Gaudium et Spes* mentions *Gravissimum Educationis* in part II, chapter II, dedicated to the promotion of progress and culture. The joint reading of these documents proves to be particularly insightful for appreciating the two dimensions that education encompasses when analyzed from the standpoint of faith, meaning its secular and theological-spiritual dimensions (*Mentum Laboris*, 2014). In this way, the Second Vatican Council takes its place as a pivotal, if not capstone, event, one O'Mally (2012) calls a changeable moment in history.

In reviewing the Council documents, one realizes the critical role of education in the life of humankind, especially as it influences culture. There is also a pastoral dimension of the role of education as it augments the mission of the Church. Over 100 years ago, the French Jesuit Caussade (2009) termed the phase "Sacrament of the Moment." While his reference was personal, it applies to this moment in history—to be more explicit, Church history. Suitably, this description frames this chapter's discussion in a more spiritual perspective. Vatican II was thus not only an event, but a spiritual event.

Remi J. De Roo (2012), a bishop for over 50 years, is one of the few prelates who attended all four sessions of the Council who is still alive. He reflected on its gatherings as an event in which the participants took part in a communal spiritual exercise. He pointed out that the Council was, in his estimation, the working of the Holy Spirit who continues to guide the Church throughout her history. In his statement from the 40th celebration of the Council, De Roo wrote: "The opening of the Second Vatican Council, in retrospect, I would describe that providential event as a prolonged exercise in communal spiritual discernment. While at times perplexing, its ultimate results were definitely positive. It remains for me a superb illustration of how the Holy Spirit continues to guide the Pilgrim People of God throughout the course of history" (De Roo, 2012, para. 1).

De Roo clearly posited two elements. The first was the collaborative nature of the deliberations, while the second was the spirituality of the experience as significant to the overall strength of the Council.

The challenges presented by the generalizations in *GE* are reflective of the Council's collaborative and spiritual nature. *GE* aptly portrays education as being of paramount importance to society and the dignity of the person, as *GE* defends the rights of Church schools to exist and the role of parents as primary educators of their children. *GE* also accords a high importance to the vocation of teaching, viewing educators as well-trained professionals with high standards.

The role of educators in Catholic schools is thereby made more complex in today's secular, materialistic, and pluralistic world, which challenges faith-based schools even as they are reaching out to non-Catholics. Still, Catholic schools serve the common good by offering instruction on conflict and peace building, on providing a preferential option for the poor even as they educate women, immigrants, those from hybrid cultures, and individuals experiencing extreme marginalization (Congregation for Catholic Education 2013).

GE: Declaration on Christian Education

Perceptions of religious life, collegiality, governance, the role of the laity, education of the laity, and social shifts in the United States from a church of immigrants to one of respectability with the election of John Kennedy impacted Catholic schools in the early 1960s. Of course, *GE* did not develop in a vacuum; it was built on earlier documents issued by the Holy See dealing with education along with international documents and the prevailing Catholic educational philosophy of the time in the shadow of World War I.

Among the many documents exemplifying the significance of education in Catholic history are the 1919 Apostolic Letter of Benedict XV, *Communes Litteras* (Acta Apostolicae Sedis, or A.S.A.); the 1930 Apostolic Encyclical of Pius XI *Divini Illius Magistri* (1930); and John XXIII's 30th anniversary message on the publication of *Divini Illius Magistri* in 1960 (A.A.S.). As noted, the United Nations contributed to the recognition on the importance of the right to education in the Universal Declaration on Human Rights (1948) and the Declaration of the Rights of Children (1959; Russo, 2010).

Also setting the stage for *GE* were the writings of Catholic philosophers and educators between 1900 and 1960, such as Jacques Maritain, John Courtney Murray, Charles L. O'Donnell, and Francis W. Howard. These authors contributed to the development of a Catholic philosophy of education grounded in the Church's scholastic intellectual tradition that dominated thinking about education in the first half of the 20th century (Veverka, n.d.).

Another important influence came from Redden and Ryan (1948), coauthors of a textbook for Catholic teacher training in the United States. Their work, *A Catholic Philosophy of Education*, engaged many serious thinkers who produced a substantial body of writing, including journal articles and multiple book-length treatments of the topic.

Conceived at a time of great change—even upheaval—in society, whether religious or secular, *GE* launched the initial discussion of the Council Fathers on education. These first rounds of debate occurred a year before *GE*'s actual proclamation. On November 17–19, 1964 (Catholic News Service [CNS], 2014a), the participants engaged in debate around what issues *GE* would address.

Originally, the Declaration on Education was to be called *De Scholis Catholicis* ("On Catholic Schools"). However, Bishop Jules Daem of Antwerp, Belgium, maintained that this would not have been as authentic because the Church's educational mission was beyond mere academics (CNS 2014a). Further, Cardinal Ritter of St. Louis supported the notion that the scope of *GE* should move beyond schooling, as expressed in an intervention he delivered before the discussion participants on November 19, 1964.

Intervention by two other Americans at this time proved noteworthy, as reflected in *GE*'s final promulgation. Archbishop Cody of New Orleans (later archbishop of Chicago), then-president of the National Catholic Education Association, reminded the Council Fathers of the importance of a declaration noting that the two greatest expenditures of nations are defense and education (CNS, 2014b). Cardinal Spellman of New York also intervened by raising the question of public support of religious schools, a major issue in the United States and subject of chapter 2 of this book (Spellman, 1946).

Against this backdrop, *De Scholis Catholicis* became *De Educatione Christiana*, "On Christian Education." This new name set a course for *GE* which would go beyond the church's mission in schools. It also was a catalyst for a new theory of Catholic education. It is interesting to note the cardinal also emphasized the need for professionals, emphasizing the role of the laity in Catholic education (Ritter, 1964) a common theme of the Council.

As *GE* emerged, it is worth noting that each commission, the body responsible for developing a Conciliar document, had a relator whose responsibility was to facilitate and sum up the proceedings of each session. The relator at the first round of sessions focused on the need to have *GE* acknowledge the rights and duties of parents, states, and the church in matters of education.

The Council Fathers joined the rights and duties with the agreements of the various interventions to form the central themes of *GE*. These key themes included parents as primary educators, religious liberty, the Catholic Church's right to maintain schools, the encouragement of student initiative, the development of faculty, global perspectives on Catholic education, and faith formation. All of these concepts have a foundation in the evolution of Christian thought on the importance of education to civil society and the Church, as expressed in *GE*'s philosophical and theological development at the Council, thereby adding to its importance.

The final voting and discussions on *GE* took place on October 13–14, 1965. *GE* passed overwhelmingly by a margin of 2,290 for and 35 against (Vatican II, n.d.). Pope Paul VI then proclaimed GE on October 28, 1965, as a Council document raising the importance of education in the scope of the Church's mission.

GE had its critics, however. Some feared that it did not go far enough as they treated the ambiguous references to higher education as wanting. This was of particular concern to Cardinal Ratzinger, later Pope Benedict XVI, who also served as a *pretri*, or theological expert, during the Council.

As early as 1966, Cardinal Ratzinger suggested that *GE* said too little about Catholic universities, particularly theology faculties and their ability to be autonomous if they are to achieve quality in their research. The prefect of the Sacred Congregation for the Doctrine of Faith, St. Pope John Paul II, would take up his concerns in two apostolic exhortations: *Sapientia Christiana* (1979) and, more explicitly, *Ex Corde Ecclesiae* (1990).

After four years the Council participants began to tire. As such, *GE* concluded with the recognition of the role of the Church in the progress and development of education. Yet the bishops realized that they would not be able to accomplish all that needed to be done. Thus, the bishops basically gave the task to what was eventually to become the Office for Schools of the Congregation of Education, with additional mandates for follow-up by episcopal conferences. This is significant because it reflected the collaborative nature of the Council and the trust the bishops had in the voices at the local level in the universal Church (*Instrumentum Laboris*, 2014).

PRESENCE

"To go forth and teach all nations" (Matt. 16:15)

This biblical imperative propels, and rationalizes all Catholic educational activity. Based on their response to external environments, Catholic schools continue to transform themselves. Consequently, it is paramount to conceptualize and provide context to the pattern, approach, and relationships Catholic schools have taken in their quest to serve, contribute, and foster the needs of quality education in the United States. Only through this framework can one appreciate how Catholic schools are a major part of the social quilt that is America.

Figure 1.1 illustrates the outline of the development of American Catholic schools (Cattaro & Cooper, 2007, p. 68). The process evolved from a total self-service enterprise in conversion to what today some may view as mediation or bringing faiths and cultures together.

From their beginnings, American Catholic schools placed a high priority on concerns for Christian justice, evidenced in liberating students through education. In this way, Catholic schools encounter, popularized by Pope Francis, indigenous peoples, immigrants, and the urban poor, providing them with the necessary academic skills to enhance their lives. The use of the cylinder as a metaphor is key because it represents an active and ongoing, rather than static, process such that conversion evangelizes and welcomes all.

CONVERSION

Pope Leo XIII's apostolic exhortation *Longinqua* (Wynne, 1903), promulgated to the bishops of the United States on the Feast of the Epiphany 1895, was designed to remind the bishops that the Catholic identity of America confirms the conversion purpose of educational endeavors. As such, it is worth briefly reviewing the historical development of Catholic education in what became the United States.

American Catholic identity grew out of the first period of Catholic education in what was formally Mexican territory during the 16th century, when the Franciscans set up mission schools. In 1528 *Doctrina Breve*, the first book published in the Western Hemisphere, encouraged these missionaries to teach the Christian faith in simple style (Buetow, 1970, p. 2). Today, many of these "missions," such as Los Angeles, San Francisco, San Diego, and Sacramento, are megaurban centers founded by virtuous men such as Father Serra, a Franciscan.

The French Jesuits also contributed to the establishment of a mission system and Catholic identity through the creation of schools in what was called New France to promote religion. In what became New York State,

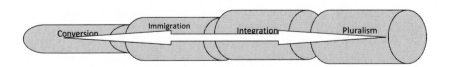

Figure 1.1.   Cyclical Development of Catholic Schools from Conversion to Pluralism

Jesuits converted more than 2,000 members of the Iroquois nation (Buetow, 1970, p. 16).

Pope Leo's intent in *Longinqua* was to serve as a reminder of how conversion led to salvation in the Catholic Church. It is thus important to recall that the witness of the French and Spanish missionaries kept true to its mission by evangelizing the first Catholics on the American shores. The assignments of these missionaries to work on the conversion process was direct: they were in North America to preach the gospel, baptize, and teach the indigenous people they encountered.

The mission of Catholic education in America since its earliest days has been primarily concerned with the tradition of justice. While exploration was at its height in the earliest days, so was exploitation. The first schools, set up at missions, were, as noted, for the Native American peoples. Black children, most of whom migrated to America by force, were also beneficiaries of Catholic education almost from the very beginning as they attended the Ursuline school in New Orleans as early as 1727 (Buetow, 1970, p. 21). Pope Leo XIII lauded these attempts by European missionaries to educate Native Americans and Africans:

> We cannot pass over in silence those whose long-continued unhappy lot implores and demands succor from men of apostolic zeal; We refer to the Indians and the negroes who are to be found within the confines of America, the greatest portion of whom have not yet dispelled the darkness of superstition. How wide a field for cultivation! How great a multitude of human beings to be made partakers of the blessing derived through Jesus Christ! (Wynne, 1903; *Longinqua*, para. 23)

The first American Catholic bishop, John Carroll (1735–1815), was consecrated in 1790. A Jesuit, Carroll continued the missionary efforts of Catholic schooling by encouraging the development of schools (McCluskey, 1968).

Unfortunately, the anti-Catholic climate during the colonial period, during which Catholics lacked status and were restricted by colonial penal laws, made the establishment of Catholic schools difficult, if not impossible. Consequently, many young Catholics, mostly men, went abroad to study (Fitzpatrick, 1958). One notable exception was the establishment of a school for girls by St. Elizabeth Ann Seton in the Catholic colony of Maryland in 1808 (Roemer, p. 128). Providentially, this institution became the forerunner of Catholic schools.

IMMIGRATION

Most of Bishop Carroll's clergy were immigrants (Fitzpatrick, 1958). Even so, he wished that all Catholics who came to the United States would lay aside national distinctions and attachments to form not French, Irish, German, or English churches, but to form a Catholic American Church. As this issue played out, a great debate, discussed below, raged between church leaders as they tackled the swarms of immigrants who were to be their charge.

Immigration played an indispensable part in this process as, for example, between 1821 and 1850, almost 2.5 million Europeans entered the country. Of this total, 1,700,000 immigrants arrived in the 1840s alone, many of whom were Catholic, and a considerable number of whom were Irish (Report on the Population, 1895).

Many priests, brothers, and nuns who were involved in the teaching apostolate also arrived on the shores of the United States in the mid-nineteenth century, making it easier for church officials to set up the foundations of their own system of education. In this way, the arrival of the Benedictine Sisters in 1852, the Religious of the Sacred Heart of Mary in 1877, the Grey Nuns in 1865, the Brothers of the Christian Schools in 1846, the Xaverian Brothers in 1854, and the Marist Brothers in 1882 (Buetow, 1970, pp. 116–17), to name a few, started a tremendous change in motion.

During this period there was a threefold increase in the Catholic population. The number grew from 6,143,222 in 1880 to 17,735,553 in 1920. This was further reflected in the development of the Catholic school system from 2,246 schools with a population of 405,234 students to 5,852 schools and 1,701,219 students during this same time period (Buetow, 1970, p. 179). Peter Guilday (1932) and John Tracy Ellis (1971), commanding historians of Catholicism in the United States, described Americanization as the question of the day.

The big question posed to the American hierarchy was whether it was the responsibility of the Catholic schools to Americanize or to encourage immigrants to continue their own national languages and faith customs. What role would schools play? If the purpose was to Americanize, were Catholic schools necessary? Should Catholics have committed to relativism where every culture was equal or assimilate, thereby reflecting a dominant culture known as American?

When immigrants arrive in the United States, the mind-set of many priests seemed to be that of protectionism. To this end, many members of the clergy acted to protect new arrivals from Protestantism. Consequently, public schools were not only seen as an enemy of the Catholic faith but also of ethnic cultures.

As this controversy played itself out, two groups emerged. The Americanists, led by Archbishop Ireland of St. Paul, Minnesota, wished to see a new world path for the Church, while the conservatives, led by Archbishop Corrigan of New York, sought to keep the status quo. The cause was further split by the Third Plenary Council of Baltimore, which mandated that every Catholic child must be in a Catholic school (Buetow, 1988, p. 152). As noted, this was a dictum that never came close to being fulfilled (McClusky, 1968, p. 105).

The Cahenslyism movement (Barry, 1953), which opposed assimilation, paved the way for anti-Americanism (liberalism). Cahenslyism (Meng, 1946) was a movement calling for the establishment of a German diocese in the United States; Germans found the English language of the Irish priest difficult, and many were converting to the Protestant faith. McAvoy (1963) reported that Americanism was most prominent in the school debate and required papal intervention. The situation became so grave that the Pope sent Archbishop Sorelli (Tyack & Hansot, 1982), his representative to resolve the issue.

Even the presence of the Papal Legate could not resolve the feud. Pope Leo XIII ended public discussion in the apostolic exhortation *Testem Benevolentiae Nostrae* (1899). Leo declared that while Catholic schools were to be promoted, it was up to local bishops as to when it was lawful and unlawful to attend public schools (Reilly, 1944). At their inception, then, Catholic schools functioned as a "fortress" protecting the immigrant population from the Protestant majority.

The Catholic Church remained something of a culturally dominated fortress until Vatican II and *GE* (O'Keefe, 2000). Even so, as new generations were born, Catholics became "Americanized" as aspects of the Old World devotional culture and theology were gradually left behind and shades of a new, more individualistic, and democratic Catholicism appeared.

INTEGRATION-MEDIATION

Catholic schools in the United States began to grow particularly in the urban centers where most of the immigrant groups settled, assimilated, and were protected by Church leaders. Short (1984) speaks of what he terms "urban villages," which had cultures of their own to provide for the needs of their populations from the womb to the tomb. In fact, many of these urban villages had protected boundaries and institutions of pluralistic complexity. Much of the growth of Catholic schools stemmed from the immigrant experience, as newcomers preferred to send their children to schools where they would be taught in the Catholic faith and their native tongue (City of St. Louis, Missouri, n.d.).

Ethnic Catholicism can be described as that special intrinsic quality of Catholicism acknowledging, accepting, and, at times, celebrating the differing sociocultural boundaries of language, nationality, and faith. For example, historical studies of the Italian-American experience in New York substantiate that the Archdiocese of New York had more than 40 Italian national parishes that had been established by the mid-1920s (Tomasi, 1978).

In what may be considered either an irony or an unintended consequence, as the urban villages and ethnic parishes started to disintegrate, immigrant groups integrated into the wider American society. This shift signaled the beginning of the end to so-called ethnic parish schools where classes were sometimes taught in Polish, German, or other ethnic languages (Buetow, 1970). Of course, a few such parishes remain sprinkled throughout the United States.

In 1946 Joseph E. Ritter was appointed as Archbishop of St. Louis. During Ritter's first year, he put pastors and leaders of Catholic schools on notice to include black children or face church discipline. Archbishop Ritter publicly said he would excommunicate any Catholic who continued to protest integration of the schools. Moreover, he instructed all pastors in the archdiocese to end racial segregation in their schools (City of St. Louis, Missouri, n.d.)

The United States Supreme Court would follow Archbishop Ritter's lead with the nation's public schools until 1954 in *Brown v. Board of Education.* Thus a new phase of Catholic school developed, where ethnic groups and racial groups were brought together in classrooms. The Bishops followed with pastoral letters—most notably, *Brothers and Sisters to Us* (NCCB, 1979)—that, for the first time, denounced racism as a sin; similar letters would follow.

Pluralism referring to religious diversity was first researched by O'Keefe (2000, pp. 66–67). He provided information about urban Catholic schools and their pluralistic religious demographics. His urban Catholic school survey studied 631 urban schools, 398 primary and 243 secondary, with respective populations of 98,467 and 138,996. His study demonstrated that 72.15% of students attending Catholic urban elementary schools were Catholic and the rest were non-Catholic.

Other studies provide data demonstrating that a large number of minority students attend Catholic schools in the dioceses known as the "Big Ten," most notably New York, Chicago, St. Louis, Cincinnati, Miami, Brooklyn, and Los Angeles (Convey, 1992). Unlike Hispanic students, who tend to be Catholic, 80% of black students who attend Catholic schools are non-Catholic.

A rise in non-Catholics attending Catholic schools can be seen at the national level. Of the 2,420,590 students enrolled in the nation's Catholic elementary and secondary schools, in 2009 nearly 14% were not Catholic, up from 11.2% in 1980 and just 2.7% in 1970 (Catholic Courier Dec. 21, 2009). The rise in non-Catholics attending Catholic schools is still growing. During the 2012–13 school year, non-Catholic students accounted for 15.9% of the total enrollment at Catholic elementary schools in the United States, according to statistics reported by the National Catholic Educational Association (McDonald & Shultz, 2014).

NATIVITY SCHOOLS: A CREATIVE RESPONSE IN THE URBAN CONTEXT

Facing contemporary challenges, Catholic schools have developed creative models and prophetical leadership in refounding concepts. These schools opened the path to new forms of Catholic education to meet the needs of urban America. The cylinder model presented in figure 1 demonstrates the ability of the Catholic school system to refound itself in service to the populations in the United States and outside and internal environments. This reinvention seems to apply to a new model of Catholic school emerging that is committed to serving the urban poor at all cost. Not surprisingly, as with past movements it rests on the shoulders of religious congregations.

Nativity model schools developed almost unnoticed. These schools do not receive governmental or diocesan subsidies to aid in their operation. Unlike more traditional Catholic schools that charge tuition, Nativity model schools are essentially free. The funding for Nativity model schools is provided by individual donors and organizations.

The Society of Jesus founded the original Nativity model school in 1971 on the Lower East Side of Manhattan. The first school was founded to provide educational, emotional, and social support to the underserved minority youth living in the Lower East Side neighborhoods. The Nativity model has been found to be so effective in serving underprivileged youth it has been replicated over 40 times in some of the neediest neighborhoods in 20 states and the District of Columbia (Smith & Cattaro, 2014).

Elements of the program components cited by Podsiadlo and Philliber (2003) can be found in each of the existing Nativity schools. In this regard, each Nativity educational center has its own distinctive identity, mission, and character; however, each is patterned on an original model developed in 1971 by the Nativity Mission Center in New York City. Among the ten key elements of schools in the Nativity Network are, most notably, being faith based, serving the economically poor and marginalized, providing holistic education, partnering with families, extending school days and years, and demonstrating commitment to their students beyond graduation.

In an unpublished study of Nativity model schools, Smith (2006) collected data from thirty-nine of the forty existing Nativity model schools. According to Smith (2006), officials in 36 out of 39 of the schools reported that they served middle-school-age students. One school indicated that it served a high-school-age population, while two noted that they served elementary-aged students. Of the 36 schools serving middle-school-age students, two schools operated a K–8 model. The remaining 34 schools served exclusively middle-school-age students ranged from grade four to six.

PROPHECY

"Where have you come from and where are you going?" Genesis 16:8

Pope Francis proposed three aspects for consideration by the participants of the meeting of the Congregation of Education on February 13, 2014. He stressed that Catholic schools must value dialogue in education, have qualified preparation of teachers and school leaders, and must express the living presence of the Gospel in education, science, and culture (Francis, 2014)

Facing the challenges presented by Pope Francis and looking toward the future, creative models and prophetical leadership are needed, as demonstrated in Arbuckle's (1997) refounding concepts. This shift is essential if leaders are to be resourceful enough to open the path to new forms of Catholic education pertaining to governance, academic quality, and maintaining presence of Catholic schools in the global sphere.

Change is occurring in Catholic schools and the world even as society is being transformed into an age of networked intelligence, a *terra incognita* (Drucker, 1992). The present, then, is a time when prophecy would certainly be advantageous, placing imagery into a world unimaginable 10 years ago. This imagery should give meaning to the life of the Church of our time those in Catholic education.

The reality is that prophecy goes to the heart of Catholic teachings, yet the Western tradition placed limits on the definition of prophecy, amplified by a culture of occultism and fortune telling rather than the transforming power of liberation. Frye (1990), in *Words with Power*, refers to this pivotal occurrence as "kerygmatic," meaning the point at which the cleavage between active speech and reception of speech are united. This was when the relationship of prophets was united with their messages.

Unequivocally, the Hebrew *nabi'* and the Latin *propheta* direct attention to the classical tradition of prophet in the Old Testament as one who speaks for another, namely God. In this legacy emerged the prophet seen as one who lifted the human condition to new heights, a role long filled by Catholic schools.

For the Catholic school leader, prophecy can be seen in ritual, beliefs, and values expressed through social relations, customs, curriculum, objects, and stories. Religious culture is thus observable, as descriptions can provide the ways in which the meanings, values, ideas, and beliefs of social groups are articulated through cultural artifacts. The question then becomes why prophecy is needed as we face a new path to the construction of identity of American Catholic schools.

The fusion of politics, policy, and prophecy paves the road to what is perceived to be one of the most complex structures of Catholic schools, namely governance. Historically, the great strength of American Catholic education has been the parish structure supporting schools. The parishes owned the property; built the buildings; had inexpensive religious sisters, brothers, and priests to teach; and a stable, loyal, local client base. In addition, many pastors, operating under the fortress model, refused to encourage non-Catholics to attend Catholic schools because they did not contribute.

With changes in demographics and technology, many Catholic families moved out of cities and have other options, including improved traditional public schools, charters, and private schools. However, the heavily bureaucratic diocesan structure, top-down control, and aging religious have been slow to adapt to these changes. Unfortunately, Catholics see school closings, mergers, and decline without a clear, viable national strategy. The political change in ownership, governance, and controls is an invitation to build bridges or, as Francis would have it, a time for dialogue instead of building walls.

Almost every discussion about the academic quality of Catholic schools relies on the work of Greeley (1967); Cibulka, O'Brien, and Zewe (1982); Bryk, Holland, Lee, and Carriedo (1984); Coleman and Hoffer (1987); and Irvine and Foster (1996). These studies reported that the social capital of these institutions provided the climate for academic success. Unfortunately, these studies are now outdated, pertained to high schools rather than elementary schools, and were conducted in urban centers instead of the suburbs. These studies also speak of a school climate relating to academic performance and values-based education, they were in a world that no longer exists. Thus, newer research is needed.

Regrettably, in today's high-stakes society Catholic schools cannot rely on the past. They need to be transparent and rely on updated research. Francis reminds Catholics to be "guided by a changing generation, and that, therefore, every educator—and the Church as a whole is an educating mother—is required to change, in the sense of knowing how to communicate with the young" (Francis, 2014, p. 171).

CONCLUSION

Since the promulgation of *Gravissimum Educationis*, Catholics have witnessed the emergence of a radically different, fluid approach to culture, theology, and philosophy (McCool, 1981, p. 33). This approach, which is drawing attention in the words of Pope Francis, can be seen as an encounter.

As change continues, Catholic schools continue to experience a crisis of meaning. This crisis emerges as schools struggle for a Catholic pedagogical identity but are caught between an identity tied to an eroding memory and the present-day secular society. Elias (1999) argued that after Vatican II there was an eclipse of a distinctive Catholic philosophy of education based on the principles of Aquinas. In fact, so infused was the principle of absolutism in Thomistic philosophy that it can be argued as one cause for the decline of a Catholic philosophy of education.

In addition the growth of analytical philosophy pragmatism phenomenology, existentialism, and even Marxism have placed strain on the dogmatic attitude of Thomism. These factors, combined with the freedom and openness developed during Vatican II (Clarke, 1979, p. 12) served as a catalyst to the erosion of the traditional Catholic philosophy of education.

What emerged, according to Elias (1999), is more of a Catholic theology of education as witnessed in such documents as *To Teach as Jesus Did* (1972). As such Elias proposed a Catholic theory of education based on the writings of two educator-philosophers of the pre– and post–Vatican II period, Bernard Lonergan (1970), a Jesuit, and Paulo Freire (1970), who was South American.

Elias would rely on Lonergan's moral and intellectual conversion as to knowing, learning, and method on the psychological and social sciences. This represents a proposed change from a rigid culture to one that is more dynamic. Elias would call on Freire's work to focus attention on the oppressed, thereby leading to a reconstruction of the development of the idea of philosophy and pedagogy.

Together, Elias, Lonergan, and Freire complement each other as to the theological, psychological, and social domains of education on the road to the development of a new theory of Catholic education. As Catholic leaders expand their concept of Catholic education to meet today's challenges, such a theory would illuminate the call of *GE* to dialogue and awareness while making room for others, such as non-Catholics and the needy. Constructing such a theory of identity would also be aligned with the concept of the ecclesiology developed after the Council exemplified in the promotion of the culture of encounter so often brought to the fore by Pope Francis.

Catholic schools are the custodians of Church culture, setting the boundaries with parents, faculty members, students, and parish members as constructs of their faith community. By emphasizing institutional integrity and identity, today's leaders can fulfill the Vatican Council's vision of Catholic schools encountering the mission of the Church.

Policy and prophecy thus provide the lens to identity while witnessing to the living Gospel in education. Dulles (1978) reminds readers that the Church of Christ consists of two inseparable dimensions: the charismatic and the institutional. The educational mission of the Church reflects this image in its schools: The Church is One, Holy, Catholic, and Apostolic.

Therefore the dual nature which Dulles describes is lived out in the Church's educational mission echoing the charismatic frame of the institution as One, Holy, Catholic, and Apostolic. Acknowledging Christ as the ONE source, promoting Holiness in sustaining worship and the spiritual nature of the school, operationalizing Catholic in openness to members of all cultures and creeds and by demonstrating the Apostolic nature of the school in service and governance. As such, Catholic schools reflect, in their outward and visible signs, these marks whereby its mission encounter society.

By their very character, Jesuit discernment (Lonergan) and South American disposition (Freire) have influenced Pope Francis to see them as part of the fabric of his reality. This openness to dialogue has enhanced the meaning of *GE* as a fluid document to be studied as leaders shape a new theory of Catholic education for the present day even as the Church is undergoing a transformation. After all, Francis reminds believers that "Catholic education is one of the most important challenges for the Church, currently committed to new evangelization in an historical and cultural context that is undergoing constant transformation" (2014, unpaginated).

APPENDIX 1

Chronological Order of Vatican II Documents

1. *Sacrosanctum Concilium*, Constitution on the Sacred Liturgy, 1963.
2. *Inter Mirifica*, Decree on the Means of Social Communication, 1963.
3. *Lumen Gentium*, Dogmatic Constitution on the Church, 1964.
4. *Orientalium Ecclesiarum*, Decree on the Catholic Churches of the Eastern Rite, 1964.
5. *Unitatis Redintegratio*, Decree on Ecumenism, 1964.
6. *Christus Dominus*, Decree Concerning the Pastoral Office of Bishops in the Church, 1965.
7. *Perfectae Caritatis*, Decree on Renewal of Religious Life, 1965.
8. *Optatam Totius*, Decree on Priestly Training, 1965.
9. *Gravissimum Educationis*, Declaration on Christian Education, 1965.
10. *Nostra Aetate*, Declaration on the Relation of the Church to Non-Christian Religions, 1965.
11. *Dei Verbum*, Dogmatic Constitution on Divine Revelation, 1965.
12. *Apostolicam Actuositatem*, Decree on the Apostolate of the Laity, 1965.
13. *Dignitatis Humanae*, Declaration on Religious Freedom, 1965.
14. *Ad Gentes*, Decree on the Mission Activity of the Church, 1965.

15. *Presbyterorum Ordinis*, Decree on the Ministry and Life of Priests, 1965.

16. *Gaudium et Spes*, Pastoral Constitution on the Church in the Modern World, 1965.

REFERENCES

Arbuckle, G. (1997). *From chaos to mission: Refounding religious life formation.* Collegeville, MI: Liturgical Press.

Barry, C. J. (1953). *The Catholic Church and German Americans.* Milwaukee, WI: Bruce.

Benedict XV. (1919, April 10). *Communes litteras. Acta Apostolicae Sedis* 11, p. 172.

Berrelleza, E., Gautier, M., & Gray, M. (2014). *Special report population trends among religious institutes of women.* Washington, DC: Center for Applied Research in the Apostolate.

Bowman, T. (n.d.). *Sr. Thea's Address to US Bishops* [Online video clip]. Available from http://link.brightcove.com/services/player/bcpid506929354001?bckey=AQ~~,AAAAdgye3dk~,p0Zv3iru3vLtuHJC18uO4sBMTKhhmskf&bctid=2781665740001

Brown v. Board of Education, 347 U.S. 483 (1954).

Bryk, A. S., Holland, P. B., Lee, V. E., & Carriedo, R. A. (1984). *Effective Catholic schools: An exploration.* Washington, DC: National Catholic Educational Association.

Buetow, H. A. (1970). *Of singular benefit: The story of Catholic education in the United States.* New York: Macmillan.

Buetow, H. A. (1988). *The Catholic school.* New York: Crossroads.

Burke, Jennifer. (2009, December 21). Schools embrace all students. *Catholic Courier.* Retrieved from http://www.catholiccourier.com/in-depth/previous-topics/schools-embrace-all-students/#sthash.wCBbPcDm.dpuf

Catholic Courier. (2009, Dec. 21). http://www.catholiccourier.com/in-depth/previous-topics/schools-embrace-all-students/#sthash.58RfAuDS.dpuf

Catholic News Service. (2014a). https://vaticaniiat50.wordpress.com/2014/11/18/background-of-council-document-on-education/

Catholic News Service. (2014b). https://vaticaniiat50.wordpress.com/2014/11/18/financial-aid-for-parents-in-choosing-schools-urged-at-council/

Cattaro, G., & Cooper, B. (2007). Developments in Catholic schools in the USA: Politics, policy, and prophesy. In G. Grace & J. O'Keefe (Eds.), *International handbook of Catholic education: Challenges for school systems in the 21st Century, part one.* Dordrecht: Springer.

Cattaro, G., & Smith, K. [AQ13] (2014). Catholic schools' enduring presence in urban America. In P. Bauch (Ed.), *Catholic schools in the public interest.* Charlotte, NC: Information Age.

Caussade, J. P. (2009). *The sacrament of the moment.* San Francisco: Harper.

Center for Applied Research in the Apostolate (CARA). (2015). *United States data over time.* Retrieved from http://cara.georgetown.edu/caraservices/requestedchurchstats.html

Cibulka, J., O'Brien, T. & Zewe, D. (1982). *Inner-city private elementary schools.* Milwaukee: Marquette University Press.

The City of St. Louis Missouri. (n.d.). A preservation plan for Saint Louis: Part I: Historical contexts. http://www.stlouis-mo.gov/government/departments/planning/cultural-resources/preservation-plan/Part-I-Education.cfm

Clarke, W. (1979). *The philosophical approach to God: A new Thomistic perspective.* Winston-Salem, NC: Wake Forest University Press.

Coleman, J. & Hoffer, T. (1987). *Public and private high schools: The impact of communities.* New York: Basic Books Press.

Coleman, J. S., Hoffer, T., & Kilgore, S. (1982). *High school achievement: Public, Catholic & private schools compared.* New York: Basic Books.

Congregation for Catholic Education. (2013). *Educating to intercultural dialogue in Catholic schools: Living in harmony for a civilization of love.* http://www.vatican.va/roman_curia/

congregations/ccatheduc/documents/rc_con_ccatheduc_doc_20131028_dialogo-intercultu-
rale_en.html

Congregation for Catholic Education. (2014). *Educating today and tomorrow: A renewing passion.* Retrieved December 9, 2014, from http://www.vatican.va/roman_curia/congrega-tions/ccatheduc/documents/rc_con_ccatheduc_doc_20140407_educare-oggi-e-domani_en.html

Convey, J. J. (1992). *Catholic schools make a difference: Twenty-five years of research.* Washington, DC: National Catholic Educational Association.

Daguns, C. (2014, October). *Pace and mission of Catholic education in Europe.* Fall meeting. Lecture conducted from European Committee for Catholic Education, Paris.

De Roo, R. (2012). *Vatican II: Voice of the Church.* http://www.vatican2voice.org/92symp/deroo.htm

Drucker, P. F. (1992). *Managing for the Future: The 1990s and Beyond.* New York: Truman Talley Books.

Dulles, A. (1978). *Models of the Church.* Image classics. New York: Doubleday.

Elias, J. (1999). Philosophy of education? *Religious Education, 94*(1), 92–110.

Ellis, J. T. (1971). The Catholic school commentator compromise? *Notre Dame Journal of Education, 2*(13), 29.

European Committee for Catholic Education (CEEC). (2014, October 10, meeting). Paris, France.

Fitzpatrick, E. A. (1958). Catholic education in colonial America. *Catholic Schools Journal 58*(October), 26–29.

Francis. (2013, June). Public audience, Vatican City: *L'Osservatore Romano Weekly Edition* in English.

Francis. (2013, November). *Evangelii Gaudium.* Apostolic exhortation. Retrieved from http://w2.vatican.va/content/francesco/en/apost_exhortations/documents/papa-francesco_esortazione-ap_20131124_evangelii-gaudium.html

Francis. (2014, February). Address of Pope Francis to participants in the plenary session of the Congregation for Catholic Education (for educational institutions). *Acta Apostolicae Sedis.* Retrieved from http://w2.vatican.va/content/francesco/en/speeches/2014/february/documents/papa-francesco_20140213_congregazione-educazione-cattolica.html

Francis. (2013). *Apostolic Exhortation, Evangelii Gaudium, of the Holy Father Francis.* Retrieved December 18, 2014, from the Holy See: http://w2.vatican.va/content/francesco/en/apost_exhortations/documents/papa-francesco_esortazione-ap_20131124_evangelii-gaudium.html

Freire, P. (1970). *Pedagogy of the oppressed.* New York: Continuum.

Frye, N. (1990). *Words with power.* New York: Harcourt Brace Jovanovich.

Geertz, C. (1971). Islam observed: Religious development in Morocco and Indonesia. Chicago: University of Chicago Press.

Greeley, A. M. (1967). *The Catholic experience: An interpretation of the history of American Catholicism.* Garden City, NY: Doubleday.

Guilday, P. (1932). *A history of the councils of Baltimore (1791–1884).* New York: The Macmillan Company.

Instrumentum Laboris. (2014). *Educating today and tomorrow: A renewing passion,* Congregation for Catholic Education. Retrieved from http://www.vatican.va/roman_curia/congrega-tions/ccatheduc/documents/rc_con_ccatheduc_doc_20140407_educare-oggi-e-domani_en.html

Irvine, J. & Foster , M. (1996). *Growing up African American in Catholic schools.* New York: Teachers College Press.

John XXIII. (1961). *Humanae Salutis.* Pope John convokes the council Christmas day 1961: Apostolic constitution. In W. Abbott (Ed.), *The documents of Vatican II,* pp. 703–09. New York: Guild Press.

John XXIII. (1960). 30th anniversary message on the publication of the encyclical letter, *Divini Illius Magistri. Acta Apostolicae Sedis* 57, p. S9.

John, P. (1979). *Sapientia Christiana*: Apostolic constitution on ecclesiastical universities and faculties. Washington, DC: United States Catholic Conference.

John Paul II. (1990). Apostolic constitution on Catholic universities ex corde. *Acta Apostolicae Sedis* 82, pp. 1475–1509.

Lonergan, B. (1970). *Method in theology*. Toronto: University of Toronto Press.

Lynch, P. (2006). *From mandated services to mandated curriculum: Institutional isomorphism and the Catholic schools of three New York State (arch)dioceses A national study* (Unpublished doctoral dissertation). Fordham University, New York.

McAvoy, T. T. (1963). *The Americanism heresy in Roman Catholicism, 1895–1900*. Notre Dame, IN: Notre Dame Press.

McCluskey, N. G. (1968). *Catholic education faces its future*. Garden City, NY: Doubleday.

McCool, G. (Ed.). (1981). *A Rahner reader*. New York: Crossroads.

McDonald, D., & Shultz, M. (2014). *The annual statistical report on schools, enrollment and staffing*. Washington, DC: National Catholic Educational Association.

Meng, J. J. (1946). Cahenslyism: The first stages: 1883–1891. *The Catholic Historical Review*, 4, 389–413.

Metzler, M. J. (1998). *United States Catholic elementary and secondary schools 1997–98*. Washington, DC.

Morrison, P. (2002). Vatican II forty years after. *National Catholic Reporter*. Retrieved from http://natcath.org/NCR_Online/archives 2/2002d/100402/100402e.htm

National Center for Educational Statistics (2013a). Table 216.20. Number and enrollment of public elementary and secondary schools, by school level, type, and charter and magnet status: Selected years, 1990–91 through 2011–12, http://nces.ed.gov/programs/digest/d13/tables/dt13_216.20.asp

National Center for Educational Statistics (2013b). Table 216.30. Number and percentage distribution of public elementary and secondary students and schools, by traditional or charter school status and selected characteristics: Selected years, 1999–2000 through 2011, http://nces.ed.gov/programs/digest/d13/tables/dt13_216.30.asp

National Conference of Catholic Bishops. (1979). *Brothers and sisters to us: US bishops' pastoral letter on racism in our day*. Washington, DC: Catholic University Press.

National Conference of Catholic Bishops. (1995). *One family under God*. Washington, DC: Catholic University Press.

O'Gorman, Robert T. (1987). *The Church that was school: Catholic identity and Catholic education in the United States since 1790*. Catholic Education Futures Project.

O'Keefe, J. (2000). The challenge of pluralism: Articulating a rationale for religiously diverse urban Roman Catholic schools in the United States. *International Journal of Education and Religion 1*, 64–88.

O'Mally, J. W. (2010). What happened at Vatican II . Cambridge, MA: Belknap Press of Harvard University Press.

O'Mally, J. (2012). Retrieved from http://vaticaninsider.lastampa.it/en/the-vatican/detail/articolo/concilio-18819/

O'Mally, J. W. (2013, February 4). *Misdirections: Ten sure-fire ways to mix up the teachings of Vatican II*. America. http://americamagazine.org/issue/article/misdirections

Paul VI. *Gaudium et Spes* (1964, November 21). *The pastoral constitution on the church in the modern world*, Retrieved from http://www.vatican.va/archive/hist_councils/ii_vatican_council/documents/vat-ii_cons_19651207_gaudium-et-spes_en.html

Paul VI. *Lumen Gentium*, (1964, November 21). *The dogmatic constitution on the church.* http://www.vatican.va/archive/hist_councils/ii_vatican_council/documents/vat-ii_const_19641121_lumen-gentium_en.html

Paul VI. (1965, October 28). *Gravissimum Educationis*. Retrieved from http://www.vatican.va/archive/hist_councils/ii_vatican_council/documents/vatii_decl_19651028_gravissimum-educationis_en.html

Pius XI. (1930). *Divini Illius Magistri*. Acta Apostolicae Sedis 22, 49–86.

Pius XII. (1946). Allocution to the youths of Italian Catholic Action, April 20, 1946: Discourses and Radio Messages, vol. 8, pp. 53–57.

Podsiadlo, J. J., & Philliber, W. W. (2003). The nativity mission center: A successful approach to the education of Latino boys. *Journal of Education for Students Placed at Risk 8*(4), 419–28.

Reilly, D. (1944). The school controversy, 1891–1893. Washington, DC: Catholic University Press.

Ratzinger, J. (2002, January 23). *The ecclesiology of Vatican II Ratzinger*. Vatican City: *L'Osservatore Romano* Weekly Edition in English, 6.

Ratzinger, J. (1966). *Theological highlights of Vatican II*. Vatican City: Libreria Editrice Vaticana.

Redden, J., & Ryan, F. (1948). *A Catholic philosophy of education*. Washington, DC: Catholic University Press.

Ritter, J. (1964, November 17). Text of Cardinal Ritter on education draft. *Catholic News Service*. Retrieved from https://vaticaniiat50.wordpress.com/2014/11/18/text-of-cardinal-ritter-on-education-draft/

Roemer, T. (1950). *The Catholic Church in the United States*. St. Louis: Herder.

Russo, C. J. (2010). Reflections on education as a fundamental human right. *Education and Law Journal, 18*(1), 87–105.

Short, J. (1984). *An introduction to urban geography*. New York: Routledge & Kegan Paul.

Spellman, F. (1946, November 17). Text of Cardinal Spellman on education draft. *Catholic News Service*. Retrieved November 18, 2014, from https://vaticaniiat50.wordpress.com/2014/11/18/text-of-cardinal-spellman-on-education-draft/

Smith, K. (2006). *Enduring presence, evolving paradigm: Presidents' perceptions of the Nativity model of inner city Catholic education: A national study* (Unpublished doctoral dissertation). Fordham University, New York.

Tomasi, S. M., & Stibili, E. C. (1978). *Italian-Americans and religion: An annotated bibliography*. New York: Center for Migration Studies.

Tyack, D., & Hansot, E. (1982). *Managers of virtue: Public school leadership in America, 1820–1980*. New York: Basic Books.

United States Conference of Catholic Bishops. (1972). *To teach as Jesus did: A pastoral message on Catholic education*. Washington, DC: United States Catholic Conference.

Vatican II (n.d.). Voice of the Church, retrieved from http://www.vatican2voice.org/4basics/sixteen.htm

Veverka, F. (n.d.). Education 1900-1960 Catholic Philosophers of Education. http://www.talbot.edu/ce20/educators/catholic/catholic_philosophers_of_education/

Wynne, J. (Ed.). (1903). The great encyclical letters of Pope Leo XIII. New York: Benzinger.

Chapter Two

A Legal History of American Roman Catholic Schools

Charles J. Russo

INTRODUCTION

The Second Vatican Council's Declaration on Catholic Education (*Gravissimum Educationis* [*GE*], literally "the Importance of Education") was one of its crowning achievements. *GE* was promulgated in 1965, a time when American Catholic elementary and secondary schools were at about their zenith in terms of student enrollments before heading into a steady decline in numbers of institutions and enrollments.

As could have been expected, *GE* was consistent with the Church's universal teaching in recognizing education as essentially a fundamental human right. Although it was unlikely to have done so intentionally, *GE* reflects from a Catholic perspective much the same message as is contained in such secular international human rights documents as the 1948 *Universal Declaration on Human Rights*, the 1959 *Declaration on the Rights of the Child*, and the 1992 *Declaration on the Rights of Persons Belonging to National or Ethnic, Religious and Linguistic Minorities*. *GE* thus recognized the right to Christian—specifically Roman Catholic—education and the authority of parents to make such free choices for their children.

According to *GE*, "Parents who have the primary and inalienable right and duty to educate their children must enjoy true liberty in their choice of schools" (*GE*, 6). The United States Supreme Court's opinion in *Pierce v. Society of Sisters of the Holy Names of Jesus and Mary* (*Pierce*, 1925), the Justices' first case involving religion and education, predated *GE* by more than 40 years. In *Pierce* the Court upheld the rights of parents to direct the upbringing of their children, presaging later developments that impacted positively on religiously affiliated non-public educational institutions, most notably for this chapter and book, Catholic schools.

Invalidating a law from Oregon that would have obligated parents to send their children to public schools, the Court reasoned in *Pierce* that "[t]he child is not the mere creature of the state; those who nurture him and direct his destiny have the right, coupled with the high duty, to recognize and prepare him for additional obligations" (p. 535). In so ruling, the Court recognized the rights of proprietors of a Roman Catholic school and a secular military academy to operate, setting the stage for further growth and development of religiously affiliated non-public elementary and secondary schools, the vast majority of which were Roman Catholic schools.

As important as *Pierce* was, especially combined with the role religion played both in American history and education, the Supreme Court did not rely on the First Amendment Religion Clauses in the fray over religiously affiliated non-public schools until 1947 in *Everson v. Board of Education* (*Everson*). Pursuant to the Religion Clauses of the First Amendment, "Congress shall make no law regarding an establishment of religion or prohibiting the free exercise thereof." *Everson* was a dispute over the costs of transporting children to their religiously affiliated, mostly Roman Catholic, non-public schools.

Following *Everson*, the Supreme Court resolved more K–12 cases on religion under the First Amendment than any other subject involving schooling. It is important to note that insofar as the litigation involving Roman Catholic schools also impacts other religiously-affiliated non-public schools, this chapter tends to use the latter term unless a case was initially litigated in one or primarily involved Catholic institutions.

Decisions of the Supreme Court have shaped the parameters of permissible aid that the Federal and state governments can provide to Catholic, and other faith-based schools. This chapter examines its major decisions. The chapter focuses largely on Supreme Court cases involving elementary and secondary education because they served to help effectuate, albeit without intending to do so, the basic principles proclaimed in *GE*.

LEGAL PREHISTORY

The 200 Roman Catholic schools in existence in 1860 grew to more than 1,300 in the next decade. Spurred on by the 1884 Third Plenary Council of Baltimore, which mandated the creation of a parish school near every Catholic Church to serve the rapidly growing immigrant population that was largely unwelcome in many public schools, by the turn of the century almost 5,000 Catholic schools operated in the United States (Mahr, 1987). During this same time, the number of Catholics in the United States rose from

7,855,000 in 1890 to an incredible 17,735,553 in 1920 (Buetow, 1970, p. 167, as cited in the *Official Catholic Directory*).

The rapid growth in the numbers of Catholics and their schools notwithstanding, they were not involved in federal litigation until *Pierce*. At the same time, though, a small number of state cases dealt with ancillary questions as, for instance, courts in New York (*O'Connor v. Hendrick*, 1906), and Pennsylvania (*Commonwealth v. Herr*, 1910) agreed that Roman Catholic nuns could not wear religious garb if they taught in public schools.

Pierce, the first Supreme Court case implicating Roman Catholic and other religiously affiliated non-public schools, relied on the Due Process Clause of the Fourteenth Amendment rather than the Establishment Clause. Later, on entering the modern era of its Establishment Clause jurisprudence in *Everson*, the Supreme Court examined two cases that significantly impacted faith-based schools and their students. In both cases, the Court relied on the Due Process Clause of the Fourteenth Amendment rather than the Establishment Clause.

Pierce v. Society of Sisters of the Holy Names of Jesus and Mary

The more far-reaching of the Supreme Court's two early cases on religion and non-public schools was *Pierce v. Society of Sisters of the Holy Names of Jesus and Mary* (*Pierce*, 1925). In *Pierce*, the proprietors of two schools in Oregon, a Roman Catholic school and a secular school (the Hill Military Academy), challenged a voter-approved initiative enacted in 1922, intended to go into effect in 1926, that made public school attendance compulsory. The law required all students who did not need what would today be described as special education between the ages of eight and sixteen to attend public schools, unless they had already completed the eighth grade. Not surprisingly, the proprietors of the schools quickly filed a suit challenging the law as presenting a threat to the continued existence of their institutions.

After a federal trial court enjoined enforcement of the statute, the Supreme Court unanimously affirmed that enforcing the law would have seriously impaired, if not destroyed, the profitability of the schools while diminishing the value of their property. Although recognizing the power of the state "reasonably to regulate all schools, to inspect, supervise, and examine them, their teachers and pupils . . . (*Pierce*, 534)," the Court focused on the schools' property rights under the Fourteenth Amendment.

The *Pierce* Court grounded its judgment on the realization that the schools sought protection from unreasonable interference with their students and the destruction of their business and property. The Court also decided that while states may oversee such important features as health, safety, and teacher qualifications relating to the operation of non-public schools, they could not do so to an extent greater than they did for public schools.

Cochran v. Louisiana State Board of Education

Cochran v. Louisiana State Board of Education (*Cochran*, 1930) involved a state law providing free textbooks for all students in the state, regardless of where they attended school. A taxpayer unsuccessfully challenged the law on the ground that it violated the Fourteenth Amendment by taking private property through taxation for a non-public purpose. As in *Pierce*, the Supreme Court resolved the dispute based on the Due Process Clause of the Fourteenth Amendment rather than the First Amendment's Establishment Clause.

In unanimously affirming the judgment of the Supreme Court of Louisiana that insofar as the students, rather than their schools, were the beneficiaries of the law, the United States Supreme Court agreed that the statute had valid secular purpose. In so doing, the Court anticipated the Child Benefit Test that emerged in *Everson v. Board of Education* (1947). As discussed below, while the Supreme Court has consistently upheld similar textbook provisions, as reflected in the companion chapter state courts have struck them down under their own more restrictive constitutions.

STATE AID TO ROMAN CATHOLIC AND OTHER RELIGIOUSLY AFFILIATED NON-PUBLIC SCHOOLS

The Supreme Court's Establishment Clause perspective on state aid to K–12 education, sometimes referred to as "parochiaid," evolved through three phases. During the first stage, beginning with *Everson v. Board of Education* in 1947 and ending with *Board of Education of Central School District No. 1 v. Allen* in 1968, the Court created the Child Benefit Test, which allows selected forms of publicly funded aid on the ground that it helps children rather than their faith-based schools.

The span between *Lemon v. Kurtzman* in 1971 (by far the leading case on the Establishment Clause in educational settings, with the Supreme Court applying it in more than thirty of its opinions), and *Aguilar v. Felton* in 1985 was the nadir from the perspective of supporters of the Child Benefit Test. This period represented the low point because during this time the Court largely refused to move beyond the limits it initiated in *Everson* and *Allen*. In *Zobrest v. Catalina Foothills School District* in 1993, the Court resurrected the Child Benefit Test, allowing it to enter a phase that extends through the present day, in which more forms of aid have been permissible.

Given this history, the remaining sections examine major Supreme Court cases involving state aid to faith-based schools and their students, essentially in the order in which they were litigated. These sections cover transportation, textbooks, secular services and salary supplements, aid to parents (divided into tuition reimbursements and income tax returns), reimbursements to faith-based schools (covering instructional materials and support services), and vouchers.

Transportation

As noted, *Everson v. Board of Education* (1947) was the first Supreme Court case on the merits of the Establishment Clause and education. *Everson* involved a law from New Jersey permitting local school boards to enter into contracts for student transportation.

After a local board authorized reimbursement to parents for the costs of bus fare for sending their children to primarily Roman Catholic schools, a taxpayer filed suit, challenging the law as unconstitutional in two respects: first, in an approach not unlike the plaintiff's unsuccessful argument in *Cochran*, he alleged that the law authorized the state to take the money of some citizens by taxation and bestow it on others for the private purpose of supporting non-public schools in contravention of the Fourteenth Amendment; second, he charged that the statute was one "respecting an establishment of religion," since it forced him to contribute to support church schools in violation of the First Amendment.

The Supreme Court rejected the plaintiff's Fourteenth Amendment claim in *Everson* in interpreting the law as having a public purpose, adding that the First Amendment did not prohibit the state from extending general benefits to all of its citizens without regard to their religious beliefs. The Court treated student transportation as another category of public services such as police, fire, and health protection.

In what became something of a Trojan Horse because of difficulties it would create for state aid to faith-based schools, the analysis in the majority opinion was proffered by Justice Hugo Black, a former member of the Ku Klux Klan (Hamburger, 2002, p. 422). Of course, the Klan hated Catholics along with African-Americans, Jews, among others. Black introduced the Jeffersonian metaphor into the Court's First Amendment analysis, writing that "[t]he First Amendment has erected a wall between church and state. That wall must be kept high and impregnable. We could not approve the slightest breach" (*Everson*, 1947, p. 18).

Following *Everson*, states had to choose whether to provide publicly funded transportation to students who attend faith-based schools. As examined in the companion chapter, lower courts, relying on state constitutional provisions, reached mixed results on this issue.

In *Wolman v. Walter* (*Wolman*, 1977), the Supreme Court considered whether public funds could be used to provide transportation for field trips for children who attended faith-based schools in Ohio. The Court held that the practice was unconstitutional because insofar as field trips were oriented to the curriculum, they were in the category of instruction rather than that of non-ideological secular services such as transportation to and from school.

Textbooks

Board of Education of Central School District No. 1 v. Allen (*Allen*, 1968), another case involving textbooks, was litigated at the Supreme Court three years after Catholic schools reached their peak enrollments in the United States. In *Allen*, the Justices relied on the First, rather than the Fourteenth, Amendment. They essentially followed the precedent from *Cochran* in affirming the constitutionality of a statute from New York that required local school boards to loan books to children in grades seven to 12 who attended non-public schools.

The law at issue in *Allen* did not mandate that the books loaned to all students had to be the same as those used in the public schools but did require that titles be approved by local board officials before they could be adopted. Relying largely on the Child Benefit Test, the Court observed that the statute's purpose was not to aid religious or non-public schools and that its primary effect was to improve the quality of education for all children.

Other than for the delivery of special education services to individual students—as in *Zobrest v. Catalina Foothills School District* (1993)—*Allen* represented the outer limit of the Child Benefit Test for large groups of children prior to the Supreme Court's ruling in *Agostini v. Felton* (1997) discussed below. The Justices upheld like textbook provisions in *Meek v. Pittenger* (1975) and *Wolman*, both of which are also examined in more detail below.

Secular Services and Salary Supplements

The Supreme Court's most important case involving the Establishment Clause and education was *Lemon v. Kurtzman* (1971). In *Lemon*, the Court invalidated a statute from Pennsylvania calling for the purchase of secular services and a law from Rhode Island that provided salary supplements for teachers in non-public schools, most of which were Roman Catholic.

The Pennsylvania law directed the superintendent of education to purchase specified secular educational services from non-public schools. Officials directly reimbursed the non-public schools for their actual expenditures for teacher salaries, textbooks, and instructional materials. The superintendent had to approve the textbooks and materials, which were restricted to the areas of mathematics, modern foreign languages, physical science, and physical education.

In Rhode Island, officials could supplement the salaries of certificated teachers of secular subjects in non-public elementary schools by directly paying them amounts not in excess of 15% of their current annual salaries; their salaries could not exceed the maximum paid to public school teachers. The supplements were available to teachers in non-public schools where average per-pupil expenditures on secular education were less than in public schools. In addition, the teachers had to use the same materials as were used in public schools.

In striking down both laws, the Supreme Court enunciated the three-part test known as the *Lemon* test. In creating this measure, the Court added a third prong to the two-part test it created in *School District of Abington Township v. Schempp* and *Murray v. Curlett* (1963), companion cases dealing with prayer and Bible reading in public schools. This third part, which dealt with excessive entanglement, came from *Walz v. Tax Commission of New York City* (1970), which upheld New York State's practice of providing state property tax exemptions for church property that is used in worship services.

According to the *Lemon* test:

> Every analysis in this area must begin with consideration of the cumulative criteria developed by the Court over many years. Three such tests may be gleaned from our cases. First, the statute must have a secular legislative purpose; second, its principal or primary effect must be one that neither advances nor inhibits religion; finally, the statute must not foster "an excessive government entanglement with religion" (*Lemon*, 1971, 612–13).

As to entanglement and state aid to faith-based schools, the Court identified three other factors: "[W]e must examine the character and purposes of the institutions that are benefitted, the nature of the aid that the State provides, and the resulting relationship between the government and religious authority" (*Lemon*, 1971, 615).

In *Lemon* the Supreme Court maintained that aid for teachers' salaries was different from secular, neutral, or non-ideological services, facilities, or materials. Reflecting on *Allen*, the Court remarked that teachers have a substantially different ideological character than books. In terms of the potential for involving faith or morals in secular subjects, the Court feared that while the content of a textbook can be identified, how a teacher covers subject matter is not.

The *Lemon* Court added that conflict can arise when teachers who work under the direction of religious officials are faced with separating religious and secular aspects of education. The Court held that the safeguards necessary to ensure that teachers avoid non-ideological perspectives give rise to impermissible entanglement. The Court concluded that an ongoing history of government grants to non-public schools suggests that these programs were almost always accompanied by varying measures of control.

Higher Education

The Supreme Court has yet to hand down a judgment directly involving Catholic higher education. In a related development, though, on the same day that it ruled in *Lemon*, the Court upheld the constitutionality of the Higher Education Facilities Act of 1963, which made construction grants available to institutions of higher education, including church-related colleges and universities. In *Tilton v. Richardson (Tilton*, 1971), a case originating in Connecticut, the Court reasoned that while the section of the law that limited recipients' obligation not to use federally financed facilities for sectarian instruction or religious worship for 20 years unconstitutionally allowed a contribution of property of substantial value to religious bodies, that section was severable.

The Supreme Court was satisfied that the remainder of the statute in *Tilton* did not violate the First Amendment. In upholding the remainder of the statute, the Justices distinguished *Tilton* from *Lemon* insofar as in *Tilton*, indoctrination was not a substantial purpose or activity of church-related colleges because the student body was not composed of impressionable children, the aid was non-ideological, and there was no excessive entanglement since the grants were one-time and single-purpose.

Two years later, in *Hunt v. McNair* (1973), the Supreme Court decided that insofar as religion was not pervasive in an institution, South Carolina was free to issue revenue bonds to benefit the church-related college. The Court was satisfied that this arrangement was acceptable because the bonds were not guaranteed by public funds.

Aids to Parents

Tuition Reimbursement

Two months after *Lemon*, the Pennsylvania legislature enacted a statute that allowed parents whose children attended non-public schools to request tuition reimbursement. The same parent as in *Lemon* challenged the new law as having the primary effect of advancing religion.

In *Sloan v. Lemon (Sloan*, 1973) the Supreme Court affirmed that the law impermissibly singled out a class of citizens for a special economic benefit. The Justices viewed this as unlike the "indirect" and "incidental" benefits that flowed to religious schools from programs that aided all parents by supplying bus transportation and secular textbooks for their children. The Court commented that transportation and textbooks were carefully restricted to the purely secular side of church-affiliated schools and did not provide special aid to their students.

The Supreme Court expanded on *Sloan*'s analysis in a case from New York, *Committee for Public Education and Religious Liberty v. Nyquist (Ny-*

quist, 1973). The Court ruled that even though the grants went to parents rather than to school officials, this did not compel a different result. The Court explained that since parents would have used the money to pay for tuition and the law failed to separate secular from religious uses, the effect of the aid unmistakably would have provided the desired financial support for non-public schools.

In so doing, the *Nyquist* Court rejected the state's argument that parents were not simply conduits because they were free to spend the money in any manner they chose since they paid the tuition and the law merely provided for reimbursements. The Court indicated that even if the grants were offered as incentives to have parents send their children to religious schools, the law violated the Establishment Clause regardless of whether the money made its way into the coffers of the religious institutions.

Income Tax

Another section of the same New York statute in *Nyquist* aided parents via income tax benefits. Under the law, parents of children who attended non-public schools were entitled to income tax deductions as long as they did not receive tuition reimbursements under the other part of the statute. The Supreme Court invalidated this provision in pointing out that in practical terms there was little difference, for purposes of evaluating whether such aid had the effect of advancing religion, between a tax benefit and a tuition grant. The Court based its judgment on the notion that under both programs qualifying parents received the same form of encouragement and reward for sending their children to non-public schools.

In *Mueller v. Allen* (*Mueller*, 1983), the Supreme Court upheld a statute from Minnesota that granted all parents state income tax deductions for the actual costs of tuition, textbooks, and transportation associated with sending their children to K–12 schools. The law afforded all parents deductions of $500 for children in grades K–6 and $700 for those in grades 7–12.

The Justices distinguished *Mueller* from *Nyquist* primarily because the tax benefit was available to all parents, not only those whose children were in non-public schools. The Court also recognized that the deduction was one among many rather than a single, favored type of taxpayer expense.

Acknowledging the legislature's broad latitude to create classifications and distinctions in tax statutes, and that the state benefited from the scheme since it promoted an educated citizenry while reducing the costs of public education, the Supreme Court was satisfied that the law met all three of *Lemon*'s prongs. The Court paid little attention to the fact that since the state's public schools were essentially free, the expenses of parents whose children attended them were at most minimal and that about 96% of taxpayers who benefited had children enrolled in religious schools.

Reimbursements to Faith-Based Schools

On the same day that it resolved *Nyquist*, in a second case from New York, the Supreme Court applied basically the same rationale in *Levitt v. Committee for Public Education and Religious Liberty* (*Levitt*, 1973). Here the Court invalidated a law allowing the state to reimburse non-public schools for expenses incurred while administering and reporting test results as well as other records. Insofar as there were no restrictions on the use of the funds, such that teacher-prepared tests on religious subject matter were seemingly reimbursable, the Court observed that the aid had the primary effect of advancing religious education because there were insufficient safeguards in place to regulate how the monies were spent.

Wolman v. Walter (1977), a case from Ohio, saw the Supreme Court uphold a law permitting reimbursement for religious schools where officials used standardized tests and scoring services to evaluate student progress. The Justices distinguished these tests from the ones in *Levitt* since the latter were neither drafted nor scored by non-public school personnel. The Court also reasoned that the law did not authorize payments to church-sponsored schools for costs associated with administering the tests.

In *Committee for Public Education and Religious Liberty v. Regan* (1980, *Regan*) the Supreme Court reexamined another aspect of *Levitt* after the New York State legislature modified the law. Under its new provisions, the statute provided reimbursements to non-public schools for the actual costs of complying with state requirements for reporting on students and for administering mandatory and optional state-prepared examinations. Unlike the law in Ohio, this statute permitted the tests to be graded by personnel in the non-public schools that were, in turn, reimbursed for these services. The law also created accounting procedures to monitor reimbursements.

The *Regan* Court conceded that the differences between the statutes were permissible, since scoring of essentially objective tests and recording their results along with attendance data offered no significant opportunity for religious indoctrination while serving secular state educational purposes. The Court concluded that the accounting method did not create excessive entanglement since the reimbursements were equal to the actual costs.

Instructional Materials

In *Meek v. Pittenger* (1975, *Meek*), the Supreme Court examined the legality of loans of instructional materials, including textbooks and equipment, to faith-based schools in Pennsylvania. Although the Court upheld the loan of textbooks, it struck down parts of the law on periodicals, films, recordings, and laboratory equipment as well as equipment for recording and projecting; the statute had the primary effect of advancing religion due to the predominantly religious character of participating schools.

The *Meek* Court was concerned because the only statutory requirement imposed on the schools to qualify for the loans was directing their curricula to offer the subjects and activities mandated by the commonwealth's board of education. The Court thought that because the church-related schools were the primary beneficiaries, the massive aid to their educational function necessarily resulted in aid to their sectarian enterprises as a whole.

The Supreme Court reached similar results in *Wolman v. Walter* (*Wolman*, 1977), upholding a statute from Ohio which specified that textbook loans were to be made to students or their parents, rather than directly to their non-public schools. The Justices struck down a provision that would have allowed loans of instructional equipment including projectors, tape recorders, record players, maps and globes, and science kits. Echoing *Meek*, the Court invalidated the statute's authorization of the loans in light of its fear that insofar as it would be impossible to separate the secular and sectarian functions for which these items were being used, the aid inevitably provided support for the religious roles of the schools.

Mitchell v. Helms (*Helms*, 2000), a Supreme Court case originating in Louisiana, expanded the boundaries of permissible aid to faith-based schools (Mawdsley & Russo, 2001). A plurality upheld the constitutionality of chapter 2 of Title I—now Title VI—of the Elementary and Secondary Education Act (2014), a federal law that permits the loans of instructional materials including library books, computers, television sets, tape recorders, and maps to non-public schools.

In *Helms*, the Supreme Court relied on the modified *Lemon* test enunciated in *Agostini v. Felton*, discussed below, by reviewing only its first two parts while recasting entanglement as one criterion in evaluating a statute's effect. Insofar as the purpose part of the test was not challenged, the plurality only considered chapter 2's effect. They concluded that it did not foster impermissible indoctrination because aid was allocated pursuant to neutral secular criteria that neither favored nor disfavored religion and was available to all schools based on secular, nondiscriminatory grounds. In its rationale, the plurality explicitly reversed those parts of *Meek* and *Wolman* that were inconsistent with its analysis on loans of instructional materials.

Support Services

In *Meek v. Pittenger* (1975), the Supreme Court invalidated a Pennsylvania law permitting public school personnel to provide auxiliary services on-site in faith-based schools. At the same time, the Court forbade the delivery of remedial and accelerated instructional programs, guidance counseling and testing, and services to aid children who were educationally disadvantaged. The Court asserted that it was immaterial that the students would have received remedial, rather than advanced, work; the required surveillance to

ensure the absence of ideology would have given rise to excessive entanglement between church and state.

Wolman v. Walter (1977) saw the Supreme Court reach mixed results on
aid. In addition to upholding the textbook loan program, the Court allowed
Ohio to supply non-public schools with state-mandated tests while allowing
public school employees to go on-site to perform diagnostic tests to evaluate
whether students needed speech, hearing, and psychological services. The
Court also allowed public funds to be spent providing therapeutic services to
students from non-public schools as long as they were delivered off-site. The
Court forbade state officials from loaning instructional materials and equipment to schools or from using funds to pay for field trips for students in non-
public schools.

The Supreme Court's 1993 decision in *Zobrest v. Catalina Foothills
School District* (*Zobrest*) was a harbinger of change to come in its Establishment Clause jurisprudence. At issue was a school board in Arizona's refusal
to provide a sign language interpreter for a student who was deaf, under the
Individuals with Disabilities Education Act, after he transferred into a Roman Catholic high school. In a suit filed as the student entered high school
but which was resolved shortly after he graduated, the Court found that an
interpreter provided neutral aid to him without offering financial benefits to
his parents or school, and that there was no governmental participation in the
instruction because the interpreter was only a conduit to effectuate his communications.

The *Zobrest* Court relied in part on *Witters v. Washington Department of
Services for the Blind* (1986), wherein it upheld the constitutionality of extending a general vocational assistance program to a blind man who was
studying to become a clergyman at a religious college. Yet the Supreme
Court of Washington later interpreted its state constitution as forbidding such
use of public funds, and the Supreme Court refused to hear a further appeal
(*Witters v. State Commission for the Blind*, 1989).

A year later, in *Board of Education of Kiryas Joel Village School District
v. Grumet* (1994), the Supreme Court reviewed a case where the New York
State Legislature enacted a statute creating a school district with the same
boundaries as an Orthodox Jewish community. The legislature created the
district in seeking to accommodate the needs of parents of children with
disabilities who wished to send them to a nearby school that would have
honored their religious customs and beliefs, particularly with regard to die-
tary practices.

On further review of state court orders invalidating the law, the Court
affirmed that it was unconstitutional. The Supreme Court maintained that
while a state may accommodate a group's religious needs by seeking to
reduce or eliminate special burdens, it went too far. Instead, the Court sug-

gested that the board could have offered an appropriate program at one of its public schools or at a neutral site near one of the village's religious schools.

Within days after the Supreme Court struck down the statute, the New York State Legislature amended the statute in an attempt to eliminate the Establishment Clause problem. Still, New York's highest court invalidated the revised law as a violation of the Establishment Clause, insofar as it had the effect of advancing one religion (*Grumet v. Cuomo*, 1997; *Grumet v. Pataki*, 1999).

Another set of conflicts arose when officials in public and non-public schools entered into cooperative arrangements. More than a decade after the Supreme Court of Michigan upheld a state constitutional amendment on shared time, officials in Grand Rapids created an extensive program. The program grew to the point where publicly paid teachers conducted 10% of classes in religious schools. Many of them worked in the religious schools. After the Sixth Circuit invalidated the plan, in *School District of City of Grand Rapids v. Ball (Ball*, 1985), the Supreme Court affirmed that the released time program was unconstitutional because it failed all three prongs of the *Lemon* test.

On the same day that it resolved *Ball*, in a more far-reaching case, the Supreme Court reviewed a dispute from New York City. In *Aguilar v. Felton (Aguilar*, 1985), the Justices considered whether public school teachers could provide remedial instruction under Title I of the Elementary and Secondary Education Act of 1965 (1965)—enacted the same year as *Gravissimum Educationis* was promulgated—in religiously affiliated non-public schools. The Title I provision of the Act, which passed with considerable support from Catholic leaders in particular (Buetow, 1970), was designed for specifically targeted children, who were educationally disadvantaged, on-site in their faith-based schools.

In *Aguilar v. Felton (Aguilar*, 1985), the Supreme Court affirmed earlier orders that the program permitting the on-site delivery of services to children in their religiously affiliated non-public schools, the vast majority of which were Roman Catholic, was unconstitutional. Even though the New York City Board of Education (NYCBOE) developed safeguards to ensure that public funds were not spent for religious purposes, the Court struck the program down based on the fear that a monitoring system to have avoided the creation of an impermissible relationship between Church and state might have resulted in the presence of excessive entanglement under the third prong of the *Lemon* test.

Twelve years later, in *Agostini v. Felton (Agostini*, 1997), the Supreme Court took the unusual step of dissolving the injunction that it upheld in *Aguilar* (Russo & Osborne, 1997). The Court reasoned that the Title I program did not violate the *Lemon* test since there was no governmental indoctrination, there were no differences between recipients based on religion, and there was no excessive entanglement. The Court thus ruled that a federally funded program that provides supplemental, remedial instruction and counseling services to disadvantaged children on a neutral basis is not invalid under the Establishment Clause when the assistance is provided on-site in faith-based schools pursuant to a program containing safeguards such as those that the NYCBOE implemented. Perhaps the most important outcome in *Agostini* was the Court's having modified the *Lemon* test by reviewing only its first two prongs, purpose and effect, while recasting entanglement as one criterion in evaluating a statute's effect.

Vouchers

Considerable controversy has arisen over the use of vouchers, with courts reaching mixed results in disputes over their constitutionality. Still, the only Supreme Court case on vouchers arose in Ohio. The Ohio General Assembly, acting pursuant to a desegregation order, enacted the Ohio Pilot Project Scholarship Program (OPPSP) to assist children in Cleveland's failing public schools. The main goal of the OPPSP was to permit an equal number of students to receive vouchers and tutorial assistance grants while attending regular public schools. Another part of the law provided greater choices to parents and children via the creation of community, or charter, schools and magnet schools. A third section featured tutorial assistance for children.

The Supreme Court of Ohio upheld the OPPSP but severed the part of the law affording priority to parents who belonged to a religious group supporting a sectarian institution (*Simmons-Harris v. Goff*, 1999). Moreover, in finding that the OPPSP violated the state constitutional requirement that every statute have only one subject, the court struck it down. Still, when the court stayed enforcement of its order to avoid disrupting the then-current school year, the Ohio General Assembly quickly reenacted a revised statute.

After lower federal courts, relying largely on *Nyquist* (1973), enjoined the operation of the revised statute as a violation of the Establishment Clause, the Supreme Court agreed to hear an appeal. In *Zelman v. Simmons-Harris (Zelman*, 2002), the Court reversed the judgment of the Sixth Circuit and upheld the constitutionality of the OPPSP (Russo & Mawdsley, 2002).

Relying on *Agostini*, the *Zelman* Court began by conceding the lack of a dispute over the program's valid secular purpose in providing programming for poor children in a failing school system. The Court examined whether it had the forbidden effect of advancing or inhibiting religion. The Court upheld the voucher program because as part of the state's far-reaching attempt to provide greater educational opportunities in a failing school system, the law allocated aid on the basis of neutral secular criteria that neither favored nor disfavored religion, was made available to both religious and secular beneficiaries on a nondiscriminatory basis, and offered assistance directly to a broad class of citizens who directed the aid to religious schools based entirely on their own genuine and independent private choices.

The *Zelman* Court was not concerned by the fact that most of the partici-pating schools were faith-based because parents chose to send their children to them insofar as surrounding public schools refused to take part in the program. If anything, the Court acknowledged that most of the children attended the religiously affiliated non-public schools, most of which were Roman Catholic, not as a matter of law but because they were unwelcomed in the public schools. The Court concluded that insofar as it was following an unbroken line of its own precedent supporting true private parental choice that provided benefits directly to a wide range of needy private individuals, its only choice was to uphold the voucher program.

CONCLUSION

Roman Catholic schools clearly have the legal right to operate but face an increasingly uncertain future in the face of declining enrollments due to a variety of factors beyond the scope of this chapter. Even so, as with most issues involving the law, the one thing to be sure of is that litigation will continue over the status of aid to Catholic schools, their students, and par-ents.

The extent to which aid may be available to Catholic schools of all levels depends on a combination of legislative action and judicial interpretation by the Supreme Court which, as demonstrated, has gone through three distinct periods of greater or lesser support for the schools. Whether the Court is willing to continue to support aid to Roman Catholic and other religiously affiliated non-public schools bears constant watching.

REFERENCES

Agostini v. Felton, 521 U.S. 203 (1997).
Aguilar v. Felton, 473 U.S. 402 (1985).
Board of Education of Central School District No. 1 v. Allen, 392 U.S. 236 (1968).
Board of Education of Kiryas Joel Village School District v. Grumet, 512 U.S. 687 (1994).
Buetow, H. A. (1970). *Of singular benefit: The story of Catholic education in the United States.* London: The Macmillan Company.
Cantwell v. Connecticut, 310 U.S. 296 (1940).
Cochran v. Louisiana State Board of Education, 281 U.S. 370 (1930).
Committee for Public Education and Religious Liberty v. Nyquist, 413 U.S. 756 (1973).
Committee for Public Education and Religious Liberty v. Regan, 444 U.S. 646 (1980).
Commonwealth v. Herr, 78 A. 68 (Pa. 1910).
Declaration on the Rights of Persons Belonging to National or Ethnic, Religious and Linguistic Minorities. (1992). Retrieved from http://www.un.org/documents/ga/res/47/a47r135.htm
Declaration on the Rights of the Child. (1959). Retrieved from http://www.un.org/cyberschool-bus/humanrights/resources/child.asp
Elementary and Secondary Education Act (Chapter 2), 20 U.S.C.A. §§ 7301–73 (2014).

Engel v. Vitale, 370 U.S. 421 (1962).

Everson v. Board of Education, 330 U.S. 1 (1947), *reh'g denied*, 330 U.S. 855 (1947).

Grumet v. Cuomo, 659 N.Y.S.2d 173 (N.Y.1997)

Grumet v. Pataki, 697 N.Y.S.2d 846 (N.Y.1999), *cert. denied*, 528 U.S. 946 (1999).

Hamburger, P. (2002). Separation of church and state. Cambridge: MA: Harvard University Press.

Hunt v. McNair, 413 U.S. 734 (1973).

Individuals with Disabilities Education Act, 20 U.S.C.A. §§ 1400 *et seq.* (2010).

Lemon v. Kurtzman, 403 U.S. 602 (1971).

Levitt v. Committee for Public Education and Religious Liberty, 413 U.S. 472 (1973).

Mawdsley, R.D. & Russo, C.J. (2001). *Mitchell v. Helms*: The Court charts new ground on state aid to religious schools. *Journal of Research in Christian Education, Vol. 10, No. 1*, 117–41.

Meek v. Pittenger, 421 U.S. 349 (1975).

Mahr, M. (Ed.). (1987). *NCEA/Ganley's Catholic schools in America*. Montrose, Colo.: Fisher Publishing Co.

Mitchell v. Helms, 530 U.S. 793 (2000), *reh'g denied*, 530 U.S. 1296 (2000), *on remand sub nom. Helms v. Picard*, 229 F.3d 467 (5th Cir. 2000).

Mueller v. Allen, 463 U.S. 388 (1983).

O'Connor v. Hendrick, 77 N.E. 612 (N.Y. 1906).

Pope Paul VI. (1965, October 28). *Gravissimum Educationis.* Retrieved October 9, 2014, from http://www.vatican.va/archive/hist_councils/ii_vatican_council/documents/va-tii_decl_19651028_gravissimum-educationis_en.html

Pierce v. Society of Sisters of the Holy Names of Jesus and Mary, 268 U.S. 510 (1925).

Russo, C. J., & Mawdsley, R.D. (2002). Equal educational opportunities and parental choice: The Supreme Court upholds the Cleveland voucher program. *Education Law Reporter, Vol. 169, No. 2*, 485–504.

School District of Abington Township v. Schempp and *Murray v. Curlett*, 374 U.S. 203 (1963).

Russo, C. J. & Osborne, A.G. (1997). *Agostini v. Felton*: Is the demise of the ghoul at hand? *Education Law Reporter, Vol. 116, No. 2*, 515–29.

School District of City of Grand Rapids v. Ball, 473 U.S. 373 (1985).

Simmons-Harris v. Goff, 711 N.E.2d 203 (Ohio 1999).

Sloan v. Lemon, 413 U.S. 825 (1973).

Tilton v. Richardson, 403 U.S. 672 (1971),

Universal Declaration on Human Rights. (1948). Retrieved from http://www.un.org/en/documents/udhr/

Walz v. Tax Commission of New York City, 397 U.S. 664 (1970).

Witters v. State Commission for the Blind, 771 P.2d 1119 (Wash. 1989), *cert. denied*, 493 U.S. 850 (1989).

Witters v. Washington Department of Services for the Blind, 474 U.S. 481 (1986).

Wolman v. Walter, 433 U.S. 229 (1977).

Zelman v. Simmons-Harris, 536 U.S. 639 (2002).

Zobrest v. Catalina Foothills School District, 509 U.S. 1 (1993).

Chapter Three

Church Documents

Vatican and US since Vatican II

John Mary Fleming

CATHOLIC EDUCATION: A BALANCE
OF THE OLD AND THE NEW

Jesus said to his disciples, "Every scribe who has been instructed in the kingdom of heaven is like the head of a household who brings from his storeroom both the new and the old" (Matt 13:52, New American Bible Revised Edition). Documents on Catholic education since *Gravissimum Educationis* have sought to encourage and inspire this balance of old and new. While looking to the past and holding on to fundamental principles, Catholic educators must also learn how to apply these principles to present situations as they look forward toward a constantly changing future. In order to face this challenge, it is necessary to know what the Church has said in relation to Catholic education and to draw out the fundamental themes that she has repeated in these documents over the past 50 years.

The following discussion presents a brief overview of the major educational documents released by the Magisterium beginning with *Gravissimum Educationis* and ending with the recent document *Educating Today and Tomorrow: A Renewing Passion*. The chapter next reflects on the four principle themes woven throughout the documents: parental rights, the role of community, the changing face of Catholic educators, and the shift from optimism to a guarded realism.

PART I: *GRAVISSIMUM EDUCATIONIS*

During the final week of October 1965, Pope Paul VI promulgated the Declaration on Christian Education, *Gravissimum Educationis* (*GE*). Among the three declarations from the Council, the other two being *Nostra Aetate* (on the relation of the Church to non-Christian religions) and *Dignitatis Humanae* (on religious freedom), *Gravissimum Educationis* stands out as a statement of principles for implementation and development of education in the practical sphere.

GE highlights the fact that education is more available and also more necessary today than ever. Committed to the entire person, as reflected in *GE*, the Church takes interest in "the progress and development of education" (Introduction, para. 4). Moreover, in laying out twelve fundamental principles for Catholic education, this document serves as the mission statement for Catholic education, then and now.

The Twelve Principles

Gravissimum Educationis' first principle is the universal right to an education: "All men of every race, condition and age, since they enjoy the dignity of a human being, have an inalienable right to an education" (*GE* 1). Within this principle the twofold goal of education is enunciated: to direct human persons to their ultimate end and to prepare them for participation in society.

Education is thus essential for both supernatural and natural ends, the supernatural end being Heaven and the natural end being threefold: the development of physical, moral, and intellectual endowments; the fostering of human maturity in all its aspects, which includes the pursuit of true freedom, a sense of responsibility, and positive and prudent sexual education; and adequate training for and promotion of the common good of society.

The second principle in *Gravissimum Educationis* addresses Christian education. According to Church teachings, all baptized Christians have a right to an education into the mysteries and practices of the Christian faith, through personal maturation and liturgical action, growing individually and as members of the body of Christ. Catechetical instruction is primary in educating people in the liturgical and intellectual aspects of the faith, and there are many aids to Christian education including many new forms of media and social associations which offer extrascholastic venues for faith education. The importance of schools as identified in *GE* highlights the special role that formal educational institutions serve.

GE's third principle focuses on the authors of education. Parents are the primary teachers of the "first school," which is the family. The family is assisted by the larger social and civic community. The Church assists in a special way, having a compelling interest in the education of the young "because she has the responsibility of announcing the way of salvation to all men" (*GE* 3).

Gravissimum Educationis clearly expounds the distinction and interplay between the different roles in the community in relation to the education of children. "Parents who have the primary and inalienable right and duty to educate their children must enjoy true liberty in their choice of schools" (*GE* 6). *GE* also calls on states to respect the rightful subsidiarity of parents in choosing the means of education for their children, going so far as declaring that to deny this right is to oppose human dignity.

GE makes it clear that this right of the parents applies most especially with regard to the moral and religious education of the child. This dimension of education embraces all who choose Catholic schools for their children, including those from different faith traditions. Further, in keeping with the respect for parental responsibility, the Church understands the varying religious expectations of non-Catholic families participating in the school system.

The final principles dealt with specifically Catholic institutions at various levels. The document recognizes that the Church respects the similarities and differences between Catholic and non-Catholic schools:

> No less than other schools does the Catholic school pursue cultural goals and the human formation of youth. But its proper function is to create for the school community a special atmosphere animated by the Gospel spirit of freedom and charity, to help youth grow according to the new creatures they were made through baptism as they develop their own personalities, and finally to order the whole of human culture to the news of salvation so that the knowledge the students gradually acquire of the world, life and man is illumined by faith. (*GE* 8)

Gravissimum Educationis highlights the different types of Catholic schools and their importance as formal institutions of learning. *GE* makes special note of factors that affect schools, such as their local situations, their school populations, and the potential need to develop non-standard schools for technical, professional, special, and religious education.

In this way, *GE* acknowledges that schools are "designed not only to develop with special care the intellectual faculties but also to form the ability to judge rightly, to hand on the cultural legacy of previous generations, to foster a sense of values, to prepare for professional life" (*GE* 5). The Catholic school prepares students for both earthly and heavenly citizenship, training them to be "a saving leaven in the human community" (*GE* 8). Therefore, in accord with the provisions of *GE*, parents have a duty to send their children to and support Catholic schools. In addition, *GE* calls on pastors to do their part in supporting Catholic schools, especially with regard to the poor in their communities.

Gravissimum Educationis makes it clear that officials at Catholic colleges and universities should stress the balance between scholarly and methodological autonomy with the need for Catholic integration at all levels. In this regard, *GE* holds up the work of St. Thomas Aquinas as a model of this fusion of faith and reason with the goal of influencing society. At the same time, *GE* requests that Catholic faculties or chairs be present at all Catholic universities, as well as calling for centers for Catholic students at non-Catholic institutions as necessary tools to assist in faith formation.

GE specifies that faculties of sacred sciences should be designed to pursue their endeavors zealously, conscientiously training priests and future theological educators. As such, the document anticipates a tendency to compartmentalize disciplines and emphasizes the importance of cooperation in the educational world. If anything, GE includes a call for coordination to be fostered in scholastic matters within schools and among other educational institutions.

Gravissimum Educationis concludes with a plea to young people to "become aware of the importance of the work of education and to prepare themselves to take it up, especially where because of a shortage of teachers the education of youth is in jeopardy" (*GE* 12). It also reminds all teachers of two global goals of education: the renewal not only of the Church but also of the world.

Looking Back and Moving Forward

Gravissimum Educationis is ambitious. Building on important Council themes, especially the universal dignity of man and the right to religious liberty, *GE* calls for a greater responsiveness to the changing conditions of the modern world. In fact, *GE* reaffirms the fundamental rights of parents as primary educators and the fundamental right to the freedom to choose Christian education for their children, regardless of state educational systems. In this way, *GE* provides a charter for all future Church educational documents, laying the foundational principles that animate magisterial teaching on education developed in its wake.

PART II: THE CONGREGATION FOR CATHOLIC EDUCATION

The Congregation for Studies at the University of Rome, established in 1588 by Pope Sixtus V, developed in size and scope until 1988, when Pope John Paul II renamed it the Congregation of Catholic Education. Following the Second Vatican Council, the Congregation for Catholic Education began to address explicitly the principles and themes introduced in *Gravissimum Educationis*. The documents produced by this Congregation are numerous and varied in scope. These following six, all of which are reviewed, are of particular importance:

- *The Catholic School* (1977)
- *Lay Catholics in Schools* (1982)
- *The Religious Dimension of Education in a Catholic School* (1988)
- *The Catholic School on the Threshold of the Third Millennium* (1997)
- *Consecrated Persons and Their Mission in Schools* (2002)
- *Educating Today and Tomorrow: A Renewing Passion* (2014).

The Catholic School (1977)

The focus of the Congregation of Catholic Education in *The Catholic School* (*CS*) is the role of education in the preaching mission of the Church. The importance of *CS* is the way in which it reaffirmed that the educational aims of the Catholic school perform "an essential and unique service for the Church herself" (*CS* 15).

CS describes Catholic schools as first and foremost as an element of the salvific mission of the Church: "Schools are a privileged means of promoting the formation of the whole man, since the school is a center in which a specific concept of the world, of man, and of history is developed and conveyed" (CS 8). *CS* adds that Catholic schools promote a Christian mentality amidst the growing pluralism of modern society.

At the same time, *CS* explains that this counterculturalism is not without particular dangers, such as a misunderstanding of the Catholic school's educational aims by society, which leads to economic discrimination and insufficient support. This is unfortunate because Catholic schools are not solely aimed at religious instruction; they seek rather to inculcate a "complete Christian formation," one that is "of special significance today because of the inadequacy of the family and society" (*CS* 45). This formation is practical as well as intellectual.

Picking up the principle of the importance of the community in education from *Gravissimum Educationis*, *The Catholic School* further develops the idea that schools provide a *community* wherein students learn to live out Gospel values for the enrichment of society, especially the poor left to the machinations of public institutions. *CS* highlights that the community is the locus of education.

How, though, is this vision of complete formation carried out in Catholic schools? Catholic schools complete this vision largely through the witness of teachers, especially the significant number of lay teachers, called into duty at the same time the Church witnessed declining religious vocations. However, teachers, are not alone, insofar as "it is the task of the whole educative community to ensure that a distinctive Christian educational environment is maintained in practice" (CS 73).

CS makes it clear that parents are primary agents in education, with teachers sharing in this role; teachers and parents work together with all "who are building a new world—one which is freed from a hedonistic mentality and from the efficiency syndrome of modern consumer society" (CS 91). Still, teachers serve as witnesses and bearers of the integrity of the purpose and mission of Catholic schools. In sum, *The Catholic School* signals a change in tone from the optimistic tone of the council document, *Gravissimum Educationis*, to a more muted one recognizing the dangers present in modern society.

Lay Catholics in Schools: Witnesses to Faith (1982)

In 1982 the Congregation of Catholic Education released *Lay Catholics in Schools* (*LCS*), declaring that "lay Catholics, both men and women, who devote their lives to teaching in primary and secondary schools, have become more and more vitally important in recent years" (*LCS* 1). The document acknowledges an array of reasons for the demographic shift in the Catholic landscape, such as greater access to education, technological and scientific advances, and a decline in vocations to the priesthood and religious life (*LCS* 3).

The changes in demographics have many causes. Even so, *LCS* begins with a theological one: "The most basic reason for this new role for Catholic laity, a role which the Church regards as positive and enriching, is theological. Especially in the course of the last century, the authentic image of the laity within the People of God has become increasingly clear" (*LCS* 2).

LCS makes it clear that the contribution of the laity is essential: "The evangelization of the world involves an encounter with such a wide variety and complexity of different situations that very frequently, in concrete circumstances and for most people, only the laity can be effective witnesses of the Gospel" (LCS 9). Additionally, *LCS* portrays lay teachers as extensions of the family in education, with parental primacy of education partly fulfilled in lay teachers' participation (*LCS* 13). *LCS* adds that numerous benefits from this extension follow, especially in cultural terms because lay people are not only transmitters of culture, but also its producers (*LCS* 20).

LCS points out that the community aspect develops through this cultural transmission, with Catholic schools flourishing as mission bases to the world. Through their participation in Catholic education, then, *LCS* views the laity as exercise both a profession and a vocation: "The life of the Catholic teacher must be marked by the exercise of a personal vocation in the Church, and not simply by the exercise of a profession" (*LCS* 37). To *LCS*, this is a key to the unique value of the Catholic school environment.

According to *Lay Catholics in Schools*, lay people have much to offer in Catholic education, and in order to fulfill properly their vocations, they should receive appropriate professional training and ongoing formation. Here *LCS* recognizes that the years of experience passed down through religious educators are no longer available (*LCS* 12). *LCS* goes on to explain that training must include both technical and personal aspects because formation does not lie merely in skills acquisition, but involves the spiritual development of the whole person.

In noting the predominance of lay teachers in schools, *LCS* reminds readers that the value of consecrated persons must not be forgotten or overlooked: "Lay Catholic educators must be very aware of the real impoverishment which will result if priests and religious disappear from the Catholic schools, or noticeably decline in number" (*LCS* 45).

As the shadows from *Gravissimum Educationis* lengthen, *Lay Catholics in Schools* notes that the role of lay Catholics in schools becomes increasingly important. In fact, in a short span of time the majority of teachers shifted from religious to lay. While *The Catholic School* had focused on external threats to Catholic education, *Lay Catholics in Schools* addresses the internal challenges, specifically the loss of identity and mission. As such, *LCS* exhorts lay Catholics to see their teaching as a vocation in need of constant professional and spiritual renewal.

The Religious Dimension of Education in a Catholic School (1988)

In 1988 the Congregation for Catholic Education released *The Religious Dimension of Education in a Catholic School: Guidelines for Reflection and Renewal* (*RDCS*). *RDCS* remains a critically important document because it offers a timeless reflection on the nature and purpose of Catholic schools by focusing on four key areas: the educational climate, the personal development of each student, the relationship established between culture and the Gospel, and the illumination of all knowledge in the light of faith (*RDCS* 1).

The Religious Dimensions of a Catholic School gives breadth and depth to a reflection about the challenges and concerns associated with maintaining the integrity of a Catholic school education with a decidedly international sensitivity. *RDCS* is pragmatic and practical in its focus in providing a framework for Catholic educators by reviewing the fundamental points about the nature and purpose of Catholic schools, such as school culture, educational goals, guidelines and curriculum, formation of teachers, religious instruction, and ecclesial and educational climate of the school.

At the time of *RDCS*' publication, the Congregation asked local ordinaries and superiors of religious congregations to "bring these reflections to the attention of all teachers and directors of Catholic schools" (*RDCS* 113). In so doing, the Congregation encouraged study, research, and experimentation in all areas that affect religious dimensions of education in a Catholic school. The Congregation also recognized that society was changing and that some schools enjoy religious freedom to integrate the academic and religious dimensions of the school, while other schools are in societies that view the instruction solely from an academic standpoint and find the school's religious dimension a cause for conflict.

The Catholic School on the Threshold of the Third Millennium (1997)

On the eve of the turn of the century, the Congregation on Catholic Education released *The Catholic School on the Threshold of the Third Millennium* (*TTM*). "On the threshold of the third millennium education faces new challenges which are the result of a new socio-political and cultural context" (*TTM* 1). *TTM* made it clear that dangerous realities in the world abound for Catholic schools: a crisis of values, subjectivism, moral relativism, and nihilism. Therefore, a "courageous renewal on the part of the Catholic school" (*TTM* 3) is needed, and there is a history of success in Catholic education involving "the evangelizing mission of the Church throughout the world, including those areas in which no other pastoral work is possible" (*TTM* 5).

As the Church looked at a new century, *The Catholic School on the Threshold of the Third Millennium* again placed the focus of education on the whole person: "The person of each individual human being, in his or her material and spiritual needs, is at the heart of Christ's teaching: this is why the promotion of the human person is the goal of the Catholic school" (*TTM* 9). For *TTM*, Catholic education is holistic; it is integrated as it avoids the compartmentalization of a relativistic interpretation of education. *TTM* in this way warns against the fragmentation of education, generic character values, false neutrality, and an "easy consensus at the price of a dangerous obscuring of content" (*TTM* 10).

While the over-specialization and hypertechnologization of modern society seek to segregate man from himself and others, *The Catholic School on the Threshold of the Third Millennium* serves as a reminder that Catholic schools provide the integral key to humanity: the person of Christ.

For *TTM*, personal formation always occurs in a communal context, connected with the Church through both ecclesial and cultural dimensions. "While respecting individual roles, the community dimension should be fostered, since it is one of the most enriching developments for the contemporary school" (*TTM* 18). This communitarian and personalistic aspect highlighted in *The Catholic School on the Threshold of the Third Millennium* is a theological and moral foundation of which teachers are reminded that they do not "write on inanimate material, but on the very spirits of human beings" (*TTM* 19).

Consecrated Persons and Their Mission in Schools (2002)

Twenty years after addressing the demographic shift in Catholic education in *Lay Catholics in Schools,* the Church turned its gaze toward the presence and purpose of consecrated persons in Catholic education in *Consecrated Persons and Their Mission in Schools* (*CP*).

CP unequivocally stipulates that if the profile of consecrated men and women is Christ, then the consecrated life is an education by Christ (*CP* 9): "The life of a consecrated person is therefore an *educational-formative* rise and fall that educates to the truth of life and forms it to the freedom of the gift of oneself, according to the model of the Easter of the Lord" (*CP* 9). This education enables consecrated persons "to promote human and spiritual bonds that promote the mutual exchange of gifts between all the members of the people of God" (*CP* 17).

Consecrated men and women in Catholic schools are thus called to be promoters of community, accompaniment, communion, and witness. "Whatever their specific task, the presence of consecrated persons in schools *infects* the contemplative glance by educating to a silence that leads to listening to God, to paying attention to others, to the situation that surrounds us, to creation" (*CP* 24).

As reflected in *CP*, consecrated persons play a decisive role in evangelization and both the vertical and horizontal dimensions of relation. Evangelically, consecrated persons offer lived examples of the Church's witness to the world, a witness that *Gravissimum Educationis* declares vital to Catholic education.

Continuing to develop the theme of community, *CP* comments on how consecrated persons guide student formation along the two great commandments: love of God and of neighbor. Vertically, for *CP*, consecrated persons offer testimony to the existential dimensions of life, asking questions of God and meaning (*CP* 50) alongside the promotion of a new culture of vocations (*CP* 56).

Horizontally, *CP* addresses how consecrated persons promote the maturity and growth of the moral responsibility in each student, actively modeling this responsibility in their consecrated life and observance. In particular, *CP* highlights how consecrated persons live out the fundamental difference and equality of men and women as the paradigm for all relationships, with special promotion of the "feminine genius" for all parts of society. In sum, for *CP*, consecrated persons have a prophetic task: forming community in schools for students and society.

Educating Today and Tomorrow: A Renewing Passion (2014)

Most recently in 2014, the Congregation published *Educating Today and Tomorrow: A Renewing Passion* (*ETT*). *ETT* offers summary reflections from two meetings celebrating the fiftieth anniversary of *Gravissimum Educationis* and the twenty-fifth anniversary of *Ex Corde Ecclesiae*. In contrast to the early educational documents, *ETT* begins with the "educational emergency" disrupting the development of individuals as well as the common good (Introduction, para. 1).

ETT recognizes the achievements in Catholic education up to the present, especially the contributions of Pope Saint John Paul II, but focuses on reaffirming the essentials. In other words, *ETT* zeroes in on both *what* one learns as well as *how* one learns it, expressed especially through the teacher-student relationship. *ETT* reaffirms the necessities of both personal and professional training for teachers, who offer a new model of holistic community to students while fighting the ever-decaying moral norms of modern society.

At the heart of this reformation in *ETT* is Christ: "Everything that happens in Catholic schools and universities should lead to an encounter with the living Christ" (*ETT* intro). In this way, *ETT* calls for redefinition of the vision of education in the face of challenges to Catholic identity, community, and dialogue with others. Specific to higher education, *ETT* identifies the challenges of new modes of schooling, internationalization of studies, and online resources.

If Catholic schools are to be important in today's society, then *ETT* exhorts educators to take these challenges as opportunities for growth and development. In fact, *ETT* declares that Catholic education today may need to look very different for tomorrow. Perhaps with an eye to past failures, ETT adds that these changes need to be appropriately timed because a society demanding quantitative results must learn that "real changes usually take a long time to happen" (*ETT* concl.).

PART III: THE UNITED STATES
CONFERENCE OF CATHOLIC BISHOPS

In the years since Vatican Council II, the United States Conference of Catholic Bishops (USCCB) has released its own educational documents. The two most notable of these documents are *To Teach as Jesus Did* (1972) and *Renewing Our Commitment to Catholic Elementary and Secondary Schools in the Third Millennium* (2005).

To Teach as Jesus Did (1972)

The American bishops issued their own response to *Gravissimum Education-is* in 1972: *To Teach as Jesus Did* (*TTJD*). This lengthy document confidently lays out principles for Catholic education, "one of the most important ways by which the Church fulfills its commitment to the dignity of the person and the building of community" (*TTJD* 13). *TTJD* announces a renewed vision of education around three points: message, community, and service. As seen throughout *TTJD* and the other Church documents, once again community surfaces as critical among the three elements of education.

TTJD proclaims the Gospel message of Christ as the foundation of Catholic education, specifying that the need for Christian identity in Catholic schools cannot be overlooked. Yet *TTJD* adds that this message must find its way in new and changing circumstances; content is eternal, but form and mode of presentation need to fit the culture in which it is proclaimed. If this enculturation is done correctly, *TTJD* declares that it can create vibrant, healthy, faith-filled communities. "Community is at the heart of Christian education not simply as a concept to be taught but as a reality to be lived" (*TTJD* 23). Education for *TTJD*, then, is about formation and discipleship, beginning with basic friendship and family structures and affecting ever broader sectors of society through a renewed participation in the political community. Further. *TTJD* views education as the vehicle for the transmission *of* a message, *to* a community, *for* service, service flowing directly from the new community amidst a people in need of help, amidst a society where faith, values, and cultures are being daily destroyed.

These three elements find practical implementation in the work of education, according to *To Teach as Jesus Did*, especially the development of continuing and adult programs of formation, so necessary in the constantly changing modern world. In this way, *TTJD* sees family education as important as well, with the rights of parents as primary educators being shared with teachers in schools. Here *TTJD* emphasizes a shared role between parents and teachers, pointing to the changing and challenging conditions of modern society and acknowledging that parents simply cannot fulfill their role without assistance, especially in religious, academic, and social instruction.

To Teach as Jesus Did was aware that Catholic lower and higher education is in need of revision and reorganization, with an emphasis on community as well as the autonomy of various disciplines within higher education. "Christian education will best be realized by programs which create the widest opportunities for students to receive systematic catechesis, experience daily living in a faith community, and develop commitment and skill in serving others" (*TTJD* 83). Moreover, *TTJD* accepts that all of these developments must be carried out with an aim toward mission: the modern world is in need of the message of Christ, and Catholic education is one of the Church's best instruments of its proclamation.

Renewing Our Commitment to Catholic Elementary and Secondary Schools in the Third Millennium (2005)

After more than thirty years of experience and reflection, the American bishops released another document on education in 2005, *Renewing Our Commitment to Catholic Elementary and Secondary Schools in the Third Millennium (ROC)*. Not surprisingly, this later intervention offers a more sober and cautious reflection on education in modern society. The optimism of early documents gives way to more guarded guidance in *ROC*.

Perhaps the most significant development in *Renewing Our Commitment* is the addition of a fourth element to the education triplet: alongside message, community, and service is placed worship. The liturgical formation of students, teaching them how to offer thanks and praise to God, balances out the service-oriented dimensions of education in *ROC*. As described in *ROC*, action in response to proclamation takes place on both vertical and horizontal dimensions, a dual emphasis mirroring the reflections of *Consecrated Persons and Their Mission in Schools*.

As promulgated in *ROC*, Catholic education must be affordable, accessible, and available to the widest population; the bishops promise to work diligently to make this a reality. Further, in *ROC* education is again seen as an extension of the primary role of parents, but this time the emphasis is on parental school choice as parents exercise their right to educate by sending their children to Catholic schools. *ROC* maintains the community that is a part of Catholic education offers an effective contribution to the harmonization of diverse populations in society, a reality that is especially the case for the growing Latino/Hispanic population who need help in social integration; Catholic education therefore offers an invaluable service to society.

These positive dimensions described in *ROC* are balanced with the serious challenges of the new millennium. *ROC* concedes that the increased diversity of people and cultures can create tensions and trials in social coherence even as the loss of religious educators through the presence of consecrated persons in the schools is particularly devastating. Without the witness of consecrated persons, *ROC* fears that the Catholic identity in many schools is weakened. Consequently, *ROC* highlights the increasing need for more programs and formation options for lay teachers if schools are to remain intentionally and intensely Catholic. For *ROC*, the internal challenge of the formation of teachers and administrators in schools—in a word, the next generation of leaders—may outweigh any external threat of diversity and economic discrimination.

PART IV: *EX CORDE ECCLESIAE*
AND CATHOLIC HIGHER EDUCATION

In describing the mission and values of Catholic higher education and requiring loyalty to the Magisterium in terms of the *mandatum* necessary to teach theology in a Catholic faculty, Pope Saint John Paul II's *Ex Corde Ecclesiae* (*ECE*) is the most significant and controversial contribution to the Church's thought on Catholic higher education.

Ex Corde Ecclesiae (1990)

As described in *ECE*, the importance of Catholic higher education could not be clearer: "Born from the heart of the Church, a Catholic University is located in that course of tradition which may be traced back to the very origin of the University as an institution" (*ECE* 1). Per *ECE*, the Catholic University combines a search for truth with certainty about the source of all truth, it consecrates itself to "the cause of truth" (*ECE* 4).

Four marks or essential characteristics of the Catholic University are outlined in *Ex Corde* are: Christian inspiration of individuals and community, continuous reflection in the light of Catholic faith on the growing knowledge of the world, fidelity to the Christian message from the Church, and an institutional commitment to serve the people of God and the whole human family (*ECE* 13). Inspiration, knowledge, fidelity, and service, then, are the marks for Catholic higher education.

But what makes a university Catholic? With theology providing the unity of disciplines, *ECE* believes that it is this integration of faith *and* reason alongside ethical and theological perspectives in all fields that makes up the identity of a truly Catholic University (*ECE* 15–17). For *ECE*, this unity of disciplines, of faith and reason, of human and divine, creates an orchestral harmony.

As proclaimed in *ECE*, there must be explicit fidelity and commitment to the Church's Magisterium on the part of Catholic theology teachers. For *ECE*, intentions are made concrete in words of affirmation through the *mandatum* given by local bishops to all who are teaching in the theology faculty. Pursuant to *ECE*, the faithful and those who are faithfully seeking must be taught by professors who are faithful to the truths of the Catholic faith in a Catholic University.

ECE views this uniting of the academic with the ecclesial as having a purpose: to engage, from a Christian missionary perspective, the "predominant values and norms of society" and "to communicate to society those *ethical and religious principles which give full meaning to human life*" (*ECE* 33). As the many educational documents have stressed, *ECE* views the university as an instrument of evangelization and so must be closely connected with, although not smothered or illegitimately bound by, the ecclesial and magisterial Church.

The Application of Ex Corde Ecclesiae *for the United States* (2000)

In 2000 the USCCB released its guidelines for application of *Ex Corde Ecclesiae*, consisting of two sections: theological and pastoral principles and particular norms. The key principles enunciated in the guidelines are those of trust and community. Due to a shared baptism and faith, dialogue and communion grounds the community of the Church and university while maintaining their distinct teaching roles. Under the guidelines, the bishops and university presidents should work together closely for mutual benefit, with the bishops providing support and assistance and the presidents providing faithful teaching and formation for seminarians and laity. The potential for authoritarianism espoused in the guidelines is avoided by close cooperation and communication.

The practical norms for implementing *ECE* in the United States focus on the Catholic identity of the university and its faculty, specifying that university officials must develop public mission statements emphasizing their Catholic vocations. *ECE* treats the bishops, for their part, as responsible for campus ministry along with providing assistance and support for Catholic students. Cooperation of the Church and the University occurs in a larger Catholic community for *ECE*, one that practices authority in communion and open dialogue.

The USCCB also published *Guidelines Concerning the Academic* Mandatum (*GAM* 2001). These guidelines explained that the *mandatum* is required of all Catholic teachers in theology faculties and it is the obligation of the individual professor, not the university, to acquire one (*GAM* 2). Local bishops must grant a *mandatum* in writing which remains in effect until explicitly withdrawn.

PART V: CONCLUDING REFLECTIONS

There are many themes and topics examined by the Church's teachings on Catholic education. Even so, four themes surface as critical to the current state of Catholic education in modern society: parental rights, the role of community, the changing face of Catholic educators, and the shift from optimism to a guarded realism.

The first theme is a developed understanding of the primary right of parents as the primary educators of their children. Parents are the first educators and their choices must be respected. *Gravissimum Educationis* identifies this right, making it clear that the state and the Church must support parents in this obligation. Yet documents following *Gravissimum Educationis,* such as *The Catholic School* and *to Teach as Jesus Did*, stress the difficulty of parents in being able to fulfill this primary role given the changing circumstances in modern society.

In the modern civil society, parents seem, at times, to be one group among many who exercise decision making in relation to schools and education. Parents may be the first decision makers about what is best for their children. Schools and teachers subtly begin to share the parental role, albeit sometimes in a supportive way, but sometimes in ways that may not fully respect the parent as *first* educator.

Gravissimum Educationis is most explicit in identifying the right of parents as first educators. As educators, parents should receive both support and resources for the educational choices they make for their children. Parents should thus have the primary right of educating *and* protecting their children against a culture no longer sympathetic to Catholic values. Parents act *as* educators *by* choosing to send their child either to a particular school or educate them at home. This means the government must respect and acknowledge the Catholic schools as an educational choice of the parent and, as such, a fundamental element of formation in society, something still very much in dispute.

A second more consistently positive development is the notion of community in schools. Although hinted at in *Gravissimum Educationis*, the notion of community becomes a dominant aspect of all later documents, whether from the congregation, bishops, or the Pope in *Ex Corde Ecclesiae*. Schools, in all of their forms, must be communities where students and teachers interact on more than professional levels and where the virtues and values of a good society are practiced and promoted. Schools need to be communities where faith and reason can be freely integrated into the practice of daily living. In a society of contrasts and contradictions, Catholic schools become prophetic communities and witnesses to the truth that the human person was made in and for communion.

A third development is perhaps the most dramatic in practice: the changing face of teachers in Catholic schools. Once the domain of religious sisters and brothers, Catholic schools are now staffed almost entirely by lay teachers who have responded to the call to serve in Catholic education. This, more than any other factor, has shaped the current state and future prospects of Catholic education in the United States. *Gravissimum Educationis* does not seem aware of this pending demographic shift in Catholic education. However, in 1977 the specific formation and training of lay teachers is identified as a critical need in *The Catholic School*.

A whole document dedicated to the challenge of the changing face of teachers in Catholic schools, *Lay Catholics in Schools*, reveals the significance of the change. Religious are, for the first, time spoken of as "leaven" in *Consecrated Persons and Their Mission in Schools*. Religious no longer serve as the backbone of the educational community but are called on to nurture community and formation of the Catholic community. There is a consistent call in the recent documents for a proper formation and training of lay teachers in the Catholic tradition. The implementation of the necessary formation remains the fundamental challenge for Catholic schools in the United States.

Finally, the trend in educational documents mirrors that of other Catholic fields from the Council to the present: an exuberant optimism gives way to a cautious realism. *Gravissimum Educationis*, while not without certain caution, tends to be highly favorable toward developments in modern society. *GE* calls for an integration of these developments into Catholic education for a renewal of the mission of schools.

Very quickly, though, the optimism of *GE* is significantly tempered by a sober reflection on social and technological advances that tend to diminish the person, damage traditional values and family structures, and threaten the practice of the faith. Still, there is a cautious realism. Of course, the new knowledge gained in society can be integrated into educational programs, but this must be done with a more tempered optimism and a realistic view to the effects on the individual and the nature and purpose of Catholic schools themselves.

The documents of the Church provide sure footing and prophetic guidance for educators standing on the shifting sands within a secular educational landscape. *Gravissimum Educationis* provided sage guidance for Catholic education in 1965; its 12 principles have given the Church a road-map for reflection over the last 50 years. Knowing the nature and purpose of Catholic education identified in the documents discussed in this chapter can assist educators to know the principles by which the Catholic school culture and identity can be articulated clearly, while still prudently applying those principles to particular communities and particular students.

The themes and trends identified here can sometimes point to a field in transition and tension between old and new. However, this is no cause for concern. The world Catholic education seeks to evangelize is in need of both the wisdom of the past and the promise of the future. Catholic schools are instruments of evangelization and mission, a "saving leaven in the human community" (*GE* 8), as *Gravissimum Educationis* puts it. This saving community, this educational community, not only has as its message, but also has as its source, the Word of God, Jesus Christ, ever ancient and ever new.

REFERENCES

Briel, D. (2008). The Declaration on Christian Education: *Gravissimum Educationis*. In Lamb, M. L., & Levering, M. (Eds.), Vatican II: Renewal within tradition (pp. 383–96). New York: Oxford University Press.

Congregation for Catholic Education. (1977, March 19). *The Catholic school.* Retrieved October 9, 2014, from http://www.vatican.va/roman_curia/congregations/ccatheduc/documents/rc_con_ccatheduc_doc_19770319_catholic-school_en.html

Congregation for Catholic Education. (1997, December 28). *The Catholic school on the threshold of the third millennium.* Retrieved October 9, 2014, from http://www.vatican.va/roman_curia/congregations/ccatheduc/documents/rc_con_ccatheduc_doc_27041998_school2000_en.html

Congregation for Catholic Education. (2002, October 28). *Consecrated persons and their missions in schools: Reflections and guidelines.* Retrieved October 9, 2014, from http://www.vatican.va/roman_curia/congregations/ccatheduc/documents/rc_con_ccatheduc_doc_20021028_consecrated-persons_en.html

Congregation for Catholic Education. (2014). *Educating today and tomorrow: A renewing passion.* Retrieved October 9, 2014, from http://www.vatican.va/roman_curia/congregations/ccatheduc/documents/rc_con_ccatheduc_doc_20140407_educare-oggi-e-domani_en.html

Congregation for Catholic Education. (1982, October 15). *Lay Catholics in schools: Witnesses to faith.* Retrieved October 9, 2014, from http://www.vatican.va/roman_curia/congregations/ccatheduc/documents/rc_con_ccatheduc_doc_19821015_lay-catholics_en.html

Congregation for Catholic Education. (1988, April 7). *The religious dimension of education in a Catholic school: Guidelines for reflection and renewal.* Retrieved October 9, 2014, from http://www.vatican.va/roman_curia/congregations/ccatheduc/documents/rc_con_ccatheduc_doc_19880407_catholic-school_en.html

Cummings, M.M., & Allen, E.A. (2012). *Behold the heritage: Foundations of education in the Dominican tradition.* Tacoma, WA: Angelico Press.

John Paul II. (1990, August 15). *Apostolic constitution on Catholic universities—Ex corde ecclesiae.* Retrieved October 9, 2014, from http://www.vatican.va/holy_father/john_paul_ii/apost_constitutions/documents/hf_jp-ii_apc_15081990_ex-corde-ecclesiae_en.html

Miller, M. (2006). *The Holy See's teaching on Catholic schools.* Manchester, NH: Sophia Institute Press.

O'Malley, J. W. (2008). What happened at Vatican II . Cambridge, MA: Belknap Press of Harvard University Press.

Pope Paul VI. (1965, October 28). *Gravissimum educationis.* Retrieved October 9, 2014, from http://www.vatican.va/archive/hist_councils/ii_vatican_council/documents/vatii_decl_19651028_gravissimum-educationis_en.html

United States Conference of Catholic Bishops. (2001, June 1). *The application of* ex corde ecclesiae *for the United States.* Retrieved October 9, 2014, from http://www.usccb.org/beliefs-and-teachings/how-we-teach/catholic-education/higher-education/the-application-for-ex-corde-ecclesiae-for-the-united-states.cfm

United States Conference of Catholic Bishops. (2001, June 15). *Guidelines concerning the academic* mandatum *(canon 812).* Retrieved October 9, 2014, from http://www.usccb.org/beliefs-and-teachings/how-we-teach/catholic-education/higher-education/guidelines-concerning-the-academic-mandatum.cfm

United States Conference of Catholic Bishops. (2005). *Renewing our commitment to Catholic elementary and secondary schools in the third millennium.* Retrieved October 9, 2012, from http://www.usccb.org/beliefs-and-teachings/how-we-teach/catholic-education/upload/renewing-our-commitment-2005.pdf

United States Conference of Catholic Bishops. (1972). *To teach as Jesus did: A pastoral message on Catholic education.* Washington, DC: United States Catholic Conference.

Chapter Four

Demographic Shifts Impacting Catholic School Education

Dale McDonald

TAKING OWNERSHIP: A STUDENT'S STORY

The school I attend is predominately white. In the sixth grade, I was the only African American student in my all-girl class. Other than keeping up with excessive homework and making friends, keeping friends was my biggest challenge. I wanted so badly to leave and go to public school. Every time I felt bad, however, there was always someone I could go to and discuss my feelings. I felt relieved that the person I adopted as my mentor at my school was African American like me. Talking to an adult who looked like me helped me to see the positive things in my school. Returning to Catholic school in the seventh grade was great. My school listens and welcomes ideas on being more welcoming. I am learning so much about my Catholic faith and realize that I have so much to give to, and receive from, our Father in heaven. I am now in the ninth grade and am looking forward to returning to the same Catholic school after my summer break. (Merritt, 2003)

Anecdotes such as this offer a glimpse into the promise and challenges of meeting the needs of Catholic school students today. Responding to the ever-increasing diversity of the student population requires new curricular approaches, greater use of technology, role models that resonate with student experience, and a mission integration of faith and culture that retains the essence of a Catholic school education for this new generation.

63

CATHOLIC SCHOOLS ROOTED IN THE IMMIGRANT CHURCH

The history of the Catholic school system in the United States follows the patterns of immigration history. The 19th-century immigrants, primarily from Western and Southern Europe, established their own nationality-based churches and schools (Byrne, 2000). These parishes and schools retained most of their ethnic and socioeconomic heritage, resulting in very little diversity or interaction with the larger surrounding culture. Following World War I, there was a shift away from ethnic identification and an increased social acceptance of the upward social mobility of American Catholics.

The waves of new immigrants coming to the United States at the end of the 20th and beginning of the 21st century continue to challenge the church and Catholic schools to be faithful to the mission of serving the new arrivals, particularly the poor and vulnerable. The mix of racial and ethnic identities, diverse socioeconomic status, language abilities, educational attainment, faith traditions and immigration status of the new immigrant populations from Central and South America, Eastern Europe, the Far East, Middle East and Africa, is impacting the demographic profile of Catholic schools across the nation.

During the past forty years, the former homogeneity of most Catholic schools has given way to accelerated enrollment diversity. This diversity requires accommodations to a newly developing environment in Catholic schools.

A NEWLY DEVELOPING ENVIRONMENT IN CATHOLIC SCHOOLS

Changing Ethnographics of Student Populations

When ethnic data were first collected by the National Catholic Educational Association (NCEA) in 1970, the national non-Caucasian student population was 10.8%. By 2014, it reached 26.2%. In the same time frame, percentages increased among the major racial and ethnic groups as participation by Asians rose from 0.5 to 5.0, African Americans from 4.8 to 7.6, and Hispanics from 13.1 to 15.0 (Bredeweg, 1970; McDonald & Schultz, 2014).

Beginning in 2012, the NCEA adopted the U.S. Census Bureau data collection format of separating ethnicity and race. Consequently, all persons must now both indicate their ethnicity as Hispanic or non-Hispanic and a race. There are some anomalies in recent NCEA data, though, because some schools do not have Hispanics choose a racial category, instead reporting their race as unknown.

Diverse ethnic enrollment in Catholic schools varies widely among regions of the nation and within dioceses. The dioceses with the largest enrollments are in large metropolitan areas that have been considered gateways or entry ports for immigrants. Most of the largest enrollments are found in old manufacturing areas in the Northeast or Midwest. At present, these regions enroll almost half (46.6%) of all Catholic school students. The percentages of Hispanic and racial minority enrollments in the six geographic areas of the nation are as follows: New England: 26.0%, Mideast: 42.3%, Great Lakes: 32.3%, Plains: 19.2%, Southeast: 32.0%, West: 62.7% (McDonald & Schultz, 2014).

From an academic perspective, Catholic schools have had a long-standing reputation for providing quality education for all students. Using empirical evidence, researchers Andrew Greeley and his associates (1976, 1982), James Coleman (1982, 1987), and others (Benson et al., 1986; Bryk et al., 1993; Manno & Graham, 2001) demonstrated higher academic achievement of Catholic school students. The National Assessment of Educational Progress (NAEP) results have shown that Catholic school students continue to score well on subject tests in mathematics, reading, science and social studies, surpassing their counterparts in public schools (Institute of Education Sciences, 2013).

Utilizing secondary analyses of national data sets and qualitative case studies of selected schools, education researchers have made a persuasive case that Catholic schools are especially effective in making a difference in closing the achievement gap for poor and minority students in urban areas (Vitullo-Martin, 1979; Bryk, Lee, & Holland, 1993).

Apart from the NAEP data, most of the findings on academic achievement date back more than 10 years and may not accurately describe the current status of student performance. There is a dearth of longitudinal research, particularly about Catholic elementary schools, that needs to be rectified in order to obtain a more accurate picture of current achievement levels.

Hispanic Students in Catholic Schools

Hispanics are the largest of the ethnic minority groups in the Catholic schools at 15.0 percent. However, Catholic schools have been inconsistent in their ability to recruit and retain Hispanics (Stevens-Arroyo & Pantoja, 2003). Currently 17% of the United States population is Hispanic. By mid-century, they are projected to be more than 30% of the total U.S. population (The University of Notre Dame Task Force, 2009).

Hispanics are pluralistic, differing in characteristics including race, national origin, and linguistic proficiency. While some Hispanic immigrants, such as Cubans in Miami, attend Catholic schools in large numbers, many other groups do not (Lawrence, 2000). Mexican-Americans, "far and away the largest U.S. immigrant group, have the lowest rate of Catholic school utilization" (Lawrence, 2000, p. 197). Lawrence points out that "obstacles or opportunities afforded by local school and parish environments seem just as important [as family income] in shaping their school-choice preferences and decisions" (2000, p. 197). In addition, financial limitations are significant. The ability to obtain bilingual services in schools plays an important role as well.

Success in serving Hispanic students has been demonstrated by new research from the Loyola Marymount University School of Education. Currently, Hispanic students constitute 48% of the Catholic school enrollment in the Archdiocese of Los Angeles. The study found that these students, among the most economically disadvantaged in Los Angeles, are completing a rigorous curriculum, outperforming their peers on national standardized tests, graduating from high school, and going to college at exceptional rates (Higareda et al., 2011). Early indications from an evaluation of the factors contributing to their successes can provide incentives and strategies for increasing the enrollment of Hispanic students in Catholic schools in other areas.

African American Students in Catholic Schools

Researchers such as Polite (2000) have discovered that Catholic schools are more effective than public schools in educating African American students because of the high quality of education offered in Catholic schools. The research has identified common characteristics of Catholic school environments that empower these students to succeed academically as well as beyond school. These factors are: a culture of high expectations that believes all students can learn and holds both students and teachers accountable, a rigorous academic curriculum, respect for diversity and support of the development of a strong African American identity of students, and attention to spiritual development.

Shields' (1996) research dispels the notion that African American students in Catholic schools are from middle-class families whose backgrounds would enable them to do well in any school. Studying a Catholic school in an urban Chicago neighborhood, he concluded that, irrespective of students' economic status, a combination of energetic and committed educators and motivated parents helps students achieve their maximum potential. However, Shields notes that on standardized achievement tests, albeit less so than in public schools, an achievement gap still persists between African American and Caucasian students. These results are similar to those concluded in the achievement data results of the evaluations of the DC Opportunity Scholarship Program (Wolf, Gutmann, & Puma, 2009), the only federally funded voucher program in the nation.

Asian Students in Catholic Schools

Research findings on Asian American students in Catholic schools are almost nonexistent. In general education literature, Asian American students are considered a "model minority" that outperform their peers in all other racial categories at advanced levels on national and international assessments such as the Program for International Student Assessment (PISA) and Trends in International Mathematics and Science Study (Sieff, 2011).

Nickerson and coauthors (2006) have identified these factors as contributing to their academic success: parental involvement, time spent on task, and study habits; they have made comparisons showing large disparities between Asian Americans and other racial groups. Hyun (2005) points to Confucian values of filial piety, the importance of family, respect for authority, communal decision making, the priority of duty over personal rights, and the suppression of feelings as the foundation of their academic achievements. Still, these characteristics may be overgeneralizations that are not indicative of all subgroups among Asian Americans, particularly for those who are Christians.

The Education Trust-West, a California education advocacy organization that works to eliminate the achievement gaps that separate low-income students and students of color from their peers, has called for the disaggregation of Asian American data (Education Trust, 2009). Researchers at Education Trust suggest that these students differ considerably in their countries of origin, languages, and socioeconomic status. The results demonstrate that Chinese, Japanese, Korean and Asian Indians perform well, while other subgroups of Asians and Pacific Islanders perform at substantially lower levels.

For Catholic school educators, the challenge of their ministry to Asian and Pacific Islanders is that of respecting and working with the diversity existing among students and their families in terms of ethnicity, language, culture, religious tradition, place of birth, recentness of arrival to the United States, and their degree of adaptation to local mores.

In their pastoral letter, *Asian and Pacific Presence: Harmony in Faith*, the United States Conference of Catholic Bishops (USCCB) wrote, "There are many Asian and Pacific communities and identities. Respect for the differences among varied cultures and historical traditions are a significant part of accepting them into U.S. society and the Church in the United States" (USCCB, 2001, Section II: Harmony Among Diverse Realities).

The letter continues, "Respect for elders and authority and sacrifice for children figure prominently in shaping their experiences. Harmony is crucial . . . faith is an important element of life. For Catholics of Asian and Pacific heritage, Catholic identity is intimately connected with family and local community. After the family, education is most valued by Asian and

Pacific peoples" (USCCB 2001, Section III: Family and Education Are Central).

Students with Special Needs

Section 504 of the Rehabilitation Act of 1973 and the Americans with Disabilities Act of 1990 are civil rights laws that, in part, prohibit discrimination in admission of students with disabilities. According to Section 504 and the Americans with Disabilities Act, "no otherwise qualified handicapped person shall, solely by reason of his/her handicap, be excluded from participation in, be denied the benefits of, or be subjected to discrimination" in any program or activity in public and private sector entities operating as public accommodations, including Catholic schools. For Catholic schools the law requires "reasonable accommodations" that would not cause undue financial burdens, fundamentally alter the programs, or result in risk of harm to the children or others, if asked to admit students with disabilities.

The Individuals with Disabilities Education Act (IDEA) is a federal education law designed to provide limited opportunities for students with disabilities who are enrolled in Catholic schools. The IDEA also provides these students with some services from their states through their local public school boards. The IDEA does not require states to spend their financial resources to serve these students as it does for children enrolled in public schools. By enrolling their children in private schools, parents forgo the child's right to a "free and appropriate public education" (U.S. Department of Education, 2008). Consequently, most students in Catholic and other private schools are not receiving publicly funded services unless the state willingly agrees to provide such and few states refuse to go beyond the federal limits.

Beyond the law, the mission of the Catholic Church and Catholic education calls for the inclusion of all God's children in programs and activities to the widest extent possible. In their *Pastoral Statement of U.S. Catholic Bishops on Persons with Disabilities*, the bishops "call upon people of good will to reexamine their attitudes toward their brothers and sisters with disabilities and promote their well-being, acting with the sense of justice and compassion that the Lord so clearly desires. Further, realizing the unique gifts individuals with disabilities have to offer the Church, we wish to address the need for their integration into the Christian community and their fuller participation in its life." (United States Conference of Catholic Bishops, 1978, paragraph 1).

Special education remains a challenge for most Catholic schools. Yet much progress has been made in accepting and serving students with special needs. At the elementary level, schools report about 11% of their student populations as having identified disabilities, while 46% have a resource teacher to assist children with disabilities and the teachers who work with these students (Cidade & Wiggins, 2014). The most common disabilities among Catholic school students are mild to moderate learning disabilities, speech impairments, and attention deficit disorders.

CATHOLIC SCHOOL STAFFING DEMOGRAPHICS

In addition to the shift from religious (3.7% in 1970) to lay (96.8% in 2014) faculty members, demographic changes are also taking place among the professionals staffing Catholic schools. Although the transition from religious to lay personnel is a significant change, school teaching and administrative personnel remain overwhelmingly female (77.3%). While faculty and administration remains overwhelmingly Caucasian (86.4%), there have been increases in the ethnic minority faculty: Hispanic, 7.1%; African American, 1.9%, and Asian, 1.1%. Other ethnic groups are less than 1% each (McDonald & Schultz, 2014).

Religious Diversity in Catholic Schools

Over the past 40 years, there has been a large increase in the number of students seeking enrollment in Catholic schools even though they are not Catholic. The closing of many schools and the decline in predominantly Catholic student enrollments during the 1960s, as well as a greater acceptance of other religious denominations in the post–Vatican II era, provided more openings for students of other faiths in the schools. In 2014 the number of non-Catholic students rose to 16.4% nationally, with many individual schools averaging significantly higher percentages. At the faculty level, approximately 14.4% of staff are not members of the Catholic faith (McDonald & Schultz, 2014).

Socioeconomic Status of Students

When analyzing a family's socioeconomic status (SES), the usual factors taken into consideration are the household income and parents' levels of education and occupations. National data have not been collected directly on the SES of the families of Catholic school students. Consequently, other indicators have been used as a proxy for SES. Among the variables used are participation in federal programs such as the Elementary and Secondary Education Act's Title I services and the U.S. Department of Agriculture's school nutrition programs (which require income eligibility criteria) and Catholic school financial assistance data.

Currently 55% of Catholic schools have students who qualify for Title I services, but only 6% of students are served. However, the funding formula for Title I limits the amount of money available to serve private school students, curtailing delivery of services to thousands of qualified students. These calculations significantly undercount the number of low-income families represented in Catholic schools. Many Catholic schools are not able to, or choose not to, participate in the federal nutrition programs for students. Although 49% of Catholic schools participate in the federal nutrition programs, serving more than 270,000 meals daily, fewer children receive such services whose SES status would qualify them for lunch or breakfast programs. These data indicate that students in Catholic schools do not represent an elitist population (McDonald & Schultz, 2014).

Tuition fees remain the single largest obstacle to the ability of parents to enroll their children in Catholic schools. The average per-pupil tuition in elementary schools is $3,880, and the mean first-year tuition in secondary schools is $9,622. These figures represent an increase of 84.8% in elementary and 99.6% in secondary school tuitions since 2000 (McDonald & Schultz, 2014).

A study focused on elementary school enrollment trends, commissioned by the National Catholic Educational Association, revealed that 44% of Catholic parents who did not enroll their children in a Catholic school cited insufficient financial assistance as the primary reason. The study found that "the central economic difference between those who enrolled a child and those who did not was not necessarily the tuition cost or the family income but rather the availability of assistance to make it an affordable option at whatever income level" (Gray & Gautier, 2006, p. 59).

Catholic schools offer financial assistance to families based on demonstrated need. The percentage of students seeking financial aid continues to rise. Currently 26% of elementary students request aid and 38% of secondary students do so. The percentage of elementary schools which report being able to meet most of the aid requests was 52%, and the percentage of secondary schools was 57% (Cidade & Wiggins, 2014; Cidade & Saunders, 2013).

MEETING THE NEEDS OF TODAY'S CATHOLIC SCHOOL STUDENTS

Catholic schools, like the rest of the American educational enterprise, are undergoing profound paradigm shifts—or should be doing so if they are to meet the needs of today's learners. The rapidly changing world of education reform requires adaptation and innovation on the part of Catholic school educators if the schools are to remain relevant and significant institutions for the education of youth in this new era. This requires strong leadership at the diocesan and local school level.

Some of the challenges Catholic schools and their learning communities—consisting of educators, students, and families—must undertake to meet current needs relate to preparing students to live and work in a global-ized and digitalized world as people whose worldview reflects the faith for-mation that has been an integral part of their Catholic schooling. The follow-ing section identifies some of the key areas that Catholic school leaders will need to pay greater attention to in multiple dimensions and in new and unfolding ways.

Faith Formation

Integration of faith and academic learning are hallmarks of Catholic educa-tion. The spiritual orientation of the school, as expressed in the formal and informal religious activities students are exposed to, should assist students in forming their own spirituality and orientation toward faith and life in the church. The academic components of faith formation and religious exercises need to be designed so students participate in ways that allow them to inte-grate the experiences and draw upon them to develop a mature faith.

Within their personal environments, students encounter differing levels of faith commitment and attachment to the church than that which they experi-ence within the school community. Helping students to navigate negative attitudes among peers and even within the family requires attention to stu-dents' expression of skepticism and disillusionment and creativity in fashion-ing responses that are relevant and true to the tenets of faith. Students whose skepticism or indifference lead them to claim to be spiritual but not religious need a strong creedal foundation to assist them in developing a faith life that can be both religiously and spiritually relevant.

Global and Multicultural Education

The cultural and religious differences among students in Catholic schools should be embraced in an environment that reflects a commitment to the Gospel values of promoting the dignity and worth of the individual. Despite social class, race, ethnicity, gender, or religious differences, all students should have an equal opportunity to learn in school.

Current educational policy in the United States is focused on closing the achievement gap between minority and economically disadvantaged students and their peers. The difference in academic achievement between minority and economically disadvantaged students and their counterparts is measured by comparison of performance on standardized tests, graduation rates and highest level of education completed.

There are no national studies pertaining to the achievement gap in Catho-lic schools. Even so, location-specific research studies have demonstrated that minority students in Catholic schools have higher achievement levels and graduation rates than public school students from similar racial and economic background (Higareda et al., 2011; Wolf, Gutman, & Puma, 2009; Bryk, Lee, & Holland, 1993; Benson et al., 1986).

The results of research studies conducted in Catholic schools have demonstrated that educators can raise academic achievement for all students by creating an environment that is conducive to learning among varied cultures. These educators succeed by adapting curricula and instructional approaches to reflect awareness, acceptance, and affirmation of cultural diversity. Catholic schools are thus called to mediate between home and school cultures by helping students develop skills, attitudes, and behaviors to succeed within their own ethnic and racial groups as well as within the school culture and global community. This may require attitudinal changes focusing on the formulized and hidden curricula and values of schools.

In addition to the curricular and pedagogical approaches, the Catholic school culture promotes attitudes which need periodic examination to ensure that they are positive for all groups. Multicultural education requires a meaningful integration of conceptual understanding and practical strategies in light of church teachings on social justice and equity issues.

Two of the challenges for Catholic school educators are adapting multiple perspectives and pedagogies in culturally sensitive ways and examining hiring practices. It is not enough to acknowledge cultural differences. Rather, differences need to be celebrated in ways that promote comfortable learning environments for all students. Likewise, educators must acknowledge differences in learning styles and implement them while promoting high expectations and standards for all.

Currently, there is more diversity among students than among faculty in Catholic schools. Hispanic, Asian, and African American student populations are 34.8% of the total while the same diversity among faculty is 9.1% (McDonald & Schultz, 2014). Students of all races and ethnic groups need good role models both within and apart from their own background. Hiring practices should be reviewed periodically to assure that efforts are being made to hire qualified minorities as faculty. Additionally, practices should be put in place to encourage and mentor current students who may be potential teachers for Catholic schools.

A New Paradigm for Teaching and Learning

Preparing students to be independent, lifelong learners will require a shift away from an emphasis on lecturing and acquisition of static skills in favor of interactive engagements that foster inquiry, experimentation, and analysis. Research (Merriman & Nicoletti, 2008) has shown that students today, part of the millennial generation, learn differently. These researchers found that students think and communicate differently because of the technology that is an integral part of their lives such that effective teaching must work with these new tools and learning environments if children are to be reached.

Educators are thus being challenged to prepare students for a future that is yet to be imagined. Today's students expect greater visual stimulation, engagement in cooperative and community-related activities, and experiential and authentic learning activities that situate them in a global community.

Today's students grew up in a digital world that developed their learning styles. These "digital natives" (Prensky, 2010) have embraced informal learning situations outside of school where they follow their own interests and passions, learning in new and different ways. Educators need to capitalize on these passions and acknowledge that web-based tools are creating an infrastructure that supports innovative teaching and learning. Technology integration requires investments of time and effort, as well as financial resources to develop the multiple platforms needed to use technology effectively. Yet not all of the work has to be done by the educators.

New learning paradigms also require administrators and teachers to use achievement data to assess student strengths and weaknesses while making instructional changes tailored to student needs. Implementing a data-driven culture in schools should focus on assisting teachers and administrators on how to use the abundance of data that is increasingly available to improve instruction as well as teaching students how to examine their own data and use it to set learning goals for themselves. Educators should be encouraged to develop longitudinal data systems and invest in the professional development and resources necessary to ensure that data are comprehensive, integrated longitudinally, relevant, and timely for effective use (Hamilton et al., 2009).

Closing the digital divide has focused on equity of access to technology resources among diverse students. Through the benefits of government programs, such as *E-Rate* and *Enhancing Education Through Technology*, and other expenditures of public funds, great progress has been made in providing students with access to advanced technology in public schools.

Catholic schools have not been as successful in accessing the federal resources as public schools and are generally not eligible for state funding. Consequently, educators in many Catholic schools, especially elementary schools, do not have the technology infrastructure needed to support advanced learning opportunities for students, many of whom do not have technology resources within their homes. Studies have shown that income, education, and ethnicity are key predictors of access to technology (Gibbs, Dosen, & Guerrero, 2008).

Catholic school leaders, mindful of the socioeconomic and racial diversity of their students, must make concerted efforts to acquire the needed technological resources to provide a digital learning environment for all students. Mayer, Mullens, & Moore (2000) found that the ability of individual schools to incorporate technology within the classroom is redefining the perception of a high-quality school as parents look at the quality and quantity of technology available to assess a school. Technology availability alone is not enough; it must be purposefully integrated into the teaching and learning experience for the students. Administrators must ensure that teachers have the time and professional development opportunities needed to make use of available resources as a teaching tool. As a group, Catholic school teachers currently use technology primarily for preparing to teach, rather than as a teaching tool (Gibbs, Dosen, Guerrero, 2008).

CONCLUSION

Catholic education, because it is rooted in the Gospel values of promoting human dignity, justice and evangelization, has embraced a long tradition of serving those children whose parents seek admittance to Catholic schools. While the context of educational institutions and the demographics of those seeking a Catholic education have changed significantly, the mission of these schools has not.

If Catholic schools are to be successful in meeting the challenges of the educational, social, cultural, and spiritual needs of all students, educational leaders must continue to adopt practices that promote interdisciplinary learning opportunities that prepare students to live and work in a globalized world.

Catholic school educators participate in the mission of Catholic education by helping students learn how to apply Catholic principles, ethics, virtues, and social teachings to moral decision-making in their own life situations and in interaction with the larger culture. Strong school leadership and the commitment of faculty and staff to professional growth, discerning the application of new methodologies, careful stewardship of available resources, and creative ingenuity in responding to ever-changing student populations and needs will ensure that Catholic schools will continue to serve all the people of God who approach their doors.

REFERENCES

Americans with Disabilities Education Act, 20 U.S.C. §§ 12101 *et seq.* (2014).

Benson, P. L., Yeager, R. L., Wood, P. K., Guerra, M. J., & Manno, B. V. (1986). *Catholic high schools: Their impact on low-income students.* Washington, DC: National Catholic Educational Association.

Bredeweg, F. 1970. *A statistical report on Catholic elementary and secondary schools for the years 1967–8 to 1969–70.* Washington, DC: National Catholic Educational Association.

Bryk, A. S., Lee, V. E., & Holland, P. (1993). *Catholic schools and the common good.* Cambridge, MA: Harvard University Press.

Byrne, J. (2000). *Roman Catholics and immigration in nineteenth-century America.* Retrieved July 12, 2011, from http://nationalhumanitiescenter.org/tserve/nineteen/nkeyinfo/nromcath.htm

Cidade, M., & Saunders, C. (2013). *Dollars and sense 2012–2013: Catholic high schools and their finances.* Washington, DC: Center for Applied Research in the Apostolate and the National Catholic Educational Association.

Cidade, M., & Wiggins, J. L. (2014). *Financing the mission: A profile of Catholic elementary schools in the United States 2013.* Washington, DC: Center for Applied Research in the Apostolate and the National Catholic Educational Association.

Coleman, J. S., & Kilgore, S. (1982). *High school achievement: public, Catholic & private schools compared.* New York: Basic Books.

Coleman, J. S., & Hoffer, T. (1987). *Public and private schools: the impact of communities.* New York: Basic Books.

Education Trust. (2009). *Closing the gaps.* Education Trust. Retrieved May 12, 2011, from http://www.edtrust.org/issues/pre-k-12/closing-the-gaps

Gibbs, M.G, Dosen, A .J., & Guerrero, R. B. (2008). Technology in Catholic schools: Are schools using the technology they have? *Catholic Education : A Journal of Inquiry and Practice 12*(2), pp. 176–92.

Gray, M., & Gautier, M. (2006). *Primary trends, challenges and outlook: A report on Catholic elementary schools.* Washington, DC: Center for Applied Research in the Apostolate.

Greeley, A. (1982). *Catholic high schools and minority students.* New Brunswick, NJ: Transaction Books.

Greeley, A. M., McCready, W. C., & McCourt, K. (1976*). Catholic schools in a declining church.* Kansas City: Sheed and Ward.

Hamilton, L., Halverson, R., Jackson, S., Mandinach, E. Supovitz, J., & Wayman, J. (2009). *Using student achievement data to support instructional decision-making.* (NCEE 2009–4067). Washington, DC: National Center for Education and Evaluation Assistance, Institute of Education Sciences, U.S. Department of Education. Retrieved March 9, 2011, from http://ies.ed.gov/ncee/ww/publications/practiceguides/

Higareda, I., Martin, S.P., Chavez, J.M., & Holyk-Casey, K. (2011). *Los Angeles Catholic schools: Impact and opportunity for economically disadvantaged students.* Los Angeles: Loyola Marymount School of Education.

Hyun, J. (2005). *Breaking the bamboo ceiling.* New York: HarperCollins.

Individuals with Disabilities Education Act, 20 U.S.C. §§ 1400 *et seq.* (2014).

Institute of Education Sciences, Center for Education Statistics, U.S. Department of Education. (2013). *National assessment of reading and mathematics at grades 4 and 8.* Retrieved October 28, 2014, from http://nces.ed.gov/nationsreportcard/subject/publications/main2013/pdf/2014451.pdf

Lawrence, S. (2000). "New" immigrants in the Catholic schools: A preliminary analysis. In Youniss, J., & Convey, J. (Eds.), *Catholic schools at the crossroads: Survival and transformation.* New York: Teachers College Press.

Manno, B. & Graham, H. (2001). Research on Catholic school effectiveness. In Hunt, T. C., Joseph, E. A., & Nuzzi, R. J. (Eds.), *Handbook of Research on Catholic Education.* Westport, CT: Greenwood Press.

Mayer, D. P., Mullens, J. E., & Moore, M. T. (2000). *Monitoring school quality: An indicators report.* (NCES 2001–030). Washington, DC: U.S. Department of Education, National Center for Education Statistics.

McDonald, D. & Schultz, M. (2014). *United States Catholic elementary and secondary schools 2013-2014: The annual statistical report on schools, enrollment and staffing.* Arlington, VA: National Catholic Educational Association.

Merriman, W., Nicoletti, A. (Eds.). (2008). *Understanding and teaching today's students.* Washington, DC: National Catholic Educational Association.

Merritt, B. (2003). Taking ownership: A student's story. *Sustaining Catholic education in and for the Black community.* The National Black Catholic Congress. Retrieved May 12, 2011, from http://www.nbccongress.org/resources/default.asp.

Nickerson, G.T., Kritsonis, W.A., & Allan, W. (2006). An analysis of the factors that impact academic achievement among Asian American, African-American, and Hispanic students. *National Journal for Publishing and Mentoring Doctoral Student Research, 3*(1), 2006.

Retrieved April 12, 2011, from http://www.maricopa.edu/studentaffairs/minoritymales/ An_Analysis_of_the_Factors.pdf

The Notre Dame Task Force on the Participation of Latino Children and Families in Catholic Schools. (2009). *To nurture the soul of a nation: Latino families, Catholic schools, and educational opportunity.* Notre Dame, IN: Alliance for Catholic Education Press at the University of Notre Dame.

Polite, V. C. (2000). Cornerstones: Catholic high schools that serve predominantly African American student populations. In Youniss, J., & Convey, J. J. (Eds.), *Catholic schools at the crossroads* (pp. 137–56). New York: Teachers College Press, Columbia University.

Prensky, M. (2010). *Teaching digital natives.* Thousand Oaks, CA: Corwin Press.

Rehabilitation Act, Section 504, 29 U.S.C. § 794(a) (2014).

Shields, P. (1996). Holy angles: Pockets of excellence. In Irvine, J. J., & Foster, M. (Eds.), *Growing up African American in Catholic schools.* New York: Teachers College Press.

Sieff, K. (2011, April 5). *Achievement gap widening between Asian American students and everyone else.* Retrieved July 12, 2011, from http://www.washingtonpost.com/local/education/achievement-gap-widening-between-asian-american-students-and-everyone-

Stevens-Arroyo, A.M., & Pantoja, S. (2003). History and inculturation: The Latino experience of Catholic education. In Augenstein, J., Kauffman, C., & Wister, R. (Eds.), *One hundred years of Catholic education: Historical essays in honor of the centennial of the National Catholic Educational Association* (pp. 257–81). Washington, DC: National Catholic Educational Association.

United States Conference of Catholic Bishops. (1978). *Pastoral statement of U.S. Catholic bishops on persons with disabilities.* Washington, DC: United States Conference of Catholic Bishops.

United States Conference of Catholic Bishops. (2001). *Asian and Pacific presence: Harmony in faith.* Washington, DC: United States Conference of Catholic Bishops. Retrieved November 6, 2014, from http://www.usccb.org/issues-and-action/cultural-diversity/asian-pacific-islander/resources/harmony-in-faith-additional-information.cfm

U.S. Department of Education, Office of Innovation and Improvement, Office of Non-Public Education. (2008). *Individuals with disabilities education act (IDEA): Provisions related to children with disabilities enrolled by their parents in private schools* . Washington, DC

Vitullo-Martin, T. (1979). *Catholic inner city schools: The future.* Washington, DC: United States Catholic Conference.

Wolf, P., Gutmann, B., & Puma, M. (2009). *Evaluation of the DC Opportunity Scholarship Program: Impacts after three years.* Washington, DC: National Center for Education Statistics.

Chapter Five

Declaration on Christian Education Encourages Catholic Schools

Lay Governance Increases to Provide Support and Leadership for Them

Regina Haney and Karen Ristau

INTRODUCTION

The Vatican II document Declaration on Christian Education, *Gravissimum Educationis* (*GE*), confirmed once again that the universal Church "proclaims anew" the importance of Catholic education for the fulfillment of the Church's mission (Abbott, 1966). *GE* expressly mentions the value Catholic schools hold to create a community dedicated to both the cultural upbringing of youth and to their formation in faith so students might be a "saving leaven in the human community" (1966, 25).

As important as *GE* is, it does not mention the need for support for the operational dimensions of Catholic schools. Truly what is taught and who is teaching are absolutes in order for Catholic (or any) schools to indeed be schools. However, other works are necessary if Catholic schools are to exist as such and fulfill the lofty ideals set forth in *Gravissimum Educationis*. These educational institutions rely on finance acumen to support salaries, buildings, and programs.

Operational and governance policies; marketing efforts; avenues for parental participation; and relationships to parishes, to local communities, and, when applicable, to sponsoring religious congregations, are all vital to the well-being of schools. Although *Gravissimum Educationis* fails to describe school governance, other Church documents touch on the topic. The most notable of these documents are the *Decree on the Apostolate of the Laity*

(1996) and *Renewing Our Commitment to Catholic Elementary & Secondary Schools in the Third Millennium* (2006). These documents highlight the importance of coresponsibility and subsidiarity for nascent school boards, a term that is used interchangeably with parish councils and commissions, in Roman Catholic schools in the United States.

School boards in Catholic schools are not extraneous or superfluous. Rather, school boards are essential because they can help educators in Catholic schools to accomplish their goals of educating children and their families while contributing to the mission of the Church in the world. In fact, "over the past two decades schools have continued to establish boards" (McDonald & Schultz, 2014, p. 11) to assist with accomplishing their goals. Moreover, at present 84.8% of the 6,594 Catholic elementary and secondary schools in the United States report having existing school boards (McDonald & Schultz, 2014).

EARLY HISTORY: BOARDS PRIOR TO 1960

As early as the mid-1880s, local groups helped local bishops to run Catholic schools. These local groups consulted and advised the schools. However, school boards were different then because they were dominated by priests rather than lay persons. Reflective of this reality, in 1863, Archbishop John B. Purcell of Cincinnati established an all-priest board of examiners to oversee the Catholic schools. The board was charged with regulating, administrating, and caring for the schools of the diocese; examining teacher candidates, both lay and religious; collecting the profit of book sales made to all schools of the diocese; and using book profits to educate poor pupils (Udoh, 1979, pp. 9–10)

An earlier outlier was Bishop John Neumann of Philadelphia, who set up a central board for education in 1852 and presided over a board made up of a pastor and two lay delegates from each parish in the city. A more common example was Bishop Dwenger of Fort Wayne, Indiana, who, in 1879, established a school board to bring all schools under general control: the control of the bishop.

The Third Plenary Council of Baltimore helped set standard rules for Catholic school boards. In 1884 the Council required each parish to build a school and each diocese to establish a diocesan commission of examination to oversee Catholic schools. These all-priest commissions assessed teachers on a written and oral examination. If teacher passed, their diplomas were valid for five years. No teacher could be hired without this document. Lay persons could serve, but evidence of their inclusion is fragmentary (Udoh, 1979, p. 12).

Superintendents and Board Growth

The addition of school superintendents slowed rather than accelerated the development of school boards. The role of the superintendent was created because bishops could not direct and supervise the schools in their care alone. They needed help, so they appointed superintendents, who were usually clerics.

One early superintendent of Catholic schools was the Reverend William Degnam of New York. Tapped as a member of an archdiocesan board that convened in 1888, he became the first diocesan inspector of schools. He represented the bishop and board in examining schools, teachers, and students. He could act on behalf of the bishop.

In other dioceses, too, superintendents oversaw schools. Where diocesan commissions existed, they advised the superintendent about policies and programs. Yet superintendents' growing power led to conflict. As Arthur Leary and John P. Breheny (1944) showed, superintendents and school boards struggled to define their roles. In fact, Sister Ruth Ward (1957) concluded that as a result of superintendents' newfound powers, most boards did not function or exist even in most large and many smaller dioceses. "For all practical purposes, they were defunct in the United States," she wrote (pp. 62–63). In two different works, Augenstein (1996, 2008) provides detailed histories of the role of superintendents in local Roman Catholic dioceses.

RESURGENCE OF THE BOARDS—
BOTH DIOCESAN AND PARISH

A variety of events helped boards of education in Catholic school to grow. Two documents from the Second Vatican Council, issued in the same year (along with statements of the American Catholic bishops), were seminal. The Declaration on Christian Education, *Gravissimum Educationis* (1966), restated the importance and value of education for the whole church. Further, the Decree on the Apostolate of the Laity, *Apostolicam Actuositatem* (1966), called on the laity to participate more in the life of the Church.

The American bishops, too, issued a powerful statement about Catholic education. In *To Teach As Jesus Did* (1972), the bishops declared that Catholic parishes should address their educational needs through representative structures. In addition, as Catholics moved out of their ethnic enclaves and became more educated, they demanded more inclusion in church governance.

Financial worries also prompted changes in Catholic schools. Broader community support was needed to pay the bills in these schools. Moreover such assistance was essential to earn the support, as financial reporting and

planning needed to be both transparent and contain advice from people besides the pastor.

> [I]f we are to divorce Catholic education from the class system imposed by
> tuition and from the inadequacies of support out of general Church funds, then
> the case must be brought to the people; they must be convinced of the need and
> they must be given a voice on policy. These things can best be accomplished
> through Boards of Education. (Voice of the Community, 1967, p. 4)

Diocesan and local school leaders looked to the government for financial
support. Because of controversies over the proper role of church and state,
Catholics grasped that a church or pastor would not receive financial assistance for parish schools. If funds became available, then lay groups had to
have the power of the purse. Michael O'Neill (1971), the superintendent of
Spokane, Washington, believed that lay school boards should be perceived as
the recipients of school funds from all sources—parents, donors, church, and
government. At the same time, diocesan leaders urged parents to work to
change laws that prohibited Catholics from receiving financial support for
the education of their children in parish schools. As a result, new kinds of
education boards governed Catholic schools as they expanded to include the
expertise of the laity.

Parish School Boards

In *Reform in Catholic School Board Governance* (2010), Gloria Ann Kalbfleisch tells the story of what may be the first parish school board:

> The model as a template for a local parish Catholic school board, St. Mary
> Parish, first was piloted under the leadership of Msgr. D'Amour. The St. Mary
> Parish community welcomed the new opportunity to elect lay members to a
> school board. These new members participated in planning, designing, and the
> construction of a new facility. They were entrusted with the responsibility to
> raise the money, purchase the land, approve the design of a school, and facili-
> tate the internal operations process necessary to provide a quality Catholic
> education. (C. De Decker, personal communication, 2005, as cited in Kalb-
> fleisch, 2010, p. 17)

Monsignor O'Neil C. D'Amour spread his ideas at the national level. In
1965 he spoke at the National Catholic Educational Association (NCEA)
convention about the value and necessity of establishing parish and diocesan
boards. Father Olin J. Murdick, superintendent of schools in Saginaw, Michigan, also urged the laity to bring their expertise to school governance. Murdick emphasized that if Catholic schools were to receive federal dollars,
someone other than the pastor needed to be in charge. In working to bring
their ideas into reality, D'Amour and Murdick chaired a committee of super-

intendents from NCEA which published an influential monograph on the board movement, *Voice of the Community* (1967).

As a result of the increased activity in the Catholic dioceses and parishes, the president of the NCEA took steps leading to the creation of a section for school boards within the Association. Father Albert C. Koob invited Monsignor D'Amour to join NCEA as a special assistant. D'Amour, a well-known figure in the board movement, oversaw a department to serve boards of education.

In 1974 the NCEA created a department of boards of education. Because of the names given to governance organizations within the church, this group was saddled with the title "National Association of Boards, Commissions, and Councils of Catholic Education (NABCCCE)." In 2006 the NCAA voted to change the name back to its originals, the Department of Boards and Councils. Today, the department's activities include research, publications, and field service for diocesan, elementary, and secondary schools. In the spirit of full disclosure, it should be noted Dr. Regina Haney, a coauthor of this chapter, directs the department.

Today's Catholic school boards differ from their 19th-century counterparts. Even so, contemporary boards wrestle with similar problems of governance. For example, the authority of school boards over schools and diocesan operations remains a challenge. In the early history of boards, school board members approved the appointment of teachers and principals in concert with the bishop. Some proposed that boards should oversee finances, hiring, curriculum, and property, almost aside from the pastor or the bishop. This was radical.

The reality is that any school calling itself Catholic is tied to the local bishop, who holds the final authority for all activity within his diocese. The same may be said of the relationship with the pastor when a school is a parish entity. Still, with the development of interparish schools, conflicts over authority issues endure. To be sure, both priests and the laity have worked collaboratively and can celebrate the results of their efforts.

O'Neil D'Amour's Vision of Lay Collaborative Boards Lived Out

Before the Second Vatican Council, Monsignor Charles O'Neil D'Amour initiated a role for the laity as members of the Roman Catholic school boards in his parish, St. Mary's in Norway, Michigan (Kalbfleisch, 2010). This model of inclusion of the laity in the governance of Catholic schools opened the doors for parishes and dioceses beyond D'Amour's locale to be more collaborative.

The boards under D'Amour's model, which included the laity, served as collaborative partners involved in working together with pastors to address challenges, demands, or meeting needs in the areas of policy, curriculum, finances, facilities, and personnel (Kalbfleisch, 2010, p. vii) to ensure the future of these Catholic schools. Yet more than half a century later, it is unclear what the fruits of D'Amour's labor have yielded. It is also unclear as to how or whether D'Amour's vision of lay collaborative boards is lived out.

For 24 years, the Department of Boards and Councils of the NCEA has recognized boards embodying D'Amour's vision of a Catholic school board. These outstanding boards provide examples, portraits of governing bodies and collaborative partnerships that contribute to the quality of the schools' Catholic education and their viability.

These exemplary boards were built from the blueprint that Sister Lourdes Sheehan provided in her seminal 1990 work, *Building Better Boards: A Handbook for Board Members in Catholic Education.* Sister Sheehan described the types of boards, the roles of administrators and boards, the committees, and the steps to ensure effective board operations. Twenty-five years later, this handbook remains the most popular go-to source for Catholic school board development.

Sheehan's work was the basis for research by Convey and Haney that identified statistically significant benchmarks or characteristics for effective boards to emulate. The results of their efforts were published in *Benchmarks of Excellence: Effective Boards of Catholic Education* (1997).

Using the research of Convey and Haney, boards could measure their contribution to the governance of a school or schools, parishes, or dioceses to self-nominate themselves for recognition through the Outstanding Board Award. Contributions may take many forms ranging from developing/revising policies, initiating or developing programs, expanding programs or grades, constructing new buildings, engaging in long-range planning, and/or improving faculty salary and benefits. This award is given at the annual NCEA convention.

Boards also need to work with identifiable benchmarks. These benchmarks can help elementary and secondary boards to "have membership that includes business people and alumni; have ownership of issues under their jurisdiction; are involved with issues pertaining to budget, policy, mission, philosophy, and planning; have goals, periodic assessments, and evaluation of board goals; have effective committees; have contact and communication with their constituents; are dedicated and committed to the school's mission; have productive meetings; train their new members and provide annual in-service for all members; and are involved in areas of planning, finance/budget management, and development/funding/marketing" (Convey & Haney, 1997, p. 44).

TYPES, MODELS, AND BOARD AUTHORITY

The 2014 Outstanding Boards selected by the Department of Boards and Councils portray boards nationally as well as a model of D'Amour's vision. First, these boards demonstrate that one size does not fit all. To this end, these boards represent varying types of authority, from advisory to consultative to limited jurisdiction. Second, these boards provide samples of models of boards or creative ways in which they are structured based on the configurations which they govern.

An illustration of one policy-making or limited jurisdictional board governs the Notre Dame Academy Schools of Los Angeles; the Sisters of Notre Dame, who sponsor both schools, have reserved powers. The Valley Catholic School Board of Directors in Beaverton, Oregon, is both a policy-making board and sponsored by a religious community. Unlike the Notre Dame school boards, who retained the separation of the schools, the Valley Catholic School Board of Directors led the effort to unify the schools into a Pre-K–12 program.

The Rapid City Catholic School System Board in South Dakota also is a board of limited jurisdiction that governs a Catholic school system serving four parishes. St. Benedict Preparatory School advisory board in Chicago, Illinois, working with its administration, leads a PK–12 school that was once a separate elementary school and a separate secondary school sponsored by two-parishes. Now the archdiocese sponsors the board.

St. Gerard Majella School Advisory Board in Kirkwood, Missouri, is a parish-sponsored elementary school. The board advises the school's pastor and administration about their educational and formative mission. These boards demonstrate the various types of authority available to boards. They are also samples of the diversity of governance models nationwide depending on the sponsorship and configuration of the institutions.

The Shift Away from a Single Parish School and Board

Of the six Outstanding Board Award winners, three are not all-parish boards or boards serving parish schools as in the days of D'Amour. One is a parish school, one is interparish, and another is a diocesan-sponsored school.

According to the NCEA's Catholic school data, the number of single-parish sponsored schools has dropped. As a result, the parish board model is falling into disuse (McDonald & Schultz, 2014). These data reveal movement toward O'Neil's vision and reform plan "for schools to move away from the parish so they would be more professional, autonomous and less parochial or insular" (Haney, 2010, p. 198).

The plan envisioned the bishops and pastors would retain authority "in matters of faith and morals" while the "decision-making boards" of parish sponsored schools would be operating under a new governance structure rather than under the parish" (Haney, 2010, p. 198). Looking at national data as well as our board award winners, D'Amour's goal of having all-parish Catholic schools that are not only governed by decision-making boards but also "less parochial or insular" (Haney, 2010, p. 198) has not been realized.

Membership

The current membership of Catholic school boards is reasonably clear. Board memberships are less clerical and more lay-run (Davies & Deneen, 1968; Murdick, 1967). A variety of the winners of the 2014 Outstanding Board Awards are lay-run entirely; others are mostly lay-run. Since the 1960s, board membership represented a diversity of professions and areas of expertise (Kalbfleisch, 2010, p. 27). Still, board members then and now share a common commitment: a strong interest in Catholic education in general and a specific commitment to the educational ministry of the school or schools they serve.

Responsibilities, Involvement with Issues, and Areas of Achievement

In the days of D'Amour, the major responsibility of Catholic school boards was to offset negative criticism of Catholic schools as mediocre while acquiring financial support from both the government and their parish communities (Sheehan, 1981; Haney, 2010). Boards today have more responsibilities. The 2014 Outstanding Boards, for example, oversee facilities, finances, policies, advancement, financial aid, construction of new school buildings and upgrading facilities, technology, and Catholic identity. This list is expanded when areas of main achievement are added: enrollment, board development, member recruitment, assistance with or hiring the head of school(s), public relations, and strategic planning.

Contact and Communication with Constituents

Contact and communication are as important for boards in Catholic schools today as in the 1960s. Members serve as goodwill ambassadors for their schools, offsetting negative criticism while promoting the value of Catholic schools and their contribution to the common good and the future church.

Contact and communication today differ from the past, though. Today's awardees published annual reports, electronic newsletters, conducted online surveys, and hosted parent focus groups. These examples represent a two-way communication model which not only gives information but solicits input from the constituents/stakeholders. One board member reported that "no matter what issues and/or obstacles this board has faced, it has demonstrated an effective line of communication internally . . . and externally with parents and the prospective community" (Haney, personal communication). This attitude goes beyond being goodwill ambassadors to being members of boards that are transparent and accountable.

Board Committees, Their Impact on Meeting Productivity and Member Ownership

As in public schools, the use of committees of Catholic school boards, whether standing or ad hoc, served to increase board productivity (Convey & Haney, 1997). Common standing committees of the 2014 Outstanding Board Awards are executive, finance, advancement/development, facilities, marketing, enrollment, communication, public relations, and strategic planning.

Pursuant to the 2014 Outstanding Board Awards reports, all board members are engaged in their assigned committees. Therefore, committee-driven boards allow members to become experts on issues that affect the schools' viability and quality. When members of committee-driven boards are asked why they attend board meetings, they say they contributed and used their time effectively; their volunteer work is appreciated and valued; they were challenged to overcome obstacles; and they feel satisfied after they overcome obstacles.

Having Goals and Periodic Board Assessment

All of the 2014 awardee school boards had goals flowing from their respective strategic plans. The boards' efforts and activities focused on the plans, which provided detailed action items and goals for each year. Yet only since the late 1990s has planning been a benchmark for an effective board (Convey & Haney, 1997). According to one 2014 awardee, "Planning helps the board not only to focus on current issues, but to look ahead to where it desires to be in years to come" (Haney, personal communication).

Board members should not plan without assessing their progress toward implementation. Periodic board assessment is essential for effectiveness (Convey & Haney, 1997). The 2014 outstanding boards continually assessed the committees' progress toward their respective goals. By way of illustration, one board reported on the board's Directors' Committee's responsibility to facilitate the board's annual self-assessment.

Training, Orientation for New Members and Annual in-Service for All Members

All 2014 Outstanding Board Award winners adhere to the idea that their members must be well versed on the mission of their schools or the charisms of the religious congregations sponsoring their schools. Individual members thus gain an understanding of their responsibilities through training. These boards require new members to participate in training in May or early June, to examine a comprehensive board binder containing materials that are updated and reviewed regularly, to participate in activities conducted at each board meeting, to outline processes for board goal setting and annual reflection, to attend retreats, and to participate in informational reports from school personnel.

The 2014 Outstanding Diocesan Board

Diocesan boards used to be oversight boards that provided "centralized diocesan school supervision" for the local Catholic schools (Walch, 2003, p. 101). Today boards are either advisory or consultative, providing support to the local schools (Convey & Haney, 1997). Like effective local boards, they take "ownership of issues under their jurisdiction, have effective committees, productive meetings, have periodic assessments, and evaluate themselves in light of their goals" (Walch, p. 64).

The archdiocesan schools' advisory council for the Archdiocese of Atlanta was recognized as a 2014 Outstanding Board along with the four local boards mentioned earlier. This outstanding model archdiocesan board reflects the support that diocesan boards nationwide provide Catholic schools in their dioceses. Some of the projects provided by the council are a marketing toolkit to help manage enrollment, an analysis of the reasons Latino families had not enrolled their children in archdiocesan schools, a viability index for all schools, assisting with in-service for new council members of local schools, reviewing and updating school policies, and formulating a transparent method of awarding financial assistance to schools. These council activities and projects support the schools in the Archdiocese of Atlanta rather than supervising them as the earlier diocesan boards did.

CONCLUSION

A shining light in the history of Catholic school boards is the creation of governance models designed to meet the needs and challenges of the times to ensure the quality and viability of American Catholic schools. In *Restructuring Catholic School Governance for a New Age* (2010), Brown challenges those involved in Catholic education to explore ideas of how to structure the schools civilly and canonically "to assure that they (schools) can continue to make the kind of significant contributions to fulfilling the Catholic church's educational mission in the United States that they have throughout history" (p. 2).

Many board members, past and present, along with others, have taken up the challenge and labored to create governance models, including the samples in this chapter that proved successful, while other models are being tested. Eventually these models will be part of the rich history of Catholic school boards on which the next generation of governance structures will be built.

REFERENCES

Augenstein, J. (2008). *Leaders in times of trial and eras of expansion*. Arlington, VA: National Catholic Educational Association.

Augenstein, J. (1996). *Lighting the way 1908–1935: The early years of Catholic school superintendency*. Arlington, VA: National Catholic Educational Association.

Breheny, J. P. (1954). *Diocesan administration of Catholic secondary education in the U.S.: Its status with a design for the future* (Unpublished doctoral dissertation). Harvard University, Cambridge, MA.

Brown, P. (2010). *Restructuring Catholic school governance for a new age: Creativity meets canon law*. Washington, DC: National Catholic Educational Association.

Convey, J., & Haney, R. (1997). *Benchmarks of excellence: Effective boards of Catholic education*. Washington, DC: National Catholic Educational Association.

Davies, D., & Deneen, J. (1968). *New patterns for Catholic education: The board movement in theory and practice*. New London, CT: Croft Educational Services.

Declaration on Christian Education (*Gravissimum Educationis*). (1966). In W. M. Abbott (Ed.), *The Documents of Vatican II*. New York: Guild Press.

Decree on the Apostolate of the Laity (*Apostolicam Actuositatem*). (1966). In W. M. Abbott (Ed.), *The Documents of Vatican II*. New York: Guild Press.

Haney, R. (2010). Design for success: New configurations and governance models for Catholic schools. *Catholic Education: A Journal of Inquiry and Practice, 14*, 195–211.

Haney, R. (2004). School Boards Provide Leadership for the Future. *Momentum* April/May. National Catholic Educational Association.

Kalbfleisch, G. (2010). *Reform in Catholic school board governance*. Pittsburgh: Dorrance.

Leary, A. M., & Breheny, J.P. (1944). *The place, function and present status of diocesan school boards* (Unpublished master's thesis). The Catholic University of America, Washington, DC.

McDonald, D., & Schultz, M. (2014). *United States Catholic elementary and secondary schools 2013–2014*. Arlington, VA: National Catholic Educational Association.

O'Neill, M. (1971). *New schools in a new Church*. Collegeville, MN: Saint John's University Press.

Renewing Our Commitment to Catholic Elementary & Secondary Schools in the Third Millennium. (2006). Washington, DC: United States Conference of Catholic Bishops.

Sheehan, L. (1990). *Building better boards: A handbook for board members in Catholic education*. Washington, DC: National Catholic Educational Association.

Udoh, S. J. (1979). *The development and testing performance standards for diocesan boards of education* (Unpublished doctoral dissertation). The Catholic University of America, Washington, DC.

United States Conference of Catholic Bishops. (1972). *To teach as Jesus did: A pastoral message on Catholic education*. Washington, DC: United States Catholic Conference.

Voice of the community: The board movement in Catholic education. (1967) Washington, DC: National Catholic Educational Association.

Walch, T. (2003). *Parish school: American Catholic parochial education from colonial times to the present*. Washington, DC: The National Catholic Educational Association.

Ward, R. O.P. (1957). *Patterns of administration in diocesan school systems* (Unpublished doctoral dissertation). The Catholic University of America, Washington, DC.

Chapter Six

American Catholic Higher Education

A Qualified Success Story

Michael J. Garanzini

INTRODUCTION

Any discussion of Catholic higher education in the United States today needs to acknowledge at least four clear and important facts. Catholic institutions of higher learning have, by and large, survived five decades of turmoil and change and have adapted to the new Catholic landscape. Of course, there are critics who complain these institutions are not Catholic enough. On the other hand, there are those who believe these institutions have not sufficiently distanced themselves from their Catholic roots to be taken seriously in the secular academy. Nevertheless, unlike Catholic elementary and secondary schools, institutions of higher education have not diminished, but have expanded.

A second reality is that Catholic institutions of higher education continue to serve the poor and those seeking to enter the ranks of the college educated. These institutions remain an attractive option for many middle-class and even poorer students. Third, these institutions play a significant role in their communities, in their local Churches, in their regions, and in the nation. Finally, Catholic institutions are not monolithic and come in a variety of sizes and shapes; there are community colleges; colleges aimed at professional education; regional, complex universities, and large research institutions.

In short, Catholic institutions of higher learning are represented in all the Carnegie institutional categories. Therefore, it is safe to say that Catholic colleges and universities are one of the most significant accomplishments of the immigrant Church in America, are still making a mark on Catholic and civic life in this country, and have perhaps benefited most among the Church's institutions from its rapprochement, its coming to terms with modernity at Vatican II.

Where Catholic primary and secondary education has seen significant erosion in numbers and impact, the opposite is true for Catholic higher education. Declines in Church-supported elementary and secondary schools have been precipitous, largely due to finances and changes in public attitude regarding the role of parishes in their lives. Colleges and universities, on the other hand, have grown. Today, Catholic institutions enroll 940,000 students, an increase of 15.1% since 2001, compared with a total enrollment of 410,000 in 1965 (Association of Catholic Colleges and Universities [ACCU], *Catholic higher education*). These institutions are academically strong, with many ranking among the country's best universities, and still more ranking among the best in their region.

Within their dioceses and local communities, dozens of these institutions are appreciated for their service in producing nurses, teachers, and professionals of all sorts. In addition, the percent of students who require financial support averages 88% of the entering class at Catholic Colleges and Universities (see ACCU website, frequently asked questions). Faculty members in these institutions produce an impressive number of journals, articles, monographs, and research reports. Their programs in the humanities, in the sciences, and in professions such as law and medicine compete with their private and public counterparts to attract high-caliber scholars and students. This achievement continues to be a success story in a landscape that has many distractions and challenges.

What accounts for the success of these institutions? Was this accomplished over and against Church support, or is this success somehow tied to cultural dynamics unleashed by the Church and the sponsoring religious communities?

In 1965, according to the Association of Catholic Colleges and Universities (ACCU), there were 240 Catholic institutions of higher learning in the United States (*Catholic higher education*). Today, there are roughly the same number of institutions in existence. While nearly 20 smaller women's colleges existed within this number, there are relatively few today. Many of these have become coeducational. The evolution or the closing of these institutions parallels the closing of private nondenominational women's colleges during this same period.

At the same time, while some predicted the increased secularization of these American institutions, paralleling their Protestant counterparts (Marsden, 1994b), this has not occurred, at least to the extent predicted. Most Catholic colleges and universities proudly display their Catholicity and see it as an advantage in the marketplace. These institutions manifest their Catholicity in public documents and on their web pages. Their lay boards select

Catholic presidents with rare exceptions (see ACCU website, section on presidents). All of the more than 30 new presidents in the 2013–14 academic year were Catholic, and they expect the mission and identity question to be high on their governance agenda.

Catholic institutions sponsor centers and programs with explicitly Catholic agendas. Their alumni are proud and often generous. And, most importantly, they continue to attract students who take on debt to attend these institutions ("Report to the Congregation for Catholic Education," American Association of Catholic Universities (ACCU) website, summer, 2014). To be sure, Catholic colleges and universities have their critics. Some bishops have complained publicly that they are too secular. These bishops object to significant numbers of non-Catholics on the faculty, large numbers of non-Catholic students, controversial speakers, and organizations such as LGBT student groups.

The criticisms go back to 1967, when a group of Catholic educators made a statement known as the Land O' Lakes Statement. That statement has engendered a bitter debate, but many trace the very flowering of Catholic higher learning to this same source and the vision of its authors. Many consider this event as the moment that Catholic universities and colleges began their journey toward integration into contemporary American academic life, even if others saw doing so as a "wholesale sell-out to the secular academy" (Gleason, 1995).

This journey toward full incorporation into mainstream American academic life has been rocky, especially in light of criticisms from the American hierarchy. A second moment of tension came in 1995, when differences over the implementation of *Ex Corde Ecclesiae*, the Church's constitution on Catholic higher education, led to heated exchanges over such issues as the *mandatum*—a kind of *nihil obstat*—required of faculty teaching Catholic theology and philosophy in Catholic institutions.

Some bishops were eager to see universities press their faculty to receive this official "mission" and approval from their local ordinaries. University presidents, by and large, took the position that the *mandatum* is a matter between bishops and theologians, and that it would be inappropriate for institutions to entangle themselves in their administration. This led to a standoff that only recently abated as leadership within the National Council of Catholic Bishops began conversations with presidents of Catholic colleges and issued a statement recognizing a short list of mutual concerns, such as the faith formation and catechesis of the present generation, the health of campus ministry programs, and the need for more support for the formation of lay Catholic leadership, while leaving the *mandatum* aside.

Yet issues such as controversial speakers, LGBT student groups, and faculty/staff benefits programs (covering reproductive procedures) remain difficult and contentious in some dioceses. For the most part, though, bishops and presidents collaborate at the local level, with the National Conference of Catholic Bishops acknowledging that most, if not all, politics are local. There is a growing consensus that the shared commitment to enhancing the Catholicity of these institutions and a common desire to leverage Catholic institutions of higher education for the benefit of the diocese and the nation outweighs some of the less significant issues.

In light of this success in such matters as growth in numbers served, in reputation, in the complexity of these institutions, in their academic standing, and in their financial security, we might ask if a document such as *Gravissimum Educationis* (Paul VI, 1965) played an important role in shaping this Catholic apostolate. Did it serve to catalyze this remarkable achievement? Can it still serve to inspire and help direct Catholic higher education in the United States? The answer, based on the course of Catholic higher education in the past 50 years as well as the shape of it in the present, is yes.

GRAVISSIMUM EDUCATIONIS (GE) AND ITS IMPACT

GE set in motion what has turned out to be a series of very positive developments in the life of the Church's higher education mission, especially in America. Without it and the direction it signaled one of several things would have happened: Catholic institutions of higher learning would have continued to be parochial in their culture and unable to make a significant mark within mainstream American higher education. Or, struggling with their cultural and social irrelevance, they would have become completely secular as they struggled to compete with their public and private counterparts.

Another option would have been be diminishment of the number of institutions to a handful of "authentically Catholic" colleges and universities. That, in fact, has become the case within the larger arena of Catholic higher education. It has become clear that the market for a more "traditional" Catholicism is a limited one. What we have today, out of the 262 total institutions, is a dozen or so institutions offering a more intensely "Catholic" educational program within the higher education community (ACCU, *FAQs*).

What has happened on a broad scale, due largely to the shock waves set off by Vatican II and its documents (such as *Gaudium et Spes*) and reinforced by *GE*, could only have been hoped for by the founders of these institutions. The institutions, which were designed to meet the needs of a newly arrived Catholic community, have evolved to address the needs of a maturing Catholic community. At the same time, these institutions are adapting to new waves of immigrants and competition with other high-quality institutions.

In order to explore this claim, three questions seem particularly relevant. First, did *GE* say anything new about education and if so, what? Second, did educators take the document seriously? I have already hinted at the Land O'

Lakes Statement. Put another way, did *GE* influence these educators or guide them in how they adjusted their institutions to a new reality under a new inspiration? Third, unlike their private counterparts founded by Protestant churches, why have Catholic institutions remained, for the most part, intentionally Catholic, even as they are increasingly led by lay educators and boards?

Did *GE* Say Anything New?

Scholars of Vatican II have noted that the documents produced by the Fathers of the Council took great pains to demonstrate their desire to be "in continuity" with past teaching. In other words, Council decrees sought to affirm, whenever possible, concerns advanced by the Church in those areas where the Church had already staked out a position. The exhortations, letters and encyclicals that influenced *GE* were not unlike those which had influenced most of the Council's decrees. From the closing days of World War I to the calling of the Council by John XXIII, successive popes spoke out about modern education and its challenges. The concerns of these exhortations and letters came out of a defensive posture and resistance to the forces that were unleashed by the modern state (Flannery, 1996).

From the turn of the century, the Church witnessed not only new forms of nationalism, with the state taking over many of the functions once relegated and directed by the Church and its structures, but especially the new role it began to play in the regulation of such matters as marriage, education, and health care. The Popes took advantage of congresses and meetings of professions such as midwives, doctors, teachers, and other groups who served the public good to present the Church's concerns. At times, the Church even created organizations and confraternities in order to exert its influence in the questions of the day, or simply to present a countervailing argument.

Forces such as communism and fascism had been successful in co-opting education, bending schools to become instruments of both the state and the ideologies undergirding them. These new totalitarian philosophies had, as their explicit aim, the weakening of the power of religion and its eventual replacement. These new forces proved to be the evil they were branded to be, having caused so much human misery in the 20th century. *GE* was meant to reinforce a response to contemporary forces inimical to freedom of conscience, even if the Church was not completely ready to advocate for "freedom of conscience" as a basic human right until this moment.

From the papacy of Benedict XV to Paul VI, then, popes had addressed the issues raised in *GE,* but Council Fathers decided to convey old ideas in a new way. What were the issues most concerning the papacy? Paramount in the minds of the Church's leaders was a desire to limit the role of the state in the moral and ethical formation of children. To counter this new authority, of course, the popes stressed the role of religion. Talks to teachers emphasized the Church's duty, and thus the duty of faithful Catholics, to resist interference of the state and other sectarian forces.

Eventually, the Popes began reflecting on the sacredness of marriage and the role of the family. As such, the nature and direction of the education of the child as a right belonging to parents by virtue of their responsibility to raise children in the Church was a consequent and late development. In speaking to organizations of Catholic teachers and other professionals, the popes urged the faithful to become active in shaping national education agendas and resisting an all-controlling state system of formation that usurped the spiritual and moral formation of children.

In addition, in exhortations to professors, heads of Catholic universities, and other professional organizations, the popes urged them to always be vigilant about guarding the deposit of faith and the formation of young minds and hearts for the Church. The popes did so over and against such forces as the state which in various forms, including democracies, assumed more and more that this right belonged to the state, given to it by the will of the majority.

Education played the role throughout the last century of driving the Church to better articulate a theory of human rights, the common good, and the principle of subsidiarity. In the endnotes for *GE*, the authors list the many speeches and decrees of popes who took up similar themes to those of *GE*. From Benedict XV's Apostolic Letter *Communes Litteras* of 1919 to John XXIII's *Pacem in Terris* of 1963, there is evidence of papal support for the critical role the Church can, and ought, to play in the education of children and the young. The fundamental role of parents; the development of the whole child, morally, physically, and intellectually; and the different, but critical, role played by institutions of higher learning are all cited in the writings of the popes, leading up to *GE*.

GE follows, then, a half-century of promotion by the Church of the significant role that Catholic lay men and women must play in education, and especially in helping shape the pedagogical philosophy that undergirds it. We usually associate the Church's interests with upholding clericalism, and indeed it did so. Yet the education of young people necessitated collaboration with lay men and women. Having seen time and again the disastrous consequences of complete state usurpation of education, the Church found itself defending the natural rights of parents, promoting the role of lay teachers, and looking to sympathetic universities to represent these issues in the wider public debate.

If the United States was somewhat out of touch with these "counter" sentiments, that was largely because it was fighting a slightly different battle, but doing so with control of its own institutions. It was busy building a system of education that went from preschool to postgraduate studies. It included a system of elementary, secondary, and tertiary institutions, which we are all well aware of as unique and of inestimable value. We can see that the issues *GE* addressed were not unfamiliar to Rome, but was there anything new?

In his well-known article "Vatican II: Did Anything Happen?," O'Malley, S.J. (2006), concluded that not only did the Council's decrees keep faith with the Church's previous teaching, they also took up new themes and set the Church off into new territory. To O'Malley and other historians of Vatican II, the Council Fathers managed at once to be "traditionalists" and also to break with tradition in remarkable ways. *GE* is one of those documents that followed such remarkable documents as *Gaudium et Spes* and did just that.

GE presented traditional themes but sent us off into new territory. It begins by describing education as "of paramount importance in people's lives" and an "ever-growing influence on the social progress of the age." And, reiterating one of its key "teachings" from Vatican II, the Council Fathers recognized a fundamental principle of our social lives: "as people become more conscious of their own dignity and responsibility, people are increasingly keen to take an active role in social life and especially in the economic and political spheres." The role of women and minority groups in these social and even religious spheres was all but predicted in these opening lines.

Reading *GE* in light of previous papal statements, with the exception of such documents as John XXIII's *Pacem in Terris*, the shift in tone and direction is quite noticeable. Speaking of the Council as a whole, O'Malley points out that Vatican II asked Catholics to look at the conditions and institutions of the contemporary world as objects and opportunities to embrace. O'Malley concluded his analysis of the Council's achievements with a reminder that the 1985 Synod of Bishops gave us norms with which to look at the Council's work, to see it in its totality and to recognize its coherence and integrity, in case, after twenty years, there was any doubt.

O'Malley urged his readers to look past the content and see the form that documents and decrees took, to see the spirit and understand what a radical break this was with the approach and words of all previous Councils. The Council spoke in what he called "a retrieved humanistic language."

According to O'Malley, the Council "engaged in a panegyric, in the *ars laudendi*, whose technical name is epideictic." This rhetorical approach aims to "heighten appreciation for a person, an event, or an institution and to excite to emulation of an ideal." By doing so, the Council intended to "excite to wonder and admiration." By helping us focus on the big issues, the Fathers of the Council sought to inspire and encourage, rather than control or direct. *GE*, like the other documents of the Council, was not meant to define concepts, explain critical elements of the teaching, or prove points. Rather, its goal was to move hearts.

One thing is then undoubtedly new. In style, there was a marked shift from content to form. That is, concerns were expressed in a new way, and, as such, yielded something new. The 1985 Synod addressing the question of how we ought to interpret Vatican II, 20 years after its conclusion, said something similar: Vatican II intended its teachings to be continuous but also fresh, even new. The Synod offered "norms" for how we are to approach the Council's work, stressing continuity and discontinuity. The sixth norm stated specifically that discontinuity with the past is a valid interpretive framework.

Anyone rereading *GE* would see it was very much in keeping with the Council's spirit of openness to the world, a shift from a defensive posture in all previous papal teachings on the subject and, at the same time, concerned with addressing a significant issue of the day. Like other documents, "It fully intended to place the Church among those who seek to contribute to "the lifting up of all peoples" (O'Malley, 2006, p. 74).

In his article expanding on O'Malley's work, Schloesser (2006) reads Vatican II as setting out deliberately to stake a claim for a new beginning and thus a certain but deliberate "discontinuity" with the past. Schloesser writes: "Looking back on the era and its great anxieties, I cannot help but notice two things: First, how painfully obvious it is that the Council not only did break from the past, but more importantly, just how much in the Cold War context such a rupture was not only possible but necessary" (pp. 276–77).

Therefore, the question that must be addressed seriously is: did the Council point the Church in a new direction? Forty years after the Council, everyone could see that it did. How else to account for the criticisms and hand-wringing that had become part of Church's political discourse, according to Schloesser (2006)?

For scholars such as Schloesser, the Council was as much a response to the world beyond the Church as it was to the accretions of practices and formulations within it. The Council Fathers were very much aware that they needed to address a world that had seen two World Wars, the Holocaust, the coming of the Atomic Age, the rise of atheistic communism, post-war existentialism, and a Cold War standoff between eastern and western Europe. He wrote:

> Some of the most poignant passages in the conciliar documents emanate from the Church's reversal of its longstanding dismissal of modernity in an attempt to take seriously the anxious concerns of contemporary humanity. The Council's call for the Church to be a humanizing force was an ethically necessary response to a century that had been, in Nietzsche's ironic phrase, "human, all too human." (Schloesser, 2006, p. 304)

The form, tone, style, and topics that the Council took in its statements and constitutions were appropriate to the context in which it found itself in 1965—"a magnanimous voice, rising above all pusillanimity, calling people back to the fundamental questions and evoking generosity and good will" (Schloesser, 2006, p. 319).

To sum up, *GE* stresses the right of families to have access to education for their children; the right of parents to educate children in the faith; the necessity that Catholic schools be places that nurture the physical, social, and intellectual lives of young people; and the call to academic excellence in our colleges and universities. *GE* offered nothing drastically new, but without placing these priorities in the context of a need to combat the state. Rather, the sentiment here is to urge the faithful to join with men and women of good will who share the same hopeful vision.

There is a new emphasis on the "embrace of the world" and the notion of sharing the same hopes and dreams for young people that Catholics share with all men and women of good will. The document then is written from the perspective that "we Christians" are already with, embedded in, and a part of a worldwide yearning for education that truly liberates the soul and enables the person to contribute to the common good and to serve the Creator.

With respect to higher education, then, what *GE* says is as important as how it says it. It affirms. *GE* entreats Catholics to become more involved in what it calls the "apostolate" of education. *GE* urges that, in whatever discipline Catholics find themselves, they should affirm the importance of taking the disciplines "on their own terms." That is, as Paul VI said, "the Church endeavors systematically to ensure that treatment of the individual disciplines is consonant with their own principles, their own methods, and with a true liberty of scientific inquiry" (1964).

If there was any suspicion that the Church was opposed to or uncomfortable with contemporary science and the scientific method, the Council Fathers did their best to affirm the Church's wholehearted embrace of the potential benefits of new knowledge and the processes producing such knowledge: "Every effort should be made in Catholic universities and faculties to develop departments for the advancement of scientific research" (Paul VI, 1965). Such language gave the American Catholic academic community a new hope and an unequivocal affirmation of their work in contributing to their disciplines and the professions.

The Council Fathers went so far as to urge the establishment of more Catholic universities to be strategically distributed throughout the world, but only if they are of quality with "high standards." Finally, the document concludes with a call for cooperation and collaboration between and among Catholic institutions of higher learning and among those working in the various disciplines, stressing that this should be for the welfare of the whole community.

Again, in terms of content, an array of papal speeches offered such sentiments in prior years. In tone and form, the gesture here is one of magnanimity and openness, even an eagerness to have the Church be seen as a contributor to the great project of building up and affirming peoples and cultures, a theme we see today echoed in the writing of the last three popes. *GE*, therefore, is not at all without precedent or context, but it does demonstrate an evolution of Catholic thought and tone.

This brings us to the question: How well have we responded to these exhortations? One way to read the enormous amount of activity over mission and identity occupying Catholic higher education today is that these institutions have taken the Council's call for academic integrity, high standards, cooperation, and collaboration, and for affirmation of the vocation of the educator in the field of higher education, quite seriously. A recent report to the Congregation for Catholic Education of the "state of our Catholic institutions" 50 years after the promulgation of *GE* and 25 years since *Ex Corde Ecclesiae* amounts to a litany of programs and projects and testimonials from the membership of the Association of Catholic Colleges and Universities (Moore, 2014).

One thing seems certain: one cannot use "orthodoxy" as a measure for answering this question. While the debate over what is authentically "Catholic" in higher education may continue, it should be said that nowhere in *GE* do the Council Fathers insist on a juridic relationship. Perhaps *GE* assumed such a relationship. But from the way the Fathers approach the variety of higher education institutions, this does not appear to be on their minds. Rather, serving the common good, openness to the role of faith, high academic standards, cooperation, and collaboration are the themes the Council Fathers stress in their exhortation.

Was the Document Taken Seriously?

A reference to the ACCU report should suffice to answer in the affirmative. Still, other defenders of this position have chronicled the steady progress made by Catholic institutions in their evolution into first-rate American academic institutions. In his highly acclaimed study of Catholic higher education's evolution after the Council, David O'Brien made the case that Catholic institutions in 1994 were closer to Ted Hesburgh's claim that these institutions were "if anything, more professedly Catholic than ever," despite a series of challenges in areas such as governance, academic freedom, and recruitment of committed Catholics to join the ranks while significantly impacting the Catholic culture of their institutions (O'Brien, 1994).

The turn, by Ted Hesburgh of Notre Dame and Paul Reinert of St. Louis University, toward lay board ownership of their respective institutions was undoubtedly a critically important step in this evolution story. Both men stated they did so precisely because Vatican II urged them to incorporate the laity, engage the world more intently, and bring a Catholic perspective into every field where the Church might conceivably make a contribution—themes echoed in *GE* (O'Brien, 1994).

Perhaps the other key moment was the gathering of 25 academics, including a number of bishops, at a retreat in Wisconsin specifically to discuss how best to implement Vatican II under the firm belief that updating and modernizing the schools would be necessary for relevance and therefore for survival. Their document, the Land O' Lakes Statement, would revolutionize the way Catholic educators at the tertiary level would come to see their vocation and the purpose of their institutions. While upbeat about the contributions that Catholic institutions could make to the American higher education landscape, the Land O' Lakes Statement was not without controversy.

Among the things the Land O' Lakes Statement embraced was the necessity of accepting academic freedom, especially freedom from all institutional and ecclesial restraint, in the modern university. In time, this document came to be seen as the opening salvo in a war of separation from the Catholic Church. What some think has been a process of renewal in the service of Vatican II's call for engaging the world was seen by others as a betrayal of an authentic Catholic allegiance (Gleason, 1987).

Led by Fr. Hesburgh, the two dozen leading university educators discussed and formalized a statement stemming from a "basic conviction that the Catholic university not only can but must be a university in the authentic sense of the word, both traditional and modern." In the Land O' Lakes Statement document's words, a Catholic university can only be a true university if it is truly Catholic. From this perspective, a Catholic university would, in fact, have something unique to contribute to the American landscape and claim to be even more authentic than its secular counterparts.

Although they are often ignored by critics, the first two of the Land O' Lakes Statement's nine sections were devoted to the articulation of a vision or theology in modern universities in order that Catholic universities might achieve their ultimate purpose. For the signers of the document, the discipline of theology gives Catholic universities their "distinct and authentically human flavor."

According to the Land O' Lakes Statement, both the Catholicity of institutions and their academic integrity are "achieved first of all and distinctively in the presence of a group of scholars in all the branches of theology." These disciplines are not only legitimate intellectual disciplines but essential. It should also be noted that these statements about the primacy of theology are bolder than the way theology's role is addressed in *Ex Corde Ecclesiae*.

The task of the Land O' Lakes Statement, then, was to explore the Catholic intellectual tradition and the "total religious heritage of the world" in order to come to the "best possible understanding of religion and revelation." In addition, the document acknowledged that theology must serve the ecumenical goals of collaboration and unity. Following this, document argued for the importance of research in all disciplines, for the public service role these institutions must play, and for their preeminent mission in preparing undergraduates to contribute to modern society by giving them "the whole world of ideas" and encouraging them to develop their full human capabilities and talents.

The Land O' Lakes Statement stressed the importance of a sound philosophical education for addressing the "pressing problems of our era." It mentions civil rights, international development and peace, and poverty as critical concerns with which a graduate of a Catholic institution ought to grapple. Moreover, it envisioned a special kind of "community" in Catholic colleges or universities, encouraging students to live out their faith "experientially and experimentally," in atmospheres where open and honest dialogue with others would contribute to a faith life with "keen interest in all human problems."

In short, the authors of Land O' Lakes envisioned a campus environment where students can learn to consecrate their talents and learning to worthy social purposes. Echoing some of the major themes of *GE*, the document reads as an application of *GE* to the American scene.

WHY DID THESE INSTITUTIONS REMAIN CATHOLIC, UNLIKE THEIR PROTESTANT COUNTERPARTS?

Catholic institutions that adapted their boards, student policies, and faculty hiring strategies even as they aimed seriously at building institutions of academic excellence did so knowing full well that there would be a risk in this sort of "secularization." Proponents of modernization support the Burtchaell thesis (1998) that Catholic institutions would head down the same path as the Ivy League schools that once began as seminaries—universities such as Harvard, Yale, Princeton, and the University of Chicago, to name some of the most prominent that have hardly a thread of relationship to their founding churches (Marsden, 1994b; Gallin, 2000).

Today, Catholic institutions, despite predictions to the contrary, are not like their formerly Protestant counterparts. Might that still happen? Perhaps, but characteristics of the Catholic experience in higher education have until now prevented such a situation from occurring. First, as Marsden points out, the Protestant churches allowed relationships with their former institutions to wither so that they eventually withdrew from official sponsorship and from control of the boards. In contrast, the American Catholic bishops and the Congregation for Education have been committed and consistent in their attempts to keep relationships strong and vital. Indeed, there remains an ongoing debate over ownership of Catholic institutions.

The St. Louis University (SLU) hospital "situation" in 1996 put a spotlight on this issue when Archbishop Rigali and Fr. Larry Biondi tangled over whether university officials had the right to sell its hospital without explicit permission of the Church since, in the Church's eyes, a formal alienation of SLU had never taken place. Ironically, Notre Dame, which was formally "alienated," is often thought of as the preeminently Catholic institution of higher learning although it is "juridically" separate—that is, not technically "owned by" the Church.

Second, as O'Brien and others have pointed out and as can be seen in Land O' Lakes, theology was never relegated to the seminary. It was kept and has been an important discipline within Catholic universities. Nearly all Catholic institutions have departments of religious studies or theology which teach Catholic doctrine alongside other religious traditions often to broaden the minds of undergraduates with "religion and revelation" and to show the important role theological ideas play in forming a coherent philosophy of life and an ethic of service.

In many Catholic universities, a legacy community still exists of religious men or religious women living on the campus itself. These sponsoring religious communities, while dwindling in numbers, contribute to the ethos and to the passing on of the particular charism of the institution. There was no parallel community in formerly Protestant institutions. Today, as in the past, these religious in Catholic institutions are available to orient their lay colleagues for major administrative positions and for service on the boards of these institutions. The special mission of institutions, including their religious character and the role of faith in the overall project of universities, are passed down from one generation to the next.

Third, almost all Catholic institutions have officers dedicated to mission and identity, orientation programs for faculty and administrators, and explicit statements of the Catholic mission are well publicized and articulated. As Georgetown's president, Tim Healy, noted in a 1991 speech, "The good effects of freedom in the Catholic University," to his fellow Jesuit educators, "We (Catholic institutions) have something unique to offer in American higher education. We did not adopt the two American heresies: that is, thinking the baccalaureate degree was for making a living, as opposed to discerning a philosophy of life, and the belief that the study of science or any academic discipline can and should be value-free" (n.p.).

Healy was adamant that Catholic universities, precisely because they are not neutral in their approach to the study of the human and divine sciences, are therefore open to scrutiny and challenge in the spirit of integrity demanded by truth-seeking. Said differently, one may no longer believe in a "hierarchy" of disciplines, but know that philosophical and theological inquiry have an essential role to play in both formation of the student and in the asking of important research questions.

Fourth, Catholic institutions have, by and large, a vibrant sacramental life readily available to everyone on their campuses including their local communities. Liturgies mark important events in the life of universities. Campus ministry programs and daily worship are seen as essential elements of community support. While other denominations have relegated worship to the interdenominational chapel, Catholic institutions often boast prominent chapel programs of rich activities related to support of faith and the spiritual growth of all members of their communities, not only for their students.

IDENTITY AND MISSION TODAY

Catholic higher education is unique insofar as its chief strength derives from a variety of factors, none more apparent than its diversity. Consider a few statistics (ACCU, *FAQs*). As noted, there are 240 Catholic degree-granting institutions, 215 of which enroll undergraduates, about 65% of whom are Catholic (ACCU, *Catholic higher education*) in programs leading to bachelor's degrees, with 10 more granting only associate degrees. Master's degrees can be earned at 209 Catholic universities. Allowing for institutions with multiple faculties, the total includes six medical schools, 46 schools of engineering, 28 law schools, 128 schools of nursing, and 184 schools of education. In sum, these institutions serve about 950,000 students (ACCU, *Catholic higher education*).

The major change over the past fifty years has been a loss of women's colleges. Today, only 14 such colleges remain. While not all of these disappeared, most became coeducational as a way to survive and remain vital. The majority of Catholic colleges and universities are still officially sponsored by their founding religious congregations, including 28 founded by the Jesuits, 16 by the Sisters of Mercy, six in the LaSallian tradition, three by the Society of Mary, and three by the Vincentians. All of these institutions are highly collaborative in nature, counting on lay men and women to continue the work begun many decades earlier.

What unites these founding charisms is an embrace of the Catholic intellectual heritage discernible in the official documents of institutions and the board selections of their presidents. In 2014 there were 27 new presidents, nearly all of whom have a background in Catholic education. Most were working within the college they were chosen to lead or came from another Catholic college or university (ACCU, *Welcome*).

The curricula and various programs and centers also display the Catholic character of institutions. Most require a core curriculum dominated by the humanities, requiring undergraduates to take courses in theology or religious studies. Likewise, courses in philosophy and morality or ethics are essential features of the standard required curricula. Almost all of these institutions have on their websites claims that Catholic values and Catholic social teaching are integrated into both curricular and cocurricular activities.

There are important ways that almost all Catholic institutions contribute to the Church and the common good. First, they educate a substantial number of middle-class and poorer students. Estimates of those who qualify for government grants meant for those in the lowest brackets of family income run from 15% to 50% at some colleges. Moreover, 95% of first-year students in Catholic colleges and universities receive some form of institutional or government aid to attend, with institutional aid amounting to 85% of the total (Day, 2011).

Institutions also educate many non-Catholics, thereby providing a rich atmosphere for Catholics and non-Catholics alike. There is research indicating that many students of other faiths, particularly Muslims, find Catholic institutions comfortable, safe places (Day, 2011). The integration of intellectual growth with leadership and spiritual growth is a hallmark of many non-academic campus programs. These objectives are woven into a variety of programs for students and take the place of organizations, such as solidarities and other devotional groups, required in the past.

Many student development directors speak of a resurgence of interest in spiritual activities as Church attendance has waned in the United States overall. Many students hunger for this type of opportunity to explore their faith. Research has shown that 59% of all Catholic university alumni say they "benefited very much from an emphasis on personal values and ethics," compared with the 16% of public university alumni who say the same (Day, 2011).

Among today's Catholic institutions exists a plethora of opportunities for informal interfaith dialogue. It is noteworthy that many Catholic institutions created formal centers for faith and spirituality exploration as well as for formation. Along with regular programming, many of these centers invite Jews, Muslims, Christians, and others as guest speakers to join in intercultural events and participate in deep and meaningful exchanges. Examples include the DePaul University Center for World Catholicism & Intercultural Theology, the Loyola University New Orleans Center for Intercultural Understanding, and the Assumption College Ecumenical Institute (ACCU, *Centers & institutes*).

Catholic business schools have a strong network of deans and faculty who meet regularly to discuss ways to help their students engage with society in a faith-filled way, specifically to form the next generation of business leaders who demonstrate professional aptitude coupled with an understanding of the true and deepest purposes of the business vocation. By way of illustration, the John A. Ryan Institute for Catholic Social Thought at the University of Saint Thomas partnered with the Pontifical Council in preparing the document "The Vocation of the Catholic Business Leader."

Catholic schools of social work, nursing, and law must embrace the Church's concern for social justice, both as an institutional priority and a curricular hallmark among the more readily identifiable characteristics of American Catholic higher education. It is safe to say that in many institutions, Catholic social teaching is applied across disciplines in ways both particular to the standards of those disciplines and as a means to foster interdisciplinary dialogue and cooperation. Within this framework, education is conducted in a service-learning style, which helps students experience solidarity with their community while developing the intellectual capabilities to confront social issues. In addition, 75% of graduates of Catholic institutions volunteer or in some other way participate in community service.

What is more difficult to measure, but is all too apparent for those who remember the pre-conciliar Catholic university, is the diversity of thought and perspectives that faculty bring to the academy. Faculty members who live their vocations in the context of Catholic colleges or universities discover a sense of community and purpose, a culture of freedom and support, and an opportunity to be an agent of transformation. Through their efforts, faculty members who embrace this vocational view can change the lives of their students, contribute to contemporary culture, and be enriched from and help advance the great tradition of Catholic thought.

To help shape and ensure the Catholic identity of their institutions, most Catholic institutions have created programs to help faculty increase their knowledge of the Catholic Intellectual Tradition and the heritages of their founding congregations. The level of urgency and success of this effort varies.

Programs such as Collegium, a summer colloquy for faith and intellectual life, is one such effort that is open to faculty from any Catholic institution. It engages faculty from all traditions to discover how they can contribute to the Catholic identity of their institutions while also respecting and taking advantage of their own spiritual perspectives and talents. The Collegium program, which is currently celebrating its 20th anniversary, counts more than 1,000 faculty as alumni.

CHALLENGES AND OPPORTUNITIES

Notable challenges for Catholic institutions of higher learning include the dwindling numbers of religious for maintaining the Catholic character and charisms of their founders. How do leaders leverage those charisms as resources in the ongoing formation of individuals on campus? Moreover, how can future institutional leaders be cultivated who are committed to the values of their founding orders and are prepared to develop and preserve those values? Catholic colleges and universities in the United States are home to approximately 1,000 scholarly centers and institutes, where faculty and other professionals explore topics as varied as ethics, justice, global studies, health sciences, interreligious studies, and many, many more.

Finally, at most institutions today, keeping the founding principles alive is a primary responsibility of the mission officer, a position that has grown rapidly in number and responsibility on Catholic campuses since the 1980s. A highly collaborative position, the mission officer is charged with maintaining and promoting the religious heritage of the institution, while remaining inclusive of people from other faith traditions and diverse backgrounds.

Dwindling financial resources have stretched many Catholic colleges. Larger, more complex institutions, some with large endowments, manage the rising cost of higher education by passing on these costs to students and with fund-raising.

The boards of trustees of Catholic colleges and universities represent both a challenge and an opportunity. These boards, made up predominantly of generous community representatives and committed alumni, have the primary responsibility for preserving and promoting the Catholic identity and mission of an institution. Nowhere else among the multitude of Catholic institutions of higher learning worldwide is this the case to the same scope and degree. This situation is a special embodiment of the results of the Second Vatican Council, Catholic tradition, and American innovation.

Recognizing the importance of the trustees' role, many universities dedicate a portion of board meeting time to augmenting members' "continuing education" in Catholic identity. In addition, seminars for Catholic university trustees held at the University of San Francisco and Notre Dame University, to name but two, reinforce the critical contribution that board members make to Catholic identity. On a number of American campuses, board members have established centers or endowments to study and enhance the charism of the institution's founders and other aspects of engaging the Catholic intellectual tradition. Chief among the board's responsibility is the selection and support of a president who understands, appreciates, and is committed to Catholic identity and mission as the driving force of the institution.

In 2006 the percentage of lay presidents at Catholic universities surpassed 50%; since then, the percentage has continued to climb, and is now above 60% (IPEDS database, multiple academic years; analysis by ACCU). Some laypeople come to the presidency without formal religious formation and lack access to the network of Church-related resources for clerics and vowed religious serving in higher education leadership. ACCU data show that in academic year 2012–13, 15 Catholic universities welcomed new presidents; in 2013–14, the number jumped to 25; and in academic year 2014–15, the number of new presidents reached 31.

Fortunately, numerous formation programs for new and aspiring presidents do exist to help cultivate the knowledge and networks that presidents

will need, unique to the Catholic mission. Efforts to groom the next generation of Catholic institutional leadership are especially vital given the role
campus presidents can play in the public arena. Observers often refer to the
"bully pulpit" of the university president, namely the authority and visibility
that the position garners. This prominence imbues campus leaders with a
responsibility, at times, to take a public stand on urgent social matters from a
position that is aligned with the Church's stance, fulfilling the call in *Ex
Corde* to "speak uncomfortable truths" (Paul II, 1990, para. 32).

A good example of this is a July 2013 letter signed by more than 100
Catholic university presidents and sent to every Catholic member of the
House of Representatives calling for comprehensive immigration reform—a
subject on which bishops have themselves been outspoken. The presidents
voiced their support for the DREAM Act, urging lawmakers to "draw wisdom and moral courage from our shared faith tradition" and recalling the
value that Catholics place on human dignity and the worth of all immigrants.

Catholic institutions of higher education enjoy generally good relations
with their bishops. Examples of collaborative initiatives between bishops and
university presidents can be found in *Promising Practices: Collaboration
Among Catholic Bishops and University Presidents* (Galligan-Stierle, 2005).
In fact, Catholic colleges and universities in the United States seek active
participation by their local bishops and genuinely open rapport between the
bishops and presidents. This relationship was the subject of study by the
Committee on Catholic Education of the United States Conference of Catholic Bishops, which released its "Final Report for the 10-Year Review of *The
Application of Ex Corde Ecclesiae for the United States*" in 2012.

Among the Committee's most positive findings, the report notes that "the
relationship between bishops and presidents on the local level can be characterized as 'positive and engaged, demonstrating progress on courtesy and
cooperation in the last ten years. Clarity about Catholic identity among college and university leadership has fostered substantive dialogues and cultivated greater mission-driven practices across the university.'" A working
group of bishops and university presidents continues the national dialogue
begun by the Committee, concentrating on such areas as hiring for mission
and the formation of trustees, faculty, and staff.

In September 2013 Boston College's Office of Institutional Research and
the ACCU published the results of a survey it conducted on the attitudes and
beliefs of Catholic college presidents concerning four key issues: leadership,
student religious formation, the Catholic intellectual tradition, and the relationship to the hierarchy. The response rate was a significant 62% of all those
who received the survey (119 presidents). The survey found that there is
significant investment in programs that address the literacy and understanding of the Catholic mission and identity of the institutions; 80% of institutions have programs. Still, the presidents cited this as a major concern.

Most college presidents said that about 25% of their students participate in retreats and religious programs. And, a vast majority—82%—said that the Catholic intellectual tradition somewhat or greatly influences teaching on campus, with about half, or 49%, stating that research was influenced by the tradition. Half of the presidents described that their relationship with their bishop as close. As many as 40% said they communicate with their bishop five or more times per year.

As might be expected, the training and background in Catholic theology of a president is largely dependent on whether the president is a religious or lay person. Lay presidents said they spent 30% or more of their time promoting the mission and identity of their institutions. This was more time and effort than their religious counterparts. Confidence that the institution will be led by someone with a commitment to the Catholic mission was high in both lay and religious groups, with lay presidents only slightly less confident (73% as opposed to 85%) that they would be replaced by someone with a deep understanding of the Catholic identity (Boston College, 2013).

The issues cited most often that give presidents pause and concern were the public perception of the Church, the impact of polarization within the Church, public infringement, and the diminishing number of priests and religious. Staffing for mission—finding people capable of advancing and promoting the Catholic character of the institution—was the chief concern and challenge cited. Second, presidents cited the problems of Church leadership, such as the small pool of qualified and interested Church leaders, the narrow agenda of many bishops, and the challenge of academic governance in a hierarchical Church—in short, ossification of the hierarchy expressed in a variety of ways.

A CLOSING NOTE

While Catholic universities have their critics, including some who insist that the designation "Catholic" should be removed from those not measuring up to their standards, the Congregation for Education and the Bishops of the United States have not seen fit to sever ties. If anything, they continue to reach out to this rich resource.

At the same time, while this country and many others question the direction, value, and practicality of higher education, it is still a prized possession, with its beneficiaries among those who have the greatest opportunities for employment, for impacting society, and for leading their communities. Catholic institutions of higher learning, at least in the United States, have won the loyalty of their communities, the respect of their colleagues and peers, and the gratitude of their alumni.

GE was instrumental in the formation of the thoughts and strategies designed to foment the flourishing of Catholic education. In the context of Vatican II, *GE* set Catholic higher education on the path of intellectual freedom, moral responsibility, religious identity, and social diversity that now mark Catholic colleges and universities.

The vision set out by *GE* has helped make Catholic institutions of higher education into sought-after destinations for students of all backgrounds and valued contributors to academic learning, society at large as well as to the Church. These institutions will continue to evolve and grow within an essentially Catholic framework. This is what those who wrote *GE* envisioned would be possible if we move forward and do not simply hold onto the past, as glorious as we might think it was.

REFERENCES

Association of Catholic Colleges and Universities. *Catholic higher education.* Retrieved from http://www.accunet.org/i4a/pages/index.cfm?pageid=3789

Association of Catholic Colleges and Universities. *FAQs: Catholic higher education.* Retrieved from http://www.accunet.org/i4a/pages/index.cfm?pageid=3797#sthash.tPM3zDi1.dpbs

Association of Catholic Colleges and Universities. *Report to the Congregation for Catholic Education.* Retrieved from http://www.accunet.org/files/public/Publications/EducatingTodayReport1.pdf, summer, 2014.

Association of Catholic Colleges and Universities. *Welcome to the Association of Catholic Colleges and Universities.* Retrieved from http://www.accunet.org/i4a/pages/index.cfm?pageid=1

Boston College. (2013). *Critical issues in Catholic higher education: Presidents' survey report.* Copy on file with author.

Burtchaell, J. T. (1998). *The dying of the light: The disengagement of colleges and universities from their Christian churches* . Grand Rapids, MI: Eerdmans Pub. Co.

Flannery, A. (Ed.). (1996). *Vatican II: Constitutions, Decrees and Declarations.* New York: Costello Press. Footnotes, especially pp. 589–91.

Galligan-Stierle, M. (Ed.). (2005). *Promising practices: Collaborations among Catholic bishops and university presidents.* Fairfield, CT: Sacred Heart University Press.

Gallin, A. (1996). *Independence and a new partnership in Catholic higher education.* Notre Dame, IN: University of Notre Dame Press.

Gallin, A. (2000). *Negotiating identity.* Notre Dame, IN: University of Notre Dame Press.

Gleason, P. (1995) *Contending with modernity: Catholic higher education in the 20th century.* New York: Oxford University Press.

Hardwick Day. (2011). *A comparative advantage alumni study for the National Catholic College Admission Association.* Retrieved from http://www.catholiccollegesonline.org/resources/pdfs/values-that-matter-2011-hardwick-day.pdf

Healy, T. (1999). *Selected Writing from Rev. Timothy S. Healy, S.J.,* Retrieved from http://visualidentity.georgetown.edu/foundational-documents/timothy-healy-selected-writings

Hesburgh, T. (1994). *The challenge and promise of a Catholic university.* Notre Dame, IN: University of Notre Dame Press.

Marsden, G. (1994a). *The soul of the American university: From Protestant establishment to established nonbelief,* Oxford.

Marsden, G. (1994b). What can Catholic universities learn from Protestant examples? In Moore, P. (Ed.), *Catholic higher education embraces efforts to assess identity.* (2014). ACCU publication "Update." Vol. XL, No. 2.

O'Brien, D. (1998). The Land o Lakes Statement. *Boston College Magazine*. Retrieved from http://www.bc.edu/content/dam/files/offices/mission/pdf1/cu7.pdf

O'Brien, D. (1994). *From the heart of the American church: Catholic higher education and American culture*. New York, Orbis Books.

O'Malley, J.W. (2006). Vatican II: Did anything happen? *Theological Studies* 67, 3–33.

Paul II. (1990). *Ex Corde Ecclesiae*. Retrieved from http://www.vatican.va/holy_father/john_paul_ii/apost_constitutions/documents/hf_jp-ii_apc_15081990_ex-corde-ecclesiae_en.html

Paul VI. *Gravissimum Educationis*. Declaration on Christian Education. 1965.

Paul VI. (1964, April). Allocution to the Academic Senate of the Catholic University of Milan. *Encyclicals and Discourses of Paul VI*, 2, Rome, pp. 438–43.

Schloesser, S. (2006). Against forgetting: Memory, History, Vatican. *Theological Studies, 67*, 275–319.

Steinfels, P. (2003). *A people adrift*. New York: Simon & Schuster.

Chapter Seven

Gravissimum Educationis at the 50-Year Mark

Catholic Schools and the Preferential Option for the Poor

Shane P. Martin and Jordan Gadd

INTRODUCTION

At the midcentury mark, Vatican II seems as inspirational and innovative in 2015 as it ever did. The documents from the Second Vatican Council still speak to a world in need of reconciliation, healing, and renewal. Adjusting for some of the language of the day, the vision that is espoused in the documents of a renewed Church firmly engaged in dialogue with the secular world resonates today as much as when the documents were written.

Among the many documents of the Second Vatican Council, the Declaration on Christian Education, *Gravissimum Educationis* has greatly influenced the development of Catholic education throughout the world. Released toward the end of the Second Vatican Council, this document provided both a framework for understanding the Church's approach to Christian education and the inspiration for further developments in Church-thinking about Catholic schools.

In 1966 Joseph Ratzinger, the future Pope Benedict XVI, referred to *Gravissimum Educationis* as an unfortunately weak document (Briel, 2008). Suggesting that the Council members were tiring as they moved toward the conclusion of their work, Ratzinger felt that the declaration was neither specific enough nor did it engage the fullness of the Council's anthropology as it could be applied to education. *Gravissimum Educationis*, though, did much to move the importance of Catholic schools to the forefront of the Church's apostolic mission in the period of renewal following the Council.

This chapter explores the declaration's influence on Catholic schools and the notion of the preferential option for the poor. The chapter first discusses the document itself in terms of the preferential option for the poor before reviewing the development of subsequent Church documents as they addressed the preferential option for the poor. Finally, the chapter discusses the practical implementation of the preferential option in Catholic education in the United States. The chapter concludes with reflections on the preferential option in light of the papacy of Pope Francis.

THE DECLARATION ON
CHRISTIAN EDUCATION: GRAVISSIMUM

Educationis, and the Preferential Option for the Poor

After addressing important issues such as liturgy, communications, ecumenism, and religious life, the Council members turned their attention to Christian education, the apostolate of the laity, religious freedom, and the relationship between the Church and the modern world. Pope Paul VI proclaimed *Gravissimum Educationis* on October 28, 1965, as part of a flurry of activity toward the end of the Council. In fact, 11 of the 16 documents of Vatican II were finalized in a 40-day period between late October and early December 1965, culminating in the magnificent and the profoundly transformational pastoral constitution *Gaudium et Spes*, on the Church in the Modern World.

In this context, *Gravissimum Educationis* was not as eye-catching, at least outside of education circles, as some of the other documents that were proclaimed at the same time. The Declaration on Christian Education engendered little debate among the bishops (Leckey, 2006). However, for Catholic educators, *Gravissimum Educationis* highlighted the importance of Catholic schools as an apostolic outreach of the Church, affirmed their vocation to the apostolate of Catholic education, and built a bridge between what Gunzer (1995, as cited in Briel, 2008) described as the "rather dark, apodictic-sounding encyclical on education by Pius XI in 1929 (*Divini Illius Magistri*)" and the modern times.

The construct of the preferential option for the poor was not implicitly mentioned in *Gravissimum Educationis*. Rather, it was first used in Church documents in 1968 by the Latin American Conference of Bishops meeting in Medellín, Colombia. Moreover, there are important notions in the declaration that definitively lay the conceptual groundwork for this notion.

Gravissimum Educationis begins with a declaration of the universal right to education held by all peoples by virtue of their dignity as human beings. The declaration continues by describing true education as teleological, in the sense that it aims at the formation of the human person in the pursuit of the ultimate end: the good of society. The notion of contributing to the common good is prevalent throughout the document, a notion that became important in the later development of Catholic schools and the option for the poor.

At its heart, *Gravissimum Educationis* affirms the notion that parents should have a choice in deciding the best educational options for their children, and that public powers have the obligation to protect and defend this right. Further, the declaration proclaims that the state must protect the right of children to an adequate school education. Additionally, *Gravissimum Educationis* supports the principle of subsidiarity and connects it to the Council's affirmation of cultural pluralism that is developed through many of its documents. It is not enough for the state to protect the rights of children to an adequate education, as mentioned above. The document asserts:

> The state . . . must always keep in mind the principle of subsidiarity so that there is no kind of school monopoly for this is opposed to the native rights of the human person, to the development and spread of culture, to the peaceful association of citizens and to the pluralism that exists today in ever so many societies. (Vatican Council II, 1965, 21)

This recognition of cultural pluralism, and the accompanying notion of *inculturation* used in other Vatican II documents and articulated in *Gaudium et Spes* as the Church's primary approach to missiology, was foundational for the development of how the poor and marginalized are perceived. The Council's anthropology affirms the importance of culture—all cultures—an idea that resonated with the Latin American bishops as they developed the notion of the preferential option for the poor.

Perhaps most significant to the development of the preferential option for the poor is *Gravissimum Educationis*'s acknowledgment that the Catholic schools are situated in local contexts, which also includes ministry to non-Catholics. This inclusive and contextualized notion of school is further developed in the exhortation to pastors and all of the faithful to

> spare no sacrifice in helping Catholic schools fulfill their function in a continually more perfect way, and *especially* in caring for the needs of those who are poor in the goods of this world or who are deprived of the assistance and affection of a family or who are strangers to the gift of Faith. (Vatican Council II, 1965, 31, emphasis added)

This direct acknowledgment of the obligation of the Church and its leaders to educate the poor—not simply the poor in faith, but also in material goods or family circumstance—is powerful in its simplicity and directness. It was to be developed in future documents while laying the groundwork for the requirement that Catholic education respond to the poor in society.

KEY VATICAN DOCUMENTS ON EDUCATION
INFLUENCED BY *GRAVISSIMUM EDUCATIONIS*

As mentioned previously, *Gravissimum Educationis* was one of the final documents of the Second Vatican Council as the Church Fathers recognized that there was further work to be done in explicating and clarifying its principles (Briel, 2008). The Church Fathers thus urged the Sacred Congregation for Catholic Education and local bishops' conferences to continue the work. The Congregation for Catholic Education delivered on this charge in subsequent documents, each of which is discussed as they developed *Gravissimum Educationis*'s commitment to the poor and marginalized.

Pope John Paul II changed the name of the Sacred Congregation for Catholic Education to the Congregation for Catholic Education in 1988. References to the Congregation in this chapter, then, reflect the name used at the time of publication of each document.

Gravissimum Educationis itself was not earth-shattering in discussing the preferential option for the poor and Catholic schools, especially in light of future developments such as the 1968 Latin American Conference of Bishops at Medellín, Colombia. Yet *Gravissimum Educationis* laid the groundwork for a profound shift in thought and practice for Catholic schools. Consequently, this section traces the influence of *Gravissimum Educationis* on subsequent Church documents on education and Catholic schools, specifically as they addressed the preferential option for the poor.

The first major post–Vatican II document to address Catholic education by the Sacred Congregation for Catholic Education was titled simply *The Catholic School*. Published in 1977, a little more than a decade after the Council, *The Catholic School* sought to develop the ideas of *Gravissimum Educationis* on Christian education specifically for the context of Catholic schools.

Noteworthy is the way *The Catholic School* builds on *Gravissimum Educationis*'s notion of the importance of cultural pluralism and introduces the notion of social justice in education. It states that a Catholic school must not be divisive or presumptuous, and should be open to others and aid in cooperation. Further, the document describes the Catholic school as having to be particularly sensitive to "the call from every part of the world for a more just society, and tries to make its own contribution towards it" (The Sacred Congregation for Catholic Education, 1977, 22). It puts the demands of justice, even in the face of local opposition, into practice in the daily life of schools.

The Catholic School goes on to address situations where Catholic schools enroll a majority of children from wealthier families, and says that in these situations the Catholic school runs the risk of giving counter-witness. Quoting *Gravissimum Educationis*, *The Catholic School* reminds its readers that first and foremost the Church offers its educational service to the poor.

Insofar as education is an important means of improving the social and economic condition of youth, if Catholic schools were to give their attention exclusively or even predominantly to those from wealthier social classes, "it could be contributing towards maintaining their privileged position, and could thereby continue to favor a society which is unjust" (The Sacred Congregation for Catholic Education, 1977, 58).

The next document by the Sacred Congregation for Catholic Education focused on the increasing role of the laity in Catholic schools. Titled *Lay Catholics in Schools: Witnesses to Faith*, the 1982 document was an affirmation of the key role of lay educators in Catholic schools "who will substantially determine whether or not a (Catholic) school realizes its aims and accomplishes its objectives" (The Sacred Congregation for Catholic Education, 1982, 1).

Lay Catholics in Schools: Witnesses to Faith primarily serves as a call to mission and identity for lay Catholic educators while addressing the synthesis of faith, culture, and life. In this section, the document calls for the lay Catholic educator to appear as a witness to faith. In line with the Vatican II spirit, it calls for the Catholic teacher to look for opportunities to engage the appropriate dialogue between culture and faith in order to bring about synthesis in the student.

Further, *Lay Catholics in Schools: Witnesses to Faith* calls on Catholic educators to engage in critical transmission of values and countervalues situated in concrete local contexts. These values generate human attitudes, including "conscientious responsibility . . . a sense of solidarity with and service towards all other persons, a sensitivity for justice, a special awareness of being called to be positive agents of change in a society that is undergoing continuous transformation" (The Sacred Congregation for Catholic Education, 1982, 30).

Lay Catholics in Schools: Witnesses to Faith added an important set of constructs to the notion of the preferential option for the poor in Catholic schools. First, it unequivocally recognized and affirmed the importance of the lay Catholic educator, which opened up possibilities for leadership and growth in ideology in Catholic education. Lay educators were much more connected to the local contexts and realities of daily life than their clerical counterparts, and this shift would influence the way Catholic schools understood their mission to the poor and marginalized.

Perhaps even more importantly, *Lay Catholics in Schools: Witnesses to Faith* introduced the importance of service in Catholic schools, along with solidarity with *all* other persons and the development of Catholic students as agents of change for social justice (The Sacred Congregation for Catholic Education, 1982, 30). These notions would lay the groundwork for social justice and service learning programs that would make their way into the curriculum of Catholic schools worldwide.

The 1988 document from the newly renamed Congregation for Catholic Education, *The Religious Dimension of Education in a Catholic School: Guidelines for Reflection and Renewal*, marks an interesting development in the understanding of Catholic education and its relationship to the preferential option for the poor. Perhaps this document is as important for what it does not say as for what it does say.

Clearly influenced by the papacy of Pope John Paul II, who is quoted throughout the document, this fairly lengthy text sets out to unmistakably establish the ecclesial authority of the institutional Church over Catholic schools and the lay people who increasingly lead them (Congregation for Catholic Education, 1988, 38). The primary missiology in the document is one of evangelization, and this is a primary purpose of the Catholic school (34).

Referencing the call to establish a universal catechism by the Second Extraordinary General Assembly of the Synod of Bishops of 1985, *The Religious Dimension of Education in a Catholic School* anticipates the new catechism. In so doing, the document calls for an approach to religious instruction that provides clear guidelines to teachers and students in Catholic schools concerning proper religious instruction.

The Religious Dimension of Education in a Catholic School opens with an overview of the present state of youth. It reads as from a deficit perspective: "Young people today are notably more depressed than in the past" (Congregation for Catholic Education, 1988, 11). The "fault" for the crises of faith that youth experience lies with the family, the parish, or the Catholic school itself (17). Therefore, clearer guidelines and better religious instruction will remedy this deficiency.

The Religious Dimension of Education in a Catholic School notes that many of today's youth "are deeply disturbed by the injustice which divides the free and the rich from the poor and the oppressed" (Congregation for Catholic Education, 1988, 20). Yet the document does little to encourage Catholic education to address the causes of injustice. It supports the work of recognized international organizations such as UNESCO and the United Nations (45), but defines justice as "the recognition of the rights of each individual" (89).

This document emphasizes obedience and service along with declaring that "All manifestations of egoism, rebellion, antipathy, jealousy, hatred, or revenge must be rooted out" (87). The most direct reference to the poor is "a preferential option for the less fortunate, the sick, the poor, the handicapped, the lonely" (89). Perhaps the careful construction of justice as an individual rather than social notion and the preferential option for those less fortunate rather than an examination of the causes of poverty were a reaction to movements in the Church such as liberation theology, which Pope John Paul II notably opposed.

The Catholic School on the Threshold of the Third Millennium served as a bridge document into the new century. The letter from the Congregation still referenced the Catholic school's "fundamental duty to evangelize" (Congregation for Catholic Education, 1997, 3) so that all men and women would "receive the gift of salvation" (3), but struck important themes that signaled the Congregation's concern with Catholic schools and the poor.

The opening of the document acknowledged the widening gap between the rich and the poor, and for the first time referenced the massive migration from underdeveloped to highly-developed countries (1). It discussed the positive aspects of multiculturalism, including an increasingly multiethnic and multireligious society, but acknowledged these as a source of further problems (1). This acknowledgment of the social nature of justice is noteworthy, for it seemed to be absent in the proceeding document from the Congregation.

The Catholic School on the Threshold of the Third Millennium provided a number of direct references to Catholic schools and the poor. It states that the Catholic school has at its root "special attention to those who are the weakest" and has "responded to the needs of the socially and economically disadvantaged" (Congregation for Catholic Education, 1997, 15). Further, the letter addressed the new poor in a spirit of love, and calls for a special focus to the poor and marginalized (15).

In *The Catholic School on the Threshold of the Third Millennium*, the Congregation affirms two important notions laid out in *Gravissimum Educationis*: the Catholic school at the service of society (16) and the principle of subsidiarity (17). In discussing these themes and focusing on the social nature of injustice, the document can be seen as contributing directly to a 21st-century understanding of the Catholic school and the preferential option for the poor.

The 2007 document *Educating Together in Catholic Schools: A Shared Mission Between Consecrated Persons and the Lay Faithful* served to call attention to the fundamental aspects of cooperation between lay faithful and consecrated persons in Catholic schools. It is noteworthy in that it addressed the challenges of globalization along with the challenges in the growing gap between the rich and the poor and the subsequent increases in migration (Congregation for Catholic Education, 2007, 1).

Educating Together in Catholic Schools: A Shared Mission Between Consecrated Persons and the Lay Faithful exhorted students in Catholic schools "to overcome individualism and to discover, in the light of faith, that they are called to live responsibly a specific vocation to friendship with Christ and in solidarity with other persons" (46). Further, youth are called to be positive in the world, focusing on "what needs to be transformed and what injustices must be overcome" (46). The document positions friendship with Christ next to solidarity with other persons, and links these to social justice, notions that further the understanding of the preferential option for the poor.

Two recent Congregation documents address Catholic education. Perhaps the most profound document on Catholic education is the Congregation's *Educating to Intercultural Dialogue in Catholic Schools: Living in Harmony for a Civilization of Love*. This document thoroughly reflects the spirit of Vatican II, specifically as connected to education, *Gravissimum Educationis*.

In language as eloquent as any Vatican II document, *Educating to Intercultural Dialogue in Catholic Schools* affirms the importance of culture and the plurality of cultures, and recommends the intercultural approach to pluralism in the modern world. The notions of poverty and justice are more thoroughly developed compared to previous documents:

> The curriculum (of the Catholic school) must help the students reflect on the great problems of our time, including those where one sees more clearly the difficult situation of a large part of humanity's living conditions. These would include the unequal distribution of resources, poverty, injustice and human rights denied. "Poverty" implies a careful consideration of the phenomenon of globalization, and suggests a broad and developed vision of poverty, in all its various forms and causes. (Congregation for Catholic Education, 2013, 66)

The second of the two most recent documents, an *Instrumentum Laboris* titled *Educating Today and Tomorrow: A Renewing Passion*, was developed in anticipation of the 50th anniversary of *Gravissimum Educationis*. Quoting *Lumen Gentium*, and in line with Pope Francis's teachings, the document calls for envisioning Christian education within the context of faith of a poor Church for the poor (Congregation for Catholic Education, 2014, 1).

Both of these documents serve as mileposts at the 50-year mark of *Gravissimus Educationis*. The documents articulate with clarity and passion the key developments of Catholic thinking about education and the preferential option for the poor. Although that precise term is not used, the vision of Catholic schools responding to the signs of the times, with a specific preference for the poor, is unmistakably clear.

THEORY INTO PRACTICE: EFFECTS OF *GRAVISSIMUM EDUCATIONIS* ON CATHOLIC SCHOOLS

Gravissimum Educationis set into motion a 50-year period of Congregation documents articulating the vision and conceptual framework for how Catholic schools should respond to the poor. Catholic schools have responded by developing numerous programs to put theory into practice. An overview of some of these programs follows.

One significant outgrowth of the Church documents emphasizing the importance of a Catholic education, particularly for underserved students, is the rise of service learning as an integral part of many Catholic high schools' mission and curriculum. One example of this is the Cristo Rey Network, a group of 28 urban high schools serving 9,000 students nationally, that includes a required work experience component be integrated into the curriculum (Cristo Rey Network, 2014).

The Cristo Rey Network only enrolls students from low-income backgrounds; nationally 96% are students of color, with an average family income of $34,000 (Cristo Rey Network, 2014). In addition to offering rigorous academics and instilling Catholic moral values in its students, the Cristo Rey schools also "integrate the learning present in its work program, classroom and extracurricular experiences for the fullest benefit of its student workers" (Cristo Rey Network, 2014). This commitment to serving students from low-income backgrounds and an emphasis on service learning aligns with the Church documents calling Catholic schools to make themselves a viable option for the poor.

In Los Angeles, the Cristo Rey model has shown great success at Verbum Dei High School, a Catholic Jesuit college and career preparatory all-boys school located in the Watts community of South Los Angeles that is a member of the Cristo Rey Network (Verbum Dei High School, 2014). Verbum Dei serves economically and educationally underserved students who are primarily African American and Latino and live in or near the community where the school is located (see Work Study: A Model for Success, Verbum Dei High School, 2014).

Verbum Dei began its Corporate Work Study Program eight years ago in partnership with local businesses, where participating organizations give Verbum Dei one "full-time equivalent" student internship for a fee of $28,000. This position is filled by four students who work five full days per month on a rotational basis in addition to their coursework and extracurricular activities that integrate the work experience into the overall curriculum (see Work Study: A Model for Success, Verbum Dei High School, 2014).

The success of this model is evident in the academics, with 100% of Verbum Dei students being accepted into college. In the work experience, the average work attendance is 99%, and 97% of students receive a performance evaluation of good or excellent (see Work Study: A Model for Success, Verbum Dei High School, 2014). Verbum Dei is a prime example of a Catholic school serving students from low-income backgrounds and integrating service to those less fortunate into the curriculum.

The Jesuit educational tradition also emphasizes the importance of service learning in its mission to educate the whole person. Many Jesuit high schools include a service learning component in the curriculum to enhance its students' understanding of and connection with underserved communities.

Loyola High School of Los Angeles, for instance, includes service in its mission and as a core value: "Informed by a faith that does justice, Loyola challenges our students to be 'men for and with others'; to serve as Jesus did, by being in companionship with, and learning from, persons who are disenfranchised, marginalized and the most in need" (Loyola High School of Los Angeles, 2014). This commitment to service is evidenced in the school's Graduate at Graduation program, where both the religious and justice aspects of service are emphasized (Loyola High School of Los Angeles, 2014).

The religion tenet at Loyola High School of Los Angeles asks students to "demonstrate an understanding of the relationship between faith in Jesus (the model for being a 'man for others') and being a 'man for others' that manifests itself through community service and a commitment to social justice," while the justice tenet asks students to "recognize the value of community service and develop a sense of social responsibility guided by compassion, confidence and accountability" (Loyola High School of Los Angeles, 2014). Loyola High School of Los Angeles is just one of many Jesuit high schools that serve the poor in numerous ways, including both academics and service.

CATHOLIC HIGHER EDUCATION RESPONDS

Catholic universities responded to the Church documents in multiple, varied ways, enhancing their own respective missions while serving Catholic K–12 schools and the underserved student populations they in turn serve. In this regard, the University of Notre Dame established the Alliance for Catholic Education (ACE) in 1993 to "sustain, strengthen, and transform Catholic schools" (University of Notre Dame, 2014).

ACE began as a teacher service program that placed teachers in underserved Catholic schools in cities across the United States. ACE was founded on the three pillars of "professional development, community-building, and spiritual growth" that shaped the organization's evolution into the wide-reaching organization it is today, working to form teachers and leaders for Catholic schools, providing professional services, and promoting outreach in support of Catholic schools (University of Notre Dame, 2014).

The success of Notre Dame's ACE program expanded to other Catholic universities interested in strengthening and supporting Catholic schools in their communities. In the late 1990s, ACE provided financial and programmatic support to other Catholic universities who started similar programs (Walch, 2013). This group of colleges and universities grew to 15 by 2005 and organized themselves as the University Consortium for Catholic Education (UCCE) (Walch, 2013).

The UCCE represented a national commitment by Catholic colleges and universities to the formation of Catholic teachers and leaders serving students from low-income backgrounds, while simultaneously reinvigorating and strengthening Catholic K–12 schools. UCCE adopted and refined ACE's three-pillar approach—academic preparation, community, and spirituality— that has been critical to its success in supporting Catholic education (Walch, 2013). UCCE now includes 13 programs with more than 400 teachers in Catholic schools across 24 states annually (The University Consortium for Catholic Education, 2014). One indicator of UCCE's success is that a majority of graduates from these programs, more than 70%, remain in education (Walch, 2013).

In Los Angeles, the ACE-like program housed at Loyola Marymount University, Partners in Los Angeles Catholic Education (PLACE Corps), has had a significant impact on the Catholic education community in the Archdiocese of Los Angeles. Founded in 2000, the program places recent college graduates in under-resourced Catholic K–12 schools, which are often in need of bright, faith-filled teachers ready to commit to serving students from low-income backgrounds.

The PLACE Corps offers evidence of the program's impact beyond the classroom. Currently nine schools in the Archdiocese of Los Angeles have a PLACE Corps alumna/us serving as principal, and an additional 25 PLACE Corps alumni serve in administrative capacities other than principal in Archdiocesan Catholic schools. Of PLACE Corps alumni, one is an ordained Archdiocesan priest, two have taken vows as brothers, and five are in religious formation. This is a testament to the three pillars of the program— professionalism, community, and spirituality—that are in alignment with the UCCE model and the founding ACE program (Loyola Marymount University, 2014).

In order to strengthen Catholic K–12 schools nationally, Loyola University Chicago, through its Andrew M. Greeley Center for Catholic Education, led a broad collaboration among Catholic educators, including "leaders and scholars in Catholic institutions of higher education, superintendents, principals, bishops, congregational sponsors, pastors, National Catholic Educational Association directors and executive committee members, and Catholic school supporters," to develop a set of national standards and benchmarks for effective Catholic K–12 schools (The Catholic School Standards Project, 2014).

The document offers all Catholic schools "a common framework of universal characteristics of Catholic identity and agreed upon criteria for Catholic school excellence" (The Catholic School Standards Project, 2014). The standards and benchmarks are organized around four core themes: mission and Catholic identity, governance and leadership, academic excellence, and operational vitality (The Catholic School Standards Project, 2014). These standards offer a roadmap forward for Catholic K–12 schools in the United

States to thrive and fulfill their mission to serve all communities, particularly the poor and underserved.

Given the focus on Latino access to Catholic K–12 schools, the Boston College Roche Center for Catholic Education launched the Two-Way Immersion Network for Catholic Schools (TWIN-CS) in 2012 to support biliteracy and bilingualism in Catholic elementary schools (Boston College, 2014). In partnership with the National Catholic Educational Association, TWIN-CS is working with 12 network schools to provide training and design support to develop two-way immersion programs that serve culturally and linguistically diverse students (Boston College, 2014). The goals of two-way immersion schools—academic excellence, bilingualism and biliteracy, and cultural competence—align with Church documents on the importance of intercultural competency and diversity for the future of Catholic K–12 education (Boston College, 2014).

In 2005 Notre Dame led an effort to develop a comprehensive strategy for higher education to strengthen and support Catholic K–12 schools in the United States that was born out of a call by the United States Conference of Catholic Bishops (University of Notre Dame, 2014). The University formed a national task force on Catholic education to "discuss the issues affecting our nation's Catholic schools" (University of Notre Dame, 2014).

Published in 2006, the final report from this task force, "Making God Known, Loved, and Served: The Future of Catholic Primary and Secondary Schools in the Untied States," identified 12 recommendations centered around the four major needs of Catholic K–12 schools outlined in the "Renewing our Commitment" pastoral statement—strengthen Catholic identity, attract and form talented leaders, ensure academic excellence, and finance Catholic schools so that they are accessible for all families (University of Notre Dame, 2006).

As follow-up to the 2006 report, Notre Dame formed a task force to examine the participation of Latino children and families in Catholic K–12 schools. This group released its report in 2009. Given the institutional context of the Catholic school system and the large demographic shifts in the United States, the task force found both tremendous challenges and opportunities for Latino student access and success.

The report identified four high-level recommendations to strengthen Latino enrollment in K–12 Catholic schools: develop demand, develop access, develop leaders, and transform Catholic schools and systems (University of Notre Dame, 2009). It is clear that there is significant overlap in these recommendations for Latino students and families with the earlier Notre Dame report and the "Renewing our Commitment" pastoral statement.

In Los Angeles, where these demographic shifts have been significantly ahead of the rest of the country, there is a specific need for research on the outcomes of Catholic schools for students of color from low-income communities. Loyola Marymount University initiated a multi-phase longitudinal study on the efficacy of inner-city Catholic schools for students living in poverty, with the first report published in 2008.

This phase found that students in Los Angeles Archdiocesan Catholic schools who received tuition assistance from the Catholic Education Foundation graduated from high school at a 98% rate compared to the state-wide public school graduation rate of 85% (Litton, Martin, Higareda, & Mendoza, 2010). Subsequently, phases two and three replicated similarly strong high school graduation rates for successive cohorts of students who received tuition assistance from the Catholic Education Foundation.

Phases two and three also expanded on the efficacy measures for inner-city Catholic schools. Efforts during these phases included completion rates for a California college preparation course, SAT sitting rates and scores, ACT sitting rates, and college acceptance and attendance rates (Higareda, Martin, Chavez, & Holyk-Casey, 2011; Huchting, Martin, Chavez, Holyk-Casey, & Ruiz, 2014).

The third phase expanded the comparison to also include comparable charter schools while the Archdiocesan Catholic schools continued to outperform both the comparable traditional public and charter schools in Los Angeles. The research on the impact of Catholic K–12 schools makes a compelling argument for including Catholic schools—a proven model with a long track record of success, particularly for our society's most marginalized and vulnerable members—in the national conversation on education reform.

CONCLUSION: CATHOLIC SCHOOLS IN THE POPE FRANCIS ERA: A CHURCH FOR THE POOR

The papacy of Pope Francis marks a decided commitment to the documents of Vatican II, and most especially the preferential option for the poor. In his simplistic way of living and apostolic outreach, the Pope models the preferential option for all to consider embracing. Pope Francis has made it clear that the poor are his preferential option: "The Pope loves everyone, rich and poor alike, but he is obliged in the name of Christ to remind all that the rich must help, respect and promote the poor" (Apostolic Exhortation, *Evangelii Gaudium*, of the Holy Father Francis, 2013, para. 58).

This is not only Francis' personal option, but the one he calls the entire Church to as Pope. "Each individual Christian and every community is called to be an instrument of God for the liberation and promotion of the poor, and for enabling them to be fully a part of society" (Francis, 2013, para. 187).

Pope Francis' vision of the Church provides a model for how Catholic education can further embrace the preferential option for the poor: "I prefer a church which is bruised, hurting and dirty because it has been out on the streets, rather than a church which is unhealthy from being confined and from clinging to its own security" (Francis, 2013, para. 49).

As Catholic schools embrace these words of Pope Francis, they show fidelity to the vision of *Gravissimum Educationis* and the document of Vatican II. It is remarkable that, at the 50th anniversary of this important document on Christian education, the Church has a pontiff who understands the vision and era of the Second Vatican Council, yet is fully immersed in the real world of modern times, especially in his love and concern for the poor. Pope Francis is the living document. Perhaps under the papacy of Francis the fullness of Vatican II and the preferential option for the poor will come to pass.

REFERENCES

Boston College. (2014). *The two-way immersion network for Catholic schools.* Retrieved December 18, 2014, from The Barbara and Patrick Roche Center for Catholic Education: http://www.bc.edu/schools/lsoe/cce/innovationinstitute.html

Briel, D. L. (2008). The declaration on christian education, *Gravissimum Educationis*. In M. Levering, & M. L. Lamb (Eds.), *Vatican II: Renewal within tradition* (pp. 385–96). Oxford: Oxford University Press.

Congregation for Catholic Education. (1997, December 28). *The Catholic school on the threshold of the third millennium.* Retrieved December 18, 2014, from The Holy See: http://www.vatican.va/roman_curia/congregations/ccatheduc/documents/rc_con_ccatheduc_doc_27041998_school2000_en.html

Congregation for Catholic Education. (2013, October 28). *Educating to intercultural dialogue in Catholic schools.* Retrieved December 18, 2014, from The Holy See: http://www.vatican.va/roman_curia/congregations/ccatheduc/documents/rc_con_ccatheduc_doc_20131028_dialogo-interculturale_en.html

Congregation for Catholic Education. (2014, April 7). *Educating today and tomorrow: A renewing passion.* Retrieved December 18, 2014, from The Holy See: http://www.vatican.va/roman_curia/congregations/ccatheduc/documents/rc_con_ccatheduc_doc_20140407_edu care-oggi-e-domani_en.html

Congregation for Catholic Education. (2007, September 8). *Educating together in Catholic schools: A shared mission between consecrated persons and the lay faithful.* Retrieved December 18, 2014, from The Holy See: http://www.vatican.va/roman_curia/congregations/ccatheduc/documents/rc_con_ccatheduc_doc_20070908_educare-insieme_en.html

Congregation for Catholic Education. (1988, April 7). *The religious dimension of education in a Catholic school: Guidelines for reflection and renewal.* Retrieved December 18, 2014, from The Holy See: http://www.vatican.va/roman_curia/congregations/ccatheduc/documents/rc_con_ccatheduc_doc_19880407_catholic-school_en.html

Cristo Rey Network. (2014). *Cristo Rey Network.* Retrieved December 18, 2014, from Cristo Rey Network: http://www.cristoreynetwork.org/page.cfm?p=356

Francis. (2013). *Apostolic Exhortation, Evangelii Gaudium, of the Holy Father Francis.* Retrieved December 18, 2014, from The Holy See: http://w2.vatican.va/content/francesco/en/apost_exhortations/documents/papa-francesco_esortazione-ap_20131124_evangelii-gaudium.html

Higareda, I., Martin, S. P., Chavez, J. M., & Holyk-Casey, K. (2011). *Los Angeles Catholic schools: Impact and opportunity for economically disadvantaged students.* Los Angeles: Loyola Marymount University.

Huchting, K., Martin, S. P., Chavez, J. M., Holyk-Casey, K., & Ruiz, D. (2014). *Los Angeles Catholic schools: Academic excellence and character formation for students living in poverty*. Los Angeles: Loyola Marymount University.

Leckey, D. R. (2006). *The laity and Christian education: Apostolicam Actuositatem, Gravissimum Educationis*. New York: Paulist Press.

Litton, E. F., Martin, S. P., Higareda, I., & Mendoza, J. A. (2010). The promise of Catholic schools for educating the future of Los Angeles. *The Journal of Catholic Education , 13*(3), 350–67.

Loyola High School of Los Angeles. (2014). *Loyola High School of Los Angeles*. Retrieved December 18, 2104, from Loyola High School of Los Angeles: http://www.loyolahs.edu/overview/

Loyola Marymount University. (2014). *About PLACE Corps*. Retrieved December 18, 2014, from LMU School of Education: http://soe.lmu.edu/admissions/programs/place/aboutplace-corps/

The Catholic School Standards Project. (2014). *National Standards and Benchmarks for Effective Catholic Elementary and Secondary Schools*. Retrieved December 18, 2014, from The Catholic School Standards Project: http://www.catholicschoolstandards.org

The Sacred Congregation for Catholic Education. (1977, March 19). *The Catholic school*. Retrieved December 18, 2014, from The Holy See: http://www.vatican.va/roman_curia/congregations/ccatheduc/documents/rc_con_ccatheduc_doc_19770319_catholic-school_en.html

The Sacred Congregation for Catholic Education. (1982, October 15). *Lay Catholics in schools: Witness to faith* . Retrieved December 18, 2014, from The Holy See: http://www.vatican.va/roman_curia/congregations/ccatheduc/documents/rc_con_ccatheduc_doc_19821015_lay-catholics_en.html

The University Consortium for Catholic Education. (2014). *History of the UCCE*. Retrieved December 18, 2014, from The University Consortium for Catholic Education: http://www.ucceconnect.com/history.html

University of Notre Dame. (2014). *Alliance for Catholic Education*. Retrieved December 18, 2014, from Alliance for Catholic Education: https://ace.nd.edu/about/the-alliance-for-catholic-education

University of Notre Dame. (2006). *Making God known, loved, and served: The future of Catholic primary and secondary schools in the United States*. Notre Dame, IN: University of Notre Dame.

University of Notre Dame. (2009). *To nurture the soul of a nation: Latino families, Catholic schools, and educational opportunity*. Notre Dame, IN: Alliance for Catholic Education Press at the University of Notre Dame.

Vatican Council II. (1965, October 28). *Declaration on Christian Education: Gravissimum Educationis*. Retrieved December 17, 2014, from The Holy See: http://www.vatican.va/archive/hist_councils/ii_vatican_council/documents/vat-ii_decl_19651028_gravissimum-educationis_en.html

Verbum Dei High School. (2014). *Verbum Dei High School: The Jesuit work study college prep in Los Angeles*. Retrieved December 18, 2014, from Verbum Dei: http://www.verbumdei.us/about/mission.html

Verbum Dei High School. (2014). *Work Study: A Model for Success*. Retrieved December 18, 2014, from Verbum Dei: http://www.verbumdei.us/workstudy/success.html

Walch, T. (2013). Conclusion: Looking backward, moving forward. In T. C. Hunt, D. J. O'Brien, & T. Walch, *Urban Catholic education: The best of times, the worst of times* (pp. 201–12). New York: Peter Lang.

Chapter Eight

Faith-Based Schools

*Ecumenical Schools and Their Implications for the
Future of American Catholic Education*

Bruce S. Cooper and Ming Zhu

INTRODUCTION

There can be little doubt that Catholic schools have long been, and continue to be, a critical force among non-public religious elementary and secondary educational institutions in the United States. Yet after reaching their peak enrollment in the mid-1960s, about the time that *Gravissimus Educationis* was promulgated, Catholic education has declined dramatically in both numbers of schools and student enrollments while other religious elementary and secondary schools have grown in size and influence.

To some degree, then, this chapter is about the ecumenical forces in American education insofar as this research and analysis examines all of non-public education across a variety of key religions and sects in the United States. A large number, even the majority, of non-public schools in the United States today have some religious identity and affiliations, whether they are, by way of illustration, Roman Catholic, Protestant (ranging from Episcopalian to Evangelical), Muslim, Jewish or another religion; for instance, Christian Science schools are called Applied Scholastics and the Ethical Culture Society runs its own schools, with all these groups sponsoring and supporting religious private schools of their own.

Ecumenism in this chapter is a broad concept, examining primarily K–12 religious schools, including, of course, those affiliated with the Roman Catholic Church. As the term "ecumenism" often refers to other Christian faiths, the term can also be used to show a concern with promoting unity among churches or religions; these can include forms of "ecumenical thinking," "ecumenical activities and actions," and "the ecumenical movement" (*Ecumenical*).

This chapter investigates four issues. First, the chapter analyzes the changing numbers of and enrollments in private and religious schools in the United States. Second, the chapter compares the trends in Catholic with ecumenical non-Catholic private schools since the late 19th century. Third, the chapter traces the decline of Catholic schools and enrollments as well as the concomitant rise in some other private schools, both religious and non-sectarian. Fourth, the chapter discusses the implications of these changes for families, education, and government in the United States while suggesting ways Catholic leaders might use these ideas to devise policies to help their schools survive and prosper.

This chapter does not ignore nondenominational private schools such as military academies for school-age students, independent schools, and non-religious schools sponsored by religious groups. Rather, the chapter focuses most closely at those K–12 schools operated and sponsored by Protestants, including born-again Evangelical Christians, Lutherans, Episcopalians, Baptists, and Seventh-day Adventists; Muslims such as at the Tarek ibn Ziyad Academy in Inver Grove Heights, Minnesota; and Jewish Talmud Torah "day schools" operated by Orthodox Jewish communities, Hasidic schools, Solomon Schechter, Conservative, Reform, and nonaffiliated schools as well as other general cross-denominational Jewish schools.

In New York City, for example, the expanding Abraham Joshua Heschel School describes itself as trans-Jewish in the following language: "The Abraham Joshua Heschel School is a pluralistic Nursery to 12th grade Jewish day school in New York City. Its two central values, *pluralism* and *egalitarianism*, create a tight-knit yet diverse community" (The Abraham Joshua Heschel School, n.d.).

The chapter also briefly includes analysis on students who are home schooled based on Cooper's (2005) *Home Schooling in Full View*. They are in the ranks of the privately educated, even though they often have no formal religious organizations. Still, home schooling families are typically Christian in outlook. Hence this framework is but one way to view, analyze, and compare the changes, trends, growth, and decline between Catholic and other ecumenical education faith-based programs in the United States over the last half-century.

Many of the types of schools examined in this chapter have also recently struggled in times of economic downturns as families sometime cannot afford their tuition and fees. Even so, overall, non-Catholic non-public schools have gained in number, size, and standing while the former have declined, closed, and lost enrollments nationally and regionally.

Besides giving a broad picture of non-public schools in the United States, this chapter analyzes which types of schools have expanded, closed, and opened. In so doing, the chapter focuses on ideas while offering practical suggestions, drawn from other growing private school types and locations, that might help the Catholic schools to become more attractive and thereby grow, as they still have a critical role to play in education and life in the United States.

The United States is a religious society, the most God-fearing and actively worshipping and prayerful nation in the modern Western world with the majority of Americans affiliated with a church, synagogue, or mosque. Moreover, the United States as a country has expended time, resources, and energy in private schools, providing good examples of these religious beliefs and practices.

The remainder of this chapter is divided into three main sections. First, the chapter reviews the growth and decline of American non-public and religious schools over the past half-century, including Catholic schools. Second, the chapter analyses non-Catholic sectarian-religious schools for K–12 students. Third, the chapter examines policy principles and practices, drawn from the growing number of private schools, which might be of use to Catholic schools, and their leadership, in helping these Catholic schools to reverse the downward trend occurring since around 1965.

BACKGROUND

The school year 1964–65, which culminated prior to the publication of *Gravissimus Educationis* in the fall of 1965, was the peak point in American history for Catholic education.

Ziegler reported, "School enrollment reached its peak during the early 1960s when there were more than 5.2 million students in almost 13,000 schools across the nation" (2011, p. 1). Depending at what point in time one starts in the 19th century, when Catholics were immigrating in large numbers to the United States from Ireland, Italy, Poland, and other European nations, we see in figure 8.1 below, in 1960, that about 5.7 million students are enrolled in 33,366 non-public schools. As Meyer reported:

> Despite a growing Catholic population (from 45 million in 1965 to almost 77 million today, making it the largest Christian denomination in the United States), Catholic school enrollment has plummeted, from 5.2 million students in nearly 13,000 schools in the 1960's to 2.5 million in 9,000 schools in 1990. After a promising increase in the late 1990s, enrollment had by 2006 dropped to 2.3 million students in 7,500 schools [continuing downward to under 1.8 million students attending Catholic schools today] (n.p.).

And the steep decline would have been even steeper if these sectarian schools had to rely on their own flock for enrollment: almost 14 percent of Catholic school enrollment is now non-Catholic, up from less than 3 percent in 1970.

When Catholic schools educated 12 percent of all schoolchildren in the United States, in 1965, the proportion of Catholics in the general population was 24 percent. Catholics still make up about one-quarter of the American population, but their schools enroll less than 5 percent of all K–12 students. (2007, p. 1)

As Arianna Prothero (2014) found more recently:

From 2004 to 2014, U.S. Catholic school enrollment dropped by 23 percent, to fewer than 2 million students, compared with 5.66 million at the pinnacle of such enrollment in the 1960s, according to data compiled by the National Catholic Educational Association, based in Arlington, Va. The decline is even more pronounced in urban areas, where a combination of changing demo-graphics, rising tuition costs, and increased competition from free, public char-ter schools, are exacting its toll on inner-city Catholic schools. (p. 55)

Since 2006–07, the decline has continued with enrollment now at about 1.8 million students in less than 6,000 Catholic schools in the United States. Further, there seems to be no "bottom" in sight yet. Consequently, in about 50 years the decline has been over two-thirds of students, with just more than half of U.S. Catholic schools closing during this time.

According to the National Catholic Education Association (NCEA):

Catholic school enrollment reached its peak during the early 1960s when there were more than 5.2 million students in almost thirteen thousand schools across the nation. The 1970s and 1980s saw a steep decline in both the number of schools and students. By 1990, there were approximately 2.5 million students in 8,719 schools. From the mid 1990s though 2000, there was a steady enroll-ment increase (1.3 per cent) despite continued closings of schools.

As further reported by the NCEA, and revealed in table 8.1, the number of Catholic schools fell from 8,146 to 6,980 between 2000 and 2010—a loss of 117 schools every year. Combined primary and secondary school enroll-ment also declined 22 percent, from 2,647,301 to 2,065,872.(NCEA).

In sum, during 2011–2012, the most recent year for which data are avail-able, 2,259,972 students enrolled in Catholic schools, constituting only 42.9% of the total private school students in U.S. non-public schools. (CAPE).

Describing this decline, Zeigler reported:

In the midst of this Catholic education boom worldwide, the Church in the United States has suffered a dramatic decline in its education apostolate. Ac-

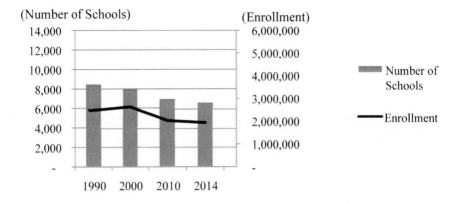

Figure 8.1. Catholic School Numbers (bar graphs) & Pupil Enrollment (line graph), between 1996 and 2014

cording to the National Catholic Education Association, the number of Catholic schools fell from 8,146 to 6,980 between 2000 and 2010—a loss of 117 schools every year. Combined primary and secondary school enrollment also declined 22 percent, from 2,647,301 to 2,065,872. (2011, p. 1)

Figure 8.2 shows the decline of Catholic school enrollments between 1995 and 2012. The figure fails to show the decline from 1966 of the Catholics and the rise of the other private and religious schools, as well as home-schooling (Cooper, 2002).

Professional Staff

Full-time equivalent professional staff in Catholic schools also showed the decline in religious (e.g., sisters, brothers, and priests) numbering: among 150,709 full-time equivalent professional staff, 97.2% are Laity (75.2% laywomen, and 22% laymen), while 2.8% are religious/clergy (1.9% sisters, 0.4% brothers, and 0.5% clergy). The numbers by level are as follows: of the 6,594 Catholic schools: 5,399 are elementary; 1,195 secondary, with 42 new schools opened, and 133 consolidated or closed. However, taking a longer view, it can be seen that the numbers dropped dramatically overall from about 5.66 million students in 1966 to around 1.9 million in 2014 (NCEA).

Catholic enrollments and schools have decreased in number. Yet the total data for all private schools is about where it was at the peak during the strongest "Catholic years" of over 5 million students in over 33,000 non-public schools in the United States (CAPE).

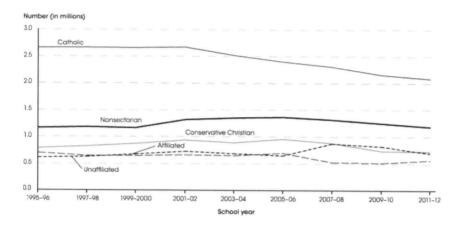

Figure 8.2.   Number of Private School Students in Prekindergarten through Grade 12, by School Type: Selected Years, 1995–96 through 2011–12. From http://nces.ed.gov/programs/coe/indicator_cgc.asp.

Quasi-Public Schools and Programs

Also, there are new quasi-private schools opening around the country, including charter, magnet, and independent schools that have private school qualities, insofar as some are privately managed while others are publicly financed and regulated by the government. Further, public vouchers are public funds allocated for families to choose, if they wish, private schools with funds following the students.

REASONS FOR THE CHANGING COMPOSITION OF ECUMENIST K–12 SCHOOLS

Research has revealed four interrelated reasons for the decline in Catholic schools and their enrollment, a discussion of which follows. The first reason for this decline is rooted in Catholic and overall urban populations in medium-sized cities. Even as New York, Los Angeles, Houston, Phoenix, and many cities in the South and Southwest have experienced population growth over the last six decades, many other cities across the Northeast and Midwest are waning. Since 1950, as Ziegler reports, Buffalo's population has declined by 310,000, Baltimore's by 312,000, Pittsburgh's by 366,000, Cleveland's by 484,000, and St. Louis's by 500,000 people. Philadelphia has lost 525,000 residents; Chicago, 770,000; and Detroit, 939,000 (2011, p. 1). Thus the drop and loss overall of population in cities with large Catholic communities could begin to explain the decline of Catholic schools in these locations.

The second reason for the decline is the loss of school endowments. Dr. Dan Peters (2013), superintendent of the Diocese of Kansas City-St. Joseph, reports: "Loss of the living *endowment* contributed by the ministry of the religious had serious financial implications for operating schools. Within the last school year, the cost of K–12 education in our diocese was more than $79 million" (p.11).

The third reason for the decline is the reduction in the composition of religious, in the form of sisters, brothers, and priests serving as teachers and administrators in Catholic schools. This serious, major decline in the numbers of sisters, brothers, and priests has raised the cost of finding, hiring, and retaining trained, qualified, loyal, and affordable teachers and principals, as well as other educational leaders. The superintendent of Catholic education in the Archdiocese of St. Louis, Missouri, Mr. George Henry, reports a move " . . . from a basically free workforce in the persons of religious priests, brothers, and women (supported by religious communities) to one comprised predominantly of the laity, who rightly must receive just wages and benefits" (2014, p. 1).

The fourth reason for the decline reflects the difficulty finding a balance between higher tuition and fees and costs to families and improved salaries for teachers. Catholic schools face a serious challenge when trying to raise enough money to pay staff decent salaries and benefits and compete with other schools, including better paying public education, without making schools so expensive that many families may have trouble (or find it impossible) to raise the tuition and fees to attend, thereby often having to drop out.

As Chris Fay, the principal of the Christian Brothers High School in Memphis, explains this great problem: "Our greatest challenge today is growing our annual fund so that we can continue to offer competitive salaries, full benefits, and a generous pension plan to our teachers, while maintaining an affordable tuition for our students' families" (Roberts, 2009, p. 4).

Likewise, as Dr. Dan Peters, the new superintendent of Catholic schools of the Kansas City-St. Joseph Diocese in Missouri, explained:

> When Catholic school enrollment peaked in 1965, no one could foresee that shifting demographics and rising operational costs would force the closing of half of all parochial schools over the next 50 years . . . These important tasks can only be accomplished with us—all parents, teachers, administrators, and the diocese—working together. (Peters, 2013, p. 4)

Clearly, the overall national picture for American Catholic schools is not good. The number of Catholic schools has dropped from over 16,000 to under 7,000, with 133 closing in 2014 and only 33 new ones opening (NCEA). At the same time, other religious and independent schools and home schooling continue to grow and expand. Figure 8.3 shows how the decline in Catholic school students (solid line) and the increase in other private school students (jagged line) affected the overall total private school enrollment in the United States (double line).

PURPOSE OF THE ANALYSIS

This analysis looks further at changes in the private and religious schools picture in the United States and analyzes the growth in other private and religious schools as the nation becomes more diverse and religion become even more important to many families and students nationwide. This analysis examines the major ecumenical and non-Catholic affiliations, including Protestant, Muslim, Jewish, and Evangelical Protestant schools along with their growing commitment to private religious education. This analysis also mentions the independent and non-religious related non-public schools, often affiliated with the National Association of Independent Schools (NAIS), plus their total numbers and enrollments across the country.

Ecumenism and Private Education in the United States

On moving from Catholic to other types of non-public schools, some important differences in growth, organization, and social and educational qualities become evident, many of which could be adopted or adapted by Catholics to help rescue their declining elementary and secondary schools in the United States. Four qualities help to explain the major differences between the Catholic school decline and the other types and ecumenical school growth and development:

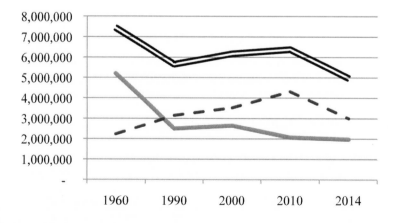

Figure 8.3.   Private Schools in the USA

Immigrant Groups and Private School Change

While Catholic schools have often served new immigrant families, including Irish, Italian, Polish, and other European groups, the arrival of large numbers of mostly Hispanics from Central and South America has changed the pattern. For unclear reasons, many Latino parents chose to send their children to public schools rather than enroll them in Catholic institutions. In contrast, other recent arriving groups to the United States, such as Jews and Muslims, have turned to their own private schools in growing numbers in the last ten years.

Declining Catholic Family Support

As Catholics have assimilated more into American life and risen in economic standing, often having moved out of inner cities to more affluent suburban public school districts, their general support of Catholic schools has waned. In part, this change is often economic. Fancy suburbs usually have higher (real estate) property taxes, based on high public school budgets locally, for the support of public schools. Moreover, some families may then be unable to afford to pay both the higher property taxes and the tuition and fees at Catholic schools.

Meanwhile, other groups opened private schools in cities and suburbs, often so their children can be brought up "in the faith." The major religious types and their schools are reviewed as follows.

Jewish K–12 School and Enrollment Growth

The increases in school numbers and enrollments in Jewish day schools and *Yeshivot* have occurred for many reasons that are key to Jewish life and childrearing. Data reveal great differentiation between and among types and practices of Jewish schools, reflecting the beliefs and practices of a variety of Jewish families and groups and their schools. At one extreme are the ultra-Orthodox Jews, the Hasidim (often men with beards and black hats), followed, in decreasing order of adherence to traditional religious teachings, mainstream Orthodox, Conservative, Reconstructionist, Reform, and other Jewish community day schools.

RAVSAK, transliterated from the Hebrew as *Reshet Batei Sefer K'hilati'im*, meaning the Network of Jewish Community Day is a New York City-based organization dedicated to helping every U.S. Jewish community of 3,000 or more Jews to open a local Jewish day school, including small Southern towns, like Greensboro, N.C., which have a growing Jewish community. Founded in 1987, RAVSAK is a New York based non-profit organization that promotes pluralistic nondenominational Jewish education, working with over 100 member schools from across North America, spanning elementary- to high school-level day school education.

These RAVSAK-initiated schools are broadly Jewish, drawing all types of Jews to them ranging from Orthodox to Jews unaffiliated with an association or synagogue. These changes are illustrated in "A Census of Jewish Day Schools in the United States 2013–2014" by Marvin Schick:

- Enrollment Growth: There were 228,174 students in Jewish Pre–K through 12th grade schools during the 2008–09 school year, a rise of 23,000—or 11%—from 2003–04, and an increase of more than 43,000 or nearly 25% since 1998–99:
- Orthodox School Growth: Jewish schools serving the most religious groups saw a 56% increase in Orthodox-Hasidic schools and a 34% increase in Yeshiva World schools over the past 10 years, in large part due to higher birth rates.
- Growth in Jewish Community Day Schools: These community day schools numbered 98 in 2008–09 as compared to 75 in 1998–99, with enrollment up over 40% during the past decade, a significant increase of students in non-Orthodox Jewish high schools.
- Nearly 25% Decrease in Enrollment in Conservative (Schechter Jewish Day) Schools: The only major declines in Jewish day schools in the United States were among Solomon Schechter Day Schools, which serve mainly the Conservative Jewish movement, over the past 10 years.
- Outside of New York and New Jersey, 47% of day school students are enrolled in non-Orthodox schools.

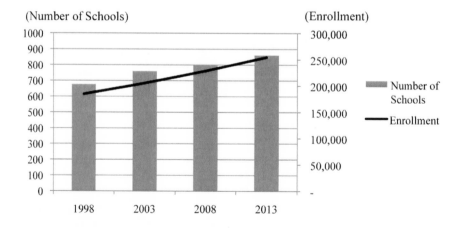

Figure 8.4.   Rise in All Jewish Day Schools and Students

Table 8.1. Jewish Day School Numbers (S) and Enrollments (E), with Percentage Changes between 1980 and 2014. From "A Census of Jewish Day Schools in the United States 2013–2014," Marvin Schick (2014).

Types	1998		2003		2008		2013		Change
	S	E	S	E	S	E	S	E	
Centrist Orthodox	80	20,504	78	18,696	72	17,650	77	18,925	-3.75%
Chabad	44	7,438	54	8,609	73	12,296	80	12,649	81.82%
Chassidic	81	39,059	101	48,446	105	60,955	137	81,940	69.14%
Community	75	14,849	95	17,416	98	20,838	97	20,413	29.33%
Immigrant/ Outreach	31	5,136	30	4,823	24	3,432	19	2,384	-38.71%
Modern Orthodox	92	26,961	87	28,720	86	29,397	83	27,217	-9.78%
Reform	20	4,485	19	4,462	17	4,569	13	3,704	-35.00%
Solomon Schechter	63	17,563	57	17,702	50	13,223	39	9,718	-38.10%
Special Education	18	695	43	1,780	33	1,967	34	2,118	88.89%
Yeshiva	172	47,643	195	54,381	244	63,985	282	75,681	63.95%
Total	**676**	**184,333**	**759**	**205,035**	**802**	**228,312**	**861**	**254,749**	**+70,416**

- Five out of six Jewish day school students in the United States attend Orthodox Jewish Day schools. Overall, enrollment declined in non-Orthodox schools 2.5% since 2003–04, yet is still 5% higher than in 1998–99.

Members of the American Jewish community have increasingly sought day schools for their children, including newcomers to the United States. They are typically from non-Orthodox families, meaning that they tend to identify with Judaism more culturally than by ritual and practice. Unlike Catholic schools, which are fairly standard, Jewish educational institutions run the gamut from ultra-Orthodox through cultural and liberal Reform Judaism, thus welcoming Jews of all levels of Orthodoxy. These schools vary in their religious practices and rituals, such as keeping kosher and separating the sexes during worship, as well as other traditions.

Protestant and Evangelical Christian Schools

Perhaps the most active new religious schools in the United States are those for Pentecostal, "born-again" Protestant children, who are often devoted Christian fundamentalists or Evangelicals. These groups are relatively new to the faith-based ranks, since the Protestants were the founders of the first "public schools" in the nation (Balmer, 2010; see also Balmer, 2000).

In fact, when the Catholics started immigrating to the United States in the early 1840s, they discovered that many of the local "public schools" were too Protestant-Christian in control and practices, such as reading and teaching the King James Bible and reciting the Lord's Prayer daily, which many Catholics did not like.

When Catholic parents complained to their Church heads, many parishes and diocesan leaders helped to open new Catholic schools for children, mainly supported by Sunday church contributions (collected often by "passing the plate"). Further, insofar as a high percentage of low-paid staff, in the form of sisters, brothers, and priests, taught in and ran Catholic schools fairly inexpensively and well, they were able to get started, grow, and expand with a modest budget and virtually no tuition charges to parents.

By the 1970s, though, because Evangelical Protestants found many public schools too liberal, "godless," undisciplined, and drug-ridden, they began to form their own Christian day schools. David Sikkink explained this process as follows: "Many conservative Protestants reserve the term 'Christian school' for schools affiliated with conservative Protestant denominations, excluding Catholic schools in particular" (2001, p. 11). As one school leader explained: "At Evangelical Christian School, we provide an outstanding learning environment. Students of all ages excel in their academic potential, extra-curricular involvement and leadership development—all within a nurturing, Christian community" (Ft. Myers Christian School, 2014).

At the same time, leaders and teachers in these schools have formed a national organization, the Association of Christian Teachers and Schools (ACTS), to spread the word, and to bring their staff together. Their association describes itself in this way: "The Association of Christian Teachers and Schools (ACTS) is a non-profit organization that strives to set new standards of Christ-centered academic excellence while assisting Christian schools to realize the highest level of educational credibility" (2015).

Like other professional organizations, ACTS sets its own goals, monitors school progress, holds conferences, accredits schools, and provides educational materials appropriate for Christian curricula. Still, the numbers of students and schools are difficult to calculate because many of these institutions are also affiliated with Protestant churches and organizations such as those supported by Evangelical Lutherans, Baptists, and Seventh-day Adventists. Yet of the 6.5 million students in American private schools, estimates are that about a million are Protestants and many of those are Evangelical Christians (CAPE).

According to the Council for American Private Education (CAPE), the total enrollment of private school is 5,268,000, of which 14% are Conservative Christian, 4.5% is Baptist, 3.6% is Lutheran, 2.1% is Episcopal, 1.1% is

Seventh-day Adventist, 0.5% is Calvinist, and 0.4% is Friends (Quakers). Therefore, up to 2012, the total enrollment of Protestant schools was 1,380,216 students (CAPE).

Muslim Private K–12 Schools

As the newest addition to faith-based schools, there is growth in Islamic schools in the United States. The Tarek ibn Ziyad Academy was one example, located in Minnesota, as it was both a charter and a Muslim school, describing its activities as:

> About 1 p.m. every school day, Tarek students stream out of classrooms, clean themselves up in the restrooms, kneel down facing the east in the assembly room or hallways, and begin to pray. Zaman says he doesn't track students' religion, but almost all children participate in the daily prayer. . . . The school's calendar and days are set up to accommodate Muslim students. Classes break during the noontime prayer; vacation days are scheduled on Muslim holidays instead of traditionally Christian ones. The cafeteria is free of pork and other foods that Islam prohibits. (Pipes, 2007, p. 1)

When a Muslim group sought to open a charter school outside Minneapolis that is supportive of and sensitive to Islamic culture, values, beliefs, and leaders, its organizers did so without classifying it as a Muslim religious charter school. This led to legal difficulties (Lemagie, 2009). Initially, the Eighth Circuit refused to allow parents to intervene to save the schools (*American Civil Liberties Union of Minnesota v. Tarek ibn Ziyad Academy*).

Later, a federal trial court in Minnesota ruled that insofar as it was religious in nature, the school's existence violated the Establishment Clause (*American Civil Liberties Union of Minnesota v. Tarek ibn Ziyad Academy*). The court rejected the school's efforts to walk the line between serving a public purpose (educating children in a sensitive, culturally specific, values-oriented program) and actually being an Islamic religious school.

According to the *Historical Dictionary of American Education* (1999), "The Clara Muhammad School, founded in Detroit in 1934 as the University of Islam, became the first full-time Islamic school. Forty-nine Islamic schools existed in 1989 . . . ; by 1994, their figures jumped to 108 and 100,000, respectively." (Altenbaugh, 1999, p. 188). See figure 8.5 below.

Table 8.2 shows the growth of Muslim schools and enrollment since their beginnings 1934 to 1999.

"A verified list of 235 schools in the United States and the U.S. Virgin Islands has now been built" (Keyworth, 2011, p. 11). This report also shows that around 32,000 students were enrolled in Islamic schools as of 2011 (p. 15). As the number of Islamic schools increases as expected, there seems to be a discrepancy as to the number of student enrollment. While Altenbaugh's

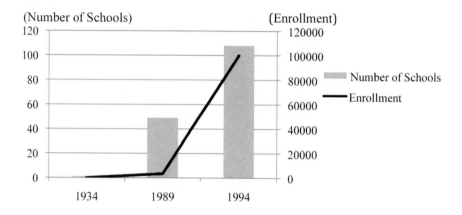

Figure 8.5.   Islamic Schools in the USA, 1934–1999

1999 citation, based on data from 1994, suggested a much greater student enrollment, there is need for further examination on the status of Islamic schools.

Table 8.2.   Islamic Schools in the USA. Adapted from Altenbaugh (1999, p. 188).

Year	Number of Schools	Enrollment
1934	1	undocumented
1989	49	3,400
1994	108	100,000

CONCLUSIONS AND PRACTICAL SUGGESTIONS

As this chapter has demonstrated, private and religious schools in the United States have had a long, important history, as indicated by the following:

1. Beliefs and hopes of families, as they immigrate and assimilate into life in the United States;
2. Changes and developments in the socioreligious qualities of a region, and how parents view and deal with these differences;
3. The importance of beliefs and religious activity, and how they affect families and their children for generations; and,
4. The needs for families to have some choices as they react to life in the public schools and their communities.

In many nations, educational funds are readily and legally available to schools that are public, private, nonsectarian and even religious. Yet the

United States has a First Amendment Constitutional divide between "church and state," religious and public schooling. Although these lines are blurring (Mulvey, Cooper, & Maloney, 2010), there can be no doubt that public, private, and religious institutions serve the education and social needs of poor, immigrant, and other children in need.

Cooper, McSween, and Murphy (2002) analyzed the "golden mean" in American public educational policy, where the public and private sectors collaborate. Such an approach would apparently both allow and demonstrate how the government and religious schools can work together to better serve the poor and underprivileged, bringing together public, private and religious agencies to carry out these important jobs. True ecumenism in action: "In God we trust."

Hence, as Catholic schools continue to decline since their peak in 1965–66, other private and religious groups have worked to open and support their schools, to a point now where the total enrollment in the private sector is just above the 5.9 million in 2013. However, while Catholic school enrollments were 89% of the total among non-public schools in the United States during the 1960s, they are around 45% today and still declining (see figure 8.3.) According to both the National Center for Education Statistics (NCES) and the U.S. Department of Education report:

> According to data provided by National Center for Education Statistics and U.S. Department of Education, in year 2011, there were approximately 4.5 million students enrolling in private schools. Even though the latest data on total private school enrollment are not up to date, according to National Center for Education Statistics, it is projected that by 2014, the number of students attending private schools will be 4.9 million. Based on data from the NCEA, the total enrollment for Catholic schools is a little over 1.9 million, which constitutes less than 40% of the total enrollment in all private schools.
>
> According to U.S. Department of Education, in 2011, an estimated 1.8 million students were homeschooled. If homeschooled students are included in this calculation, the total enrollment in the private sector in 2011 was approximately 6.3 million. Catholic school enrollment was barely 30% of the total enrollment in the private sector. (NCES; NCEA; U.S. Department of Education)

WHAT CATHOLIC SCHOOLS CAN DO

This chapter now offers five concrete, practical suggestions to Church and public leaders designed to help Catholic schools survive, grow, and prosper as critical education programs in the nation. Leaders in Catholic education should consider adopting the following recommendations.

First, Catholic leaders should become active in the policy-making programs to privatize and support education. Perhaps in the future, with some help from vouchers and even charter school status, the Catholic school community will rise again, and become leaders in the religious and ecumenical community in support of non-public schooling. Clearly, "privatization" in education in the United States is here to stay. As such, Catholics must get organized and focused to help that movement again. After all, by 1965, Catholics comprised close to 90% of all of the roughly six million children who were attending non-public education programs in the United States but have now fallen to enrolling about 45% of all non-public school students as the decline continues.

Providing vouchers to families who select a Catholic school seems to work more simply, without "blurring the lines" between church and state from the First Amendment. Chartering religious schools may be more effective—although more legally difficult and controversial (Russo & Cattaro, 2010) And, as this volume demonstrates, help may be on the way as many states are creating public voucher and charter school programs, with Catholics joining the effort, even though the legal issues are confounding the process.

As Prothero (2014) explained:

> Leaders at a private Roman Catholic school in St. Louis are preparing for a big change: They are planning to give up the inner-city institution's religious identity to become a public charter school, so they can serve more low-income families.
>
> An issue examined by the Friedman Foundation for Educational Choice involved the experience of 18 former Catholic schools in three metropolitan areas—Indianapolis, Miami, and Washington—that turned into charters between 2008 and 2010. It found that enrollment increased dramatically after the change, as did the proportion of minority students served.
>
> Several experts said they were not aware of data identifying how many Catholic or other private schools have converted to charters. And, in fact, it appears the volume has slowed as the economy has improved. In New Jersey, a pair of non-Catholic private schools recently applied to become charters next school year, although only one was approved by the state. (p. 23)

Second, Catholic educational leaders should concentrate on bringing recent American immigrants—for example, those from Hispanic America—into Catholic schools. These leaders should consider recruiting Hispanic children into Catholic schools, reaching for the best and most gifted students while also serving the neediest.

For example, Adam Emerson (2013) reported that "as charter enrollment exceeded Catholic school enrollment for the first time this school year (in 2011–12), each sector had about the same number of students. Catholic school enrollment *dropped* 1.5 percent to 2,001,740 students, while charter school enrollment *increased* 13 percent to 2,326,542 students. From here on, any graph plotting student numbers in each sector likely will look like a pair of open scissors" (p. 1).

Educational and religious leaders should accordingly work hard to contact, recruit, and enroll Latino students into their schools. In fact, as revealed by the growth described by Sister Dale McDonald in chapter 4, *Demographic Shifts Impacting Catholic School Education*, of this book, an argument can be made that the future of the Church in the United States greatly depends on the education, commitment, and religious practices of the next generation of Central and South American families to help keep it the vibrant force it has long been in American life.

Third, leaders should seek to open new schools in every Catholic community. Using examples of the RAVSAK program for Jewish schools, Catholic leaders should seek to open and maintain a Catholic school or schools in every Catholic community of a specified size in every state to bring families together.

As is happening in developments between and among neighboring parishes in many places, perhaps Catholic leaders could build schools that straddle towns and dioceses so that more children have an opportunity to attend a Catholic school in their towns or regions/neighborhoods. Greater collaboration is necessary, and perhaps a national commission could do a demographic analysis and make Catholic schools more available in areas where larger numbers of Catholic families reside or work.

Fourth, leaders should strive to use public funds wherever and whenever possible, including vouchers and charters, if and when they are legal and available. Another possible future would be more like the European approach, where Catholic groups would seek vouchers for families to help parents pay tuition and fees at Catholic schools, and be able to open new charter schools together. While these chartering options may be considered unconstitutional, it's time to continue testing the process.

Fifth, leaders should organize alumni and other groups to raise funds and build support for American Catholic schools. The whole Catholic Church should become involved so the community is able to have the necessary leadership, energy, and resources to "save" the Catholic schools from shrinking, closing and extinction. Now is the time. Where's the leadership?

As the *New York Daily News* explained about New York City Catholic schools,

> Two-dozen city Catholic schools shut their doors last year, including Blessed Sacrament in the Bronx, NY. Supreme Court Justice Sonia Sotomayor, valedictorian of the Class of 1968, lamented her alma mater's closing and stated: "Do you know how important those eight years were? It was a road of opportunity for kids with no other alternative."
>
> Gotham City's [New York City's] Catholic schools have been helping poor kids like Sotomayor—originally Irish and Italian immigrants; today,

mostly low-income black and Hispanic kids—for more than 150 years. Many aren't even Catholic. (Sahm & Stern, 2013, pp. 22–23)

CONCLUSION

So, spurred on by *Gravissimus Educationis*, life goes on 50 years later. Catholic school leaders and families, along with U.S. policy makers and policy analysts should continue to study and research ways to build positive school leadership and pay for and ensure the future of Catholic education and other ecumenical groups for the next generations of our children and Catholics. God bless us all!

REFERENCES

Altenbaugh, R. J. (1999). *Historical dictionary of American education .* Westport, CT: Greenwood Press.

American Civil Liberties Union of Minnesota v. Tarek ibn Ziyad Academy, 788 F. Supp.2d 950 (D. Minn. 2011).

American Civil Liberties Union of Minnesota v. Tarek ibn Ziyad Academy, 643 F.3d 1088 (8th Cir. 2011).

Association of Christian Teachers and Schools. Retrieved January 2, 2015, from http://www.actsschools.org/index.html

Balmer, R. (2000), *Blessed assurance: A history of Evangelicalism in America.* New York: Beacon Press.

Balmer, R. (2010), *The making of Evangelicalism: From revivalism to politics and beyond.* Waco, TX: Baylor University Press.

Cooper, B. S. (2005). *Home schooling in full view: A reader.* Charlotte, NC: Information Age Publishing.

Cooper, B. S., McSween, R. B., & Murphy, P. (2002). Finding a golden mean in education policy: Centering religious and public schools. *Peabody Journal of Education, 87*(1), 368–82.

Council for American Private Education. *Facts and studies.* Retrieved January 2, 2015, from http://www.capenet.org/facts.html

Ecumenical. Retrieved from http://www.thefreedictionary.com/ecumenical

Emerson, A. (2013). Time for more generous vouchers and Catholic charter schools. Retrieved from http://edexcellence.net/commentary/education-gadfly-daily/choice-words/2013/time-for-more-generous-vouchers-and-catholic-charter-schools.html

Ft. Myers Christian School. (2014). Retrieved January 2, 2015, from http://www.goecs.org/

Henry, G. (2014, April 23). Retiring superintendent George Henry receiving several honors in April. *St. Louis Review*, p. 1.

Keyworth, K. (2011). *Islamic schools of the United States: Data-based profiles.* Institute for Social Policy and Understanding. Retrieved Jan 4, 2014 from http://www.ispu.org/pdfs/609_ISPU%20Report_Islamic%20Schools_Keyworth_WEB.pdf.

Lemagie, S. (2008, May 28). State orders charter school to correct 2 areas tied to Islam. *Star Tribune.* Retrieved Jan 4, 2014 from http://m.startribune.com/local/south/19076119.html

Meyer, P. (2007). Can Catholic schools be saved? Lacking nuns and often students, a shrinking system looks for answers. *Education Next. 7*(2), 1–3.

Mulvey, J. D., Cooper, B. S., & Maloney, Arthur T. (2011). *Blurring the lines between church, state and education.* Charlotte, NC: Information Age Publishing.

National Catholic Educational Association. *United States Catholic elementary and secondary schools 2014–2015: The annual statistical report on schools, enrollment, and staffing.* Retrieved January 2, 2015, from http://www.ncea.org/data-information/catholic-school-data

National Center for Education Statistics. *Digest of education statistics.* Retrieved from http://nces.ed.gov/programs/digest/d13/tables/dt13_105.20.asp

Paul VI. (1965, October 28). *Gravissimum educationis.* Retrieved January 2, 2015, from http://www.vatican.va/archive/hist_councils/ii_vatican_council/documents/vatii_decl_19651028_gravissimum-educationis_en.html

Peters, D. (2013). *Now faith is being sure of be of what we hope for and certain of what we do not see.* The Catholic Diocese of Kansas City-St. Joseph.

Pipes, D. (2007). *Tarek ibn Ziyad Academy: An Islamic charter school in Minnesota? Middle East Forum,* Lion's Den: Daniel Pipes Blog. March 8, 2007.

Prothero, A. (2014). Converting Catholic schools to charters draws scrutiny. *Education Week 30*(1), pp. 55–56.

Roberts, J. (2009). For the first time, Christian Brothers High School principal is a layperson. *The Commercial Appeal.* July 29, 2009, pp. 2–4.

Russo, C. J., & Cattaro, G. M. (2010). Faith-based charter schools: An idea whose time is unlikely to come. *Journal of Catholic Education, 13*(4), 32–44.

Sahm, C., & Stern, S. (July 31, 2014). Pray we can save our Catholic schools. *New York Daily News,* pp. 21–22.

Schick, M. (2014). *A census of Jewish day schools in the United States 2013-2014.* Retrieved January 2, 2015, from http://avichai.org/knowledge_base/a-census-of-jewish-day-schools-in-the-united-states-2013-14-2014/

Sikkink, D. (2001). Diversity in Christian schools. *Education Next,* Summer 2001.

U.S. Department of Education. Retrieved January 2, 2015, from http://www2.ed.gov/about/offices/list/oii/nonpublic/statistics.html

Ziegler, J. J. (2011, May 31). The state of Catholic schools in the U.S.: Signs of hope despite a bleak prognosis. *Catholic World Report.* Special Report, pp. 1–11.

Chapter Nine

Catholic Schools
and the Common Good

John J. Convey

INTRODUCTION

The common good consists of all facets of society intended to enable individuals to flourish humanly and spiritually. Humans are social beings who live in communities. As such, all persons share mutual responsibility for one another. Individuals who are productive members of society contribute to the common good by using their talents to help foster, among other things, community development and economic growth, which in turn makes the world a better place in which to live. The common good requires productive people who work to serve and promote a well-functioning society.

According to ancient and modern philosophers and political theorists, the common good of society also requires the presence of individuals with character who possess personal virtue and an understanding of justice. After the family, the school is the institution that plays the most important role in the development of character, virtue, and justice. Catholic schools are thus uniquely situated to contribute to the common good since they provide an education of body, mind and soul; they educate the whole person. Against this background, this chapter examines the variety of ways that Catholic schools contribute to the common good.

THE NOTION OF THE COMMON GOOD

Ancient writers to those of modern days, including philosophers, theologians, political theorists, and Church leaders, have offered their thoughts about the common good and what it entails. Early Greek philosophers considered the importance of the common good and identified its constitutive elements as community, justice and virtue.

Plato related the common good to justice and a political order that promotes cooperation and friendship among different social groups, each adding to the common good and benefiting from it. Aristotle described man as political beings by nature who contribute to the common good through their participation as citizens in their communities in *Politics*. In the *Nicomachean Ethics*, Aristotle argued that the good of the individual is inseparable from the good of the community.

Aristotle's *Nicomachean Ethics* provided the foundation for Thomas Aquinas's theory of the common good. Aquinas was concerned with the ultimate common good, God. Aquinas understood the temporal common good by analogy to the ultimate common good (Lewis, 2006; Sherwin, 1993). Among the natural human inclinations for Aquinas are seeking the good, including the highest good, which is eternal happiness with God, and living in community (*Summa Theologica*, Question 94, Article 2).

Aquinas believed that society and individuals share a common end, which, similar to Aristotle, is to live virtuously and, Aquinas added, through virtuous living to attain the possession of God. Aquinas therefore raised the stakes by arguing that the primary common good consists of knowing, loving and serving God, while not diminishing the importance of other common goods that contribute to an individual's happiness.

The writings of Aquinas furnish the foundation and justification for the mission of Catholic schools to educate the whole person, including the exploration of the transcendent. Catholic schools accomplish this through the establishment of the faith community, the teaching of religion, and the integration of Catholic teachings into the curriculum to the extent that they naturally apply.

CATHOLIC SOCIAL TEACHING AND THE COMMON GOOD

The common good is a prominent theme in Church documents and Catholic social teaching. In the Vatican II Apostolic Constitution, *Gaudium et Spes* ("The Church in the Modern World"), the common good is seen as "the sum of those conditions of social life, which allow groups and individuals to reach their fulfillment more fully and more easily" (Vatican Council II, 1965a, #26) and to attain perfection more adequately and more readily (#74). Two notions are present here: the fulfillment of groups and individuals (the temporal common good) and in the sense of Aquinas, the attainment of perfection, the ultimate common good.

The Apostolic Constitution *Gaudium et Spes* further emphasizes the importance to society of educated persons with good character when it decries illiteracy and a lack of responsible activity as preventing people from assisting in the promotion of the common good (#60). "The obligations of justice and love are fulfilled only if each person, contributing to the common good, according to his own abilities and the needs of others, also promotes and assists the public and private institutions dedicated to bettering the conditions of human life" (Vatican Council II, 1965a, #30).

The *Compendium of the Social Doctrine of the Church* reiterates that the common good is an end goal of human life (Pontifical Council for Justice and Peace, 2004): "The goal of life in society is in fact the historically attainable common good" (#168). The *Compendium* emphasizes that the common good "stems from the dignity, unity and equality of all people" (#164): "The common good, in fact, can be understood as the social and community dimension of the moral good" (#164).

The essential characteristics and requirements for the common good are illustrated in a variety of the seven themes of Catholic social teaching summarized by the United States Conference of Bishops (United States Conference of Catholic Bishops, 2005). In the theme *Call to Family, Community and Participation*, the bishops stress the social aspect of the person, the centrality of the social institutions of marriage and the family, the right and duty of people to seek together the common good and the well-being of all, especially the poor and vulnerable.

In *Solidarity*, the bishops emphasize the unity of the human family and the priority of working for justice and peace. In *Care for God's Creation*, the bishops underscored the responsibility for stewardship of creation so that the planet will remain hospitable for the common good of future generations. For each of these ends, the bishops wrote, the proper social formation of the person, the central place of the family in the community, working for justice and peace, and stewardship of creation becomes part of the domains of education necessary in Catholic schools.

SCHOOLS AND THE COMMON GOOD

How do Catholic schools contribute to the common good? The promotion of the common good requires educated people who understand the constitutive elements of the common good and have the knowledge, skills, and will to support and maintain it. Through their academic programs, schools provide the basic education to help individuals develop knowledge and skills. However, an academic education, in itself a desired good, is not sufficient to contribute fully to and support the common good.

Aquinas and the ancients argued that the interdependency and mutual responsibility of individuals in society in promoting the common good requires people of virtue and character. Education and schooling are moral enterprises; as such, they are major contributors to the formation of character and virtue needed to prepare individuals to contribute the common good.

"Moral" here is understood as virtuous, ethical, conforming to a standard of right behavior, and the development of character. The purpose of schooling is the formation of all dimensions of a person. In addition to developing academic and intellectual skills, schools play an essential role in the social, cultural, and moral development of persons. Not all schools have the attainment of these characteristics as specific goals. Catholic schools certainly do.

CATHOLIC SCHOOLS AND THE COMMON GOOD

The contributions of Catholic schools to the common good are evident in their provision of a high quality academic education to prepare students to be productive citizens in the workplace; their programs of religious education that assist parents in the formation of their children's religious identity and values; their emphasis on civic participation, principles of social justice, and community service that help students understand their responsibility to help others; their inclusion of non-Catholic students whereby Catholic schools demonstrate their commitment to the democratic ideal; and their education of generations of immigrants to prepare them for life in the United States and to contribute to the nation's welfare.

In today's society, Catholic schools contribute to the common good beyond what public schools can do. In writing about the common good, DeFiore (2006) notes that Catholic schools "serve needs beyond the individual" (p. 109) by providing children with a holistic education designed to serve as a model for all schools. While all schools provide an academic education, Catholic school educators can talk about God and the relationship between faith and reason. Catholic schools provide a liberal education in the classical sense of the term, helping individuals to become fully integrated human beings, which is essential to their understanding of themselves as well as how they ought to live, both as individuals and members of society.

In a real sense, educators in Catholic schools have the best of both worlds. In addition to teaching academic subjects, educators in Catholic schools foster the religious and moral formation of their students within faith communities—especially through the teaching of religion—but also by integrating, when appropriate, Catholic teachings and values into the other areas of the curriculum. The schools' emphasis on religious formation and moral values contributes to the development of virtue and character needed for the common good.

The Vatican II document on Christian education, *Gravissimum Educationis*, that is examined throughout this volume exhorts educators in Catholic schools to help their students develop the fullness of their capabilities so they can take their part in social life. To this end, *Gravissimum Educationis* encourages educators to "become actively involved in various community organizations, open to discourse with others and willing to do their best to promote the common good" (Vatican Council II, 1965b, #1).

Catholic schools work for the common good in order to build up the Kingdom of God (Sacred Congregation for Catholic Education, 1977, #60). The duties of schools and their teachers are to cultivate human values, respect for the state and its representatives, the observance of just laws, and a search for the common good (Congregation for Catholic Education, 1988, #45). Therefore, the goals of Catholic schools should include the transmission of traditional civic values such as freedom, justice, the nobility of work, and the need to pursue social progress (#45).

One of the tasks of Catholic schools is to provide a synthesis of faith and life, which is achieved by the "growth of the virtues characteristic of the Christian" (Sacred Congregation for Catholic Education, 1977, para. 37). Catholic schools, then, are places where the complete formation of the person occurs, the development of knowledge, affect, values, character, community involvement and service, all of which contribute to the common good.

Socialization of Immigrants

A major contribution of Catholic schools to the common good has been the socialization of immigrants. A large number of Catholic schools in the United States were founded in the latter part of the 19th and first third of the 20th century to serve Catholic immigrants from Ireland, Germany, Poland, France, Italy, and other countries. As ethnic parishes were established to provide for the liturgical and sacramental needs of these immigrant populations, most parishes also established Catholic schools to provide for the academic and religious education needs of the new immigrants as well as their transition to a new country.

The overall effectiveness of these immigrant schools in educating and socializing immigrants has been remarkable, given that Catholics now comprise one of the best educated and financially secure groups in the United States. The early history of Catholic schools in the United States and their economic impact to this day has been well documented (Buetow, 1970, 1988; Neal, 1997; Sage Policy Group, 2010).

The role of Catholic schools in educating and socializing the immigrants who came in large numbers from Southeast Asia and Central and South America during the latter half of the 20th century and the first decade of the 21st century is still developing. While some children from these immigrant populations have been able to attend Catholic schools, most have not, often because of cultural and/or financial reasons. Ironically, as the number of these immigrants increased, the number of Catholic schools has decreased nationwide.

A challenge facing Catholic school educators today is how to provide adequately for the education of these children in the newest wave of immigration, especially in the light of the growing Latino population in the United States. Catholic schools can make a substantial contribution to the common good by providing excellent educations for these children, but only if they are able to find Catholic schools nearby that are welcoming and affordable.

Inclusion of Non-Catholics

Catholic schools have historically enrolled non-Catholic students. During the past 50 years, though, the number of students who are non-Catholics but are enrolled in Catholic schools increased from 144,000 in 1964 to over 323,000 in 2013. In 2013 non-Catholics constituted over 14% of the enrollment in Catholic elementary school and over 21% of the enrollment in Catholic secondary schools (McDonald & Schultz, 2014, p. 22). The increase in the number of non-Catholics has been particularly significant given that the total enrollment in Catholic schools over the past half century has declined by over 3.6 million students, from 5.6 million in 1964 to just under 2.0 million in 2013.

Studies have shown that the inclusion of non-Catholics in Catholic schools, particularly those from disadvantaged backgrounds, resulted in Catholic schools being better integrated and, in a sense, more egalitarian than public schools. The sociologist James Coleman (Coleman, Hoffer, & Kilgore, 1982; Coleman & Hoffer, 1987) argued that Catholic schools exemplify the ideal of the common school because of the diversity of the students they served.

Donlevy (2008) pointed out that the liberal concepts of the common good, identified as personal autonomy, individual rights and freedoms, and the principles of fairness, justice, equality and respect for diversity, are evident in the policy of Catholic schools to admit non-Catholics. Donlevy concluded that Catholic schools in their practices of inclusion serve as exemplars for a democratic society.

Findings from Research

What does research reveal about the efforts of Catholic schools to contribute to the common good and their effectiveness in doing so? What factors enable Catholic schools to help their students to contribute to the common good? This section presents findings from the research that deal with the constitutive elements of the common good, the mechanisms in place that help Catholic schools be a viable instrument for the common good, and the success of

Catholic schools in producing outcomes that are necessary to maintain the common good.

Building of Community

A strong community is a constitutive element of the common good. Catholic schools have been particularly effective in creating well-functioning communities (Bryk, Lee & Holland, 1993; Coleman & Hoffer, 1987; Convey, 1992). A Catholic school's culture is enriched by the perspective of faith. "What makes the Catholic school distinctive is its attempt to generate a community climate in the school that is permeated by the Gospel spirit of freedom and love" (Congregation for Catholic Education, 1988, #1). The faith community of a Catholic school is a moral community that facilitates the development of students' academic, religious, and social personalities, all keys to their ability to contribute to and advance the common good.

The most compelling evidence for the contribution of the communal element of a Catholic school to its effectiveness comes from the research of Coleman and his associates (Coleman et al., 1982; Coleman & Hoffer, 1987). Coleman's concept of a functional community—a community in which a common set of values is not only shared, but also, more importantly, one that produces efficacious results because of the nature of the relationships within the community—is a microcosm of the community envisioned as necessary for the common good. Coleman maintained that the functional community of a Catholic school plays a major role in its effectiveness. Later, Bryk and his associates (1993) would observe the same in their book, *Catholic Schools and the Common Good.*

Research demonstrates that Catholic schools develop their functional faith communities intentionally through the leadership of the principal and the support of teachers who have a commitment to assist in the development of the faith community (Benson & Guerra, 1985; Ciriello, 1996; Convey, 2010, 2012; Yeager, Benson, Guerra, & Manno, 1985). The core components of a strong communal school identified by Bryk and Driscoll (1988) of shared values, a common agenda of activities, and a pattern of social relationships enable Catholic schools to develop and sustain their faith communities.

Catholic School Teachers

The mission-related motivation and high commitment of Catholic school teachers help to advance the common good because teachers play such a major role in the formation of the character and values of their students. Catholic school teachers contribute to fostering the common good by their example and witness of life. The Church is clear in its teachings regarding the role of teachers in Catholic schools (Congregation for Catholic Education, 1988, 1997; Sacred Congregation of Catholic Education, 1977, 1982).

In addition to teaching academic subjects and imparting values, Catholic schools contribute to the religious formation of their students, which assists in the development of virtue and character, constitutive elements necessary for the common good. The Church refers to teachers in Catholic schools as "witnesses to faith" (Sacred Congregation for Catholic Education, 1982) and identifies teachers as having the "prime responsibility for creating this unique Christian school climate . . . , as individuals and as a community" (Congregation for Catholic Education, 1997, paragraph 19).

The presence of mission-orientated teachers is essential to maintaining the culture of a Catholic school (Congregation for Catholic Education, 1997; Convey, 1992). Many teachers choose to work in Catholic schools because of their desire to minister to the faith community in the schools. Studies have found that Catholic elementary school teachers who reported high mission-related commitment are more satisfied with their work than are other teachers (Tarr, Ciriello, & Convey, 1992; Convey, in press).

Academic Achievement

Catholic schools contribute to the common good by providing a quality academic education that produces well-educated graduates who have the skills necessary to be productive citizens. Catholic schools generally have focused curricula, including a strong commitment to core academic programs; hold high expectations for all students; and have environments characterized by discipline and order, all of which contribute to their effectiveness in preparing students to further the common good.

Studies using longitudinal data from national studies sponsored by the United States Department of Education in the 1980s provide the best evidence for the academic excellence of Catholic schools, particularly Catholic high schools. The most publicized studies using data from the longitudinal study *High School and Beyond* were conducted by James Coleman, Tony Bryk, and their colleagues (Bryk et al., 1993; Coleman et al., 1982; Coleman & Hoffer, 1987). Their studies revealed that, after controlling for differences in family background, students in Catholic high schools have better verbal skills and higher achievement in mathematics in both the sophomore and senior years than did their counterparts in public schools.

It is also worth noting that Catholic schools were found to be particularly effective for minority students and those from disadvantaged backgrounds, an important contribution to the common good (Cibulka, O'Brien, & Zewe, 1982; Greeley, 1982). Researchers attributed the better performance of students in Catholic schools to the strong functional communities, high expectations of the teachers, and the structured curriculum that characterized these schools. A review of these studies demonstrated that the outcomes of the commitment of Catholic schools to academic quality are clearly evident: more time is spent doing homework, attendance is better, dropouts are fewer, and interest and effort are higher (Convey, 1992).

Some recent studies have not found a Catholic school advantage, particularly when statistical controls are applied for demographic differences or potential selection bias (Lubienski & Lubienski, 2006). However, most studies, including recent investigations on the effects of voucher programs (Howell, Wolf, Campbell, & Peterson, 2002), show the effectiveness of Catholic schools for producing good academic outcomes for students, especially for those students who come from disadvantaged backgrounds.

The benefit provided for these students who often are not helped by attending public schools in terms of their academic achievement and upward mobility provides the best evidence for the contribution of Catholic schools to the common good. Catholic schools help disadvantaged students move out of poverty to the mainstream of American life and in doing so contribute to the stability, safety and economic growth of the community (Bauch, Cooper, & O'Keefe, 2014).

Moral Development and Values

The common good requires individuals who have a properly formed system of values. How, then, do Catholic schools communicate values? Innes (1992) in her dissertation research documented three forms of sharing of values that occur in virtually every Catholic school: personal and conscious sharing of values by the faculty and staff and modeled in their daily lives; imparting of values through the curriculum; and informal sharing of values, primarily through the type and quality of everyday interpersonal interactions. The imparting of values and development of character are fostered through rituals of daily prayer and periodic Eucharistic liturgies; the presence of religious symbols and religious messages in the halls and classrooms; a school's welcoming posture; and discussions of contemporary moral issues in religion, science, and social studies classes.

How successful have Catholic schools been in communicating the values promoting the common good, transmitting the fundamental knowledge about the faith, and producing graduates who are constant in their religious practice? Undoubtedly, the common good is strengthened by individuals with strong family values, who have a concern for others and are willing to help those in need and act accordingly, who actively seek to strengthen their communities through active participation in them, and who have respect for the environment.

Studies show that students in Catholic schools have strong family values and generally place these values in their hierarchy of values higher than goals that equate success in life with having a good job and making a lot of money (Benson, Yeager, Wood, Guerra, & Manno, 1986; Convey, 2010; Kraushaar, 1972; Neuwien, 1966). In addition, consistent with the outcomes resulting from the strong functional communities in these schools, studies demonstrate that students from Catholic schools generally embrace family-related values to a greater extent than do their peers who attended other schools (Convey, 1992, 2010; Greeley & Rossi, 1966; Guerra, Donahue, & Benson, 1990; Kraushaar, 1972).

Individuals with concern for others and a willingness to help others in need also contribute to the common good when they act on these values. Studies over the past 50 years have shown that students from Catholic schools, often more than Catholic students from other schools, demonstrate high levels of concern for others (Convey, 1992, 2010); express concern about those suffering from hunger (Convey & Thompson, 1999) and about friends who were having problems with drugs or alcohol (Convey, 2010); select working for the improvement of society and the benefit of others as important life goals (Kraushaar, 1972); reject attitudes that reflected a self-centered and selfish point of view (Guerra et al., 1990); acknowledge the importance of making a contribution to society as a way of making a difference in their lives (Convey, 2010); and indicate their willingness to make financial sacrifices to help the poor in other countries (Benson et al., 1986).

Religious Outcomes

While Catholic schools, like other schools that provide a good education, contribute to the common good through their academic programs, an additional objective of Catholic schools is religious formation, which provides yet another avenue for development of values. The common good is undoubtedly strengthened by the presence of individuals who are knowledgeable about their faith and practice their religion faithfully.

Catholic schools in their religion classes and when appropriate in other classes are in a privileged position to pose questions to students about the nature of persons, their relationship to society, and their moral obligation to be good citizens. Studies have linked religion with adolescent moral development, correct value orientation, promotion of positive social behaviors, participation in civic activities, and willingness to perform volunteer service, all of which further the common good (Benson et al., 1989; Donahue & Benson, 1995; Kerestes, Youniss, & Metz, 2004; King & Furrow, 2004; Youniss, McLellan, Su, & Yates, 1999).

Catholic schools have played a major role in developing the religious knowledge of Catholic students. There has been a lot of research, beginning with the Notre Dame Study on Catholic Education in the mid-1960s (Neuwien, 1966), extending through the work of Andrew Greeley and his associates

(Greeley & Rossi, 1966; Greeley, McCready, & McCourt, 1976) and culminating in studies sponsored by the National Catholic Educational Association (Benson et al., 1986), particularly those that used data from ACRE, the religious education assessment from the National Catholic Educational Association (Convey, 2010; Convey & Thompson, 1999) and its predecessor (Thompson, 1982). These studies show that students in Catholic schools, including non-Catholic students, score higher on religious knowledge outcomes than do Catholic students in parish religious education programs.

Many factors influence the extent to which students practice their religion. Even so, the research has been clear over the past 50 years that Catholics who attended Catholic schools report more regular practice of their religion than Catholics who attended other schools (Convey, 1992; Convey & Thompson, 1999). The measures of religious practice typically used by studies include attendance at Mass, regular prayer, and reception of the sacraments. The effects of Catholic school attendance in influencing the religious practice of young people remain, even when other factors are controlled.

Civic Responsibility

Catholic schools contribute to the common good by preparing students to be good citizens and to carry out their civic obligations. Catholic schools, particularly high schools, have been proactive in providing service-related activities and opportunities for their students. In the most comprehensive study of Catholic high schools in the past 50 years, *The Catholic High School: A National Portrait*, principals reported the presence of service projects and activities that incorporate justice-related values, concepts, and skills into the curriculum (Yeager et al., 1985). Moreover, more than half of Catholic high school teachers who participated in a national survey indicated that helping students develop a commitment to promoting social justice and encouraging students to participate in service projects were extremely important or very important goals (Benson & Guerra, 1985).

Research shows that Catholic schools produce graduates who are engaged in civic affairs, committed to service as adults, and vote in elections (Campbell, 2001; Dee, 2005; Neal, 1997; Yates & Youniss, 1998). In *Catholic Schools in Action*, most students demonstrated high levels of concern for others (Neuwien, 1966). In Kraushaar's (1972) survey, almost half the students from Catholic high schools selected "working for the improvement of society and the benefit of others" as one of their two most important life goals. In the ACRE assessment, Catholic school students, as well as those in parish religious education programs, acknowledged a personal responsibility for making the world a better place to live (Convey, 2010).

Another important value for fostering the common good is active participation in the community. The sentiments toward involvement in community activities among Catholic school students have improved since the mid-1960s due to the emphasis that Catholic schools, particularly Catholic high schools, place on service learning and volunteering, which has increased the awareness among Catholic school students of the need and importance of community service. Indeed the results from ACRE show that Catholic school students acknowledge the emphasis that their religion programs place on volunteer work (Convey & Thompson, 1999) and that they understand that they have a personal responsibility for making the world a better place, including caring for the environment (Convey, 2010).

Reinders and Youniss (2006), using longitudinal data from two Catholic high schools, found participation in service directed toward people in need altered the self-awareness of students, increasing the likelihood of their involvement in future volunteer service, participation in civic activities, and voting. These results are consistent with research using national longitudinal data from NELS:88, the federally-sponsored longitudinal study beginning in 1988, that shows high school community service, whether required or on a volunteer basis, predicts adult voting and volunteering (Hart, Donnelly, Youniss, & Akins, 2007).

Tolerance

The common good of society requires equal treatment of individuals without regard to their gender, race, or ethnicity. Catholic schools contribute to the common good when they honor diversity and promote tolerance. Studies show that students in Catholic schools generally have had more favorable attitudes toward gender equality than toward racial equality; however, attitudes toward the latter have improved over the past 40 years.

As to gender equality, past studies have revealed that most Catholic school students, particularly females, reject sexism while endorsing equal pay and career opportunities for both men and women (Benson et al., 1986; Guerra et al., 1990). Further, in the low-income-serving schools studied by Benson and his associates (Benson et al., 1986), black and Hispanic students were more likely than were white students to endorse equal opportunity for members of both genders. The overwhelming number of students who participated in the ACRE assessment administered during the 1994–95 school year indicated that women and men can be equally effective as leaders and should be treated equally in their jobs (Convey & Thompson, 1999).

The support of Catholic school students for equal opportunity for individuals from different racial and ethnic groups has varied from study to study. This variation partly reflects changing societal attitudes. For example, in the 1966 study *Catholic Schools in Action*, while the majority of the students rejected prejudicial statements concerning African Americans, enough responded in a prejudicial manner to prompt the author, Reginald Neuwien (p.

223), to challenge the leadership of Catholic schools to examine how the schools teach the principles of racial equality. About the same time, Greeley and Rossi (1966) found that only about one in four of the Catholics interviewed responded in an unbiased manner to statements measuring their racial attitudes.

Later surveys (Fee, Greeley, McCready, & Sullivan, 1981; Greeley et al., 1976; Guerra et al., 1990) revealed that Catholics educated in Catholic schools improved in their racial attitudes, yet still only about half the students in the NCEA study on low-income-serving Catholic schools (Benson et al., 1986) rejected statements that represented racial prejudice. In the ACRE assessment of 1994–1995, over 85% of students rejected the exclusion of individuals because of race or national background (Convey & Thompson, 1999), and in the ACRE assessment of 2004–05, students in Catholic schools reported lower incidences of racism in their schools than did Catholics who attended other schools (Convey, 2010). Greene (1998) discovered similar results regarding sentiments toward racial tolerance by Catholic school students using data from the longitudinal study NELS:88.

CONCLUSION

Over the past 50 years, Catholic schools have contributed to the common good through their high-quality programs of academic preparation and religious formation by mission-motivated and committed teachers within a communal environment. As a result, Catholic schools have produced well-educated graduates with well-formed values who are productive citizens serving the public good through their work, their commitment to community service, and their efforts to make the world a better place in which to live.

Catholic schools have thus contributed to the common good by educating immigrants and helping with their socialization as well as by welcoming all students, regardless of their religion. Catholic schools have been successful in increasing the likelihood that disadvantaged students will graduate from high school and attend college. Finally, graduates of Catholic schools are more likely than public school graduates to vote, engage in civic affairs, tolerate diverse views, and commit to community service dedicated to the common good.

REFERENCES

Bauch, P. A., Cooper, B. S., & O'Keefe, J. M. (2014). Summary and conclusion: The innovative road ahead. In P. A. Bauch (Ed.), *Catholic schools in the public interest: Past, present and future directions.* Charlotte, NC: Information Age Publishing, Inc.

Benson, P. L., & Guerra, M. J. (1985). *Sharing the faith: The beliefs and values of Catholic high school teachers.* Washington, DC: National Catholic Educational Association.

Benson, P. L., Yeager, R. J., Wood, P. K., Guerra, M. J., & Manno, B. V. (1986). *Catholic high schools: Their impact on low-income students.* Washington, DC: National Catholic Educational Association.

Bryk, A. S., & Driscoll, M. E. (1988). *The high school as community: Contextual influences, and consequences for students and teachers.* Madison, WI: Wisconsin Center for Education Research.

Bryk, A. S., Lee, V. E., & Holland, P. B. (1993). *Catholic schools and the common good.* Cambridge, MA: Harvard University Press.

Buetow, H. A. (1970). *Of singular benefit.* New York: Macmillan.

Buetow, H. A. (1988). *The Catholic school: Its roots, identity and culture.* New York: Crossroads.

Campbell, D. E. (2001). Making democratic education work. In P. E. Peterson & D. E. Campbell (Eds.), *Charters, vouchers, and public education.* Washington, DC: Brookings Institution Press.

Cibulka, J. G., O'Brien, T. J., & Zewe, D. (1982). *Inner-city private elementary schools.* Milwaukee: Marquette University Press.

Ciriello, M. J. (Ed.). (1996). *Formation & development for Catholic school leaders: Volume II: The principal as spiritual leader.* Washington, DC: United States Conference of Catholic Bishops.

Coleman, J. S., Hoffer, T., & Kilgore, S. (1982). *High school achievement: Public, Catholic, and private schools compared.* New York: Basic Books.

Coleman, J.S., & Hoffer, T. (1987). *Public and private high schools: The impact of communities.* New York: Basic Books.

Congregation for Catholic Education. (1988). *The religious dimension of education in a Catholic school.* Washington, DC: United States Catholic Conference.

Congregation for Catholic Education. (1997). *The Catholic school on the threshold of the Third Millennium.* Washington, DC: United States Conference of Catholic Bishops.

Convey, J. J. (1992). *Catholic schools make a difference: Twenty-five years of research.* Washington, DC: National Catholic Educational Association.

Convey, J. J. (2012). Perceptions of Catholic identity: Views of Catholic school administrators and teachers. *Catholic Education: A Journal of Inquiry and Practice, 16(1),* 195–222.

Convey, J. J. (in press). Motivation and job satisfaction of Catholic school teachers. *The Journal of Catholic Education.*

Convey, J. J. (2010). *What do our children know about their faith? Results from the ACRE assessment.* Arlington, VA: National Catholic Educational Association.

Convey, J. J., & Thompson, A. D. (1999). *Weaving Christ's seamless garment: Assessment of Catholic religious education.* Washington, DC: National Catholic Educational Association.

Dee, T. S. (2005). The effects of Catholic schooling on civic participation. *International Tax and Public Finance, 12(5),* 605–25.

DeFiore, L. (2006). Catholic schools and the common good. *Current Issues in Catholic Higher Education, 25(1),* 109–19.

Donahue, M. J., & Benson, P. L. (1995). Religion and the well-being of adolescents. *Journal of Social Issues, 51,* 145–60.

Donlevy, J. K. (2008). The common good: the inclusion of non-Catholic students in Catholic schools. *Journal of Beliefs & Values, 29(2),* 161–71.

Fee, J. L., Greeley, A. M., McCready, W. C., & Sullivan, T. A. (1981). *Young Catholics: A report to the Knights of Columbus.* New York: Sadlier.

Greeley, A. M. (1982). *Catholic high schools and minority students.* New Brunswick: Transaction Books.

Greeley, A. M., & Rossi, P. B. (1966). *The education of Catholic Americans.* Chicago: Aldine Publishing Company.

Greeley, A. M., McCready, W. C., & McCourt, K. (1976). *Catholic schools in a declining church.* Kansas City: Sheed and Ward.

Greene, J. (1998). Civic values in public and private schools. In P. Peterson & B. C. Hassel (Eds.), *Learning from school choice* (pp. 83–106). Washington, DC: Brookings Institution Press.

Guerra, M. J., Donahue, M.J., & Benson, P. (1990). *The heart of the matter: Effects of Catholic high schools on student values, beliefs and behaviors.* Washington, DC: National Catholic Educational Association.

Hart, D., Donnelly, T. M., Youniss, J., & Atkins, R. (2007). High school community service as a predictor of adult voting and volunteering. *American Educational Research Journal, 44(1),* 197–219.

Howell, W. G., Wolf, P., Campbell, D., & Peterson, P. (2002). School vouchers and academic performance: Results from three randomized field trials. *Journal of Policy Analysis and Management, 21(2),* 191–217.

Innes, D. L., CSA. (1992). *Mechanisms by which values are imparted in a Catholic elementary school: A qualitative study.* (Doctoral Dissertation, The Catholic University of America, Washington, DC). *Dissertation Abstracts International,* Order No. 9220775.

Kerestes, M., Youniss, J., & Metz, E. (2004). Longitudinal patterns of religious perspective and civic integration. *Applied Developmental Science, 8(1),* 39–46.

King, P. E., & Furrow, J. L. (2004). Religion as a resource for positive youth development: Religion, social capital, and moral outcomes. *Developmental Psychology, 40(5),* 703–18.

Kraushaar, O. F. (1972). *American nonpublic schools: Patterns of diversity.* Baltimore: The Johns Hopkins University Press.

Lewis, V. B. (2006). The common good in classical political philosophy. *Current Issues in Catholic Higher Education, 25(1),* 25–41.

Lubienski, S. T., & Lubienski, C. (2006). School sector and academic achievement: A multilevel analysis of NAEP mathematics data. *American Educational Research Journal, 43(4),* 651–98.

McDonald, D., & Schultz, M. M. (2014). *United States Catholic elementary and secondary schools 2013–2014.* Arlington, VA: National Catholic Educational Association.

Neal, D. (1997). The effects of Catholic secondary schooling on educational achievement. *Journal of Labor Economics, 15(1),* 98–123.

Neuwien, R. (1966). *Catholic schools in action.* Notre Dame: The University of Notre Dame Press.

Pontifical Council for Justice and Peace (2004). *Compendium of the Social Doctrine of the Church.* Vatican City.

Reinders, H., & Youniss, J. (2006). School-based required community service and civic development in adolescents. *Applied Developmental Science, 10(1),* 2–12.

Sacred Congregation for Catholic Education (1977). *The Catholic school.* Washington, DC: United States Catholic Conference.

Sacred Congregation for Catholic Education (1982). *Lay Catholics in schools: Witnesses to faith.* Washington, DC: United States Catholic Conference.

Sage Policy Group (2010). *The economic benefits produced by Archdiocese of Baltimore Catholic Schools & their graduates.* Baltimore: Sage Policy Group, Inc.

Sherwin, M. (1993). St. Thomas and the common good: The theological perspective. An invitation to dialogue. *Angelicum, 70(3),* 307–28.

Summa theological by St. Thomas Aquinas. Translated by Fathers of the English Dominican Province. Westminster, MD.: Christian Classics, 1981.

Tarr, H. C., Convey, J. J., & Ciriello, M. J. (1993). Commitment and satisfaction among parochial school teachers: Findings from Catholic education. *Journal of Research in Christian Education, 2,* 41–63.

Thompson, A. D. (1982). *That they may know you.* Washington, DC: National Catholic Educational Association.

United States Conference of Catholic Bishops (2005). *Seven themes of Catholic social teaching.* Washington, DC: United States Conference of Catholic Bishops. Retrieved on June 30, 2014, from http://www.usccb.org/beliefs-and-teachings/what-we-believe/catholic-social-teaching/seven-themes-of-catholic-social-teaching.cfm

Vatican Council II. (1965a). *Gaudiem et spes.* [*The Church in the modern world*]. Retrieved on June 30, 2014, from http://www.vatican.va

Vatican Council II. (1965b). *Gravissimum educationis* [*Declaration on Christian education*]. Retrieved on June 30, 2014, from http://www.vatican.va.

Yates, M., & Youniss, J. (1998). Community service and political identity development in adolescence. *Journal of Social Issues, 54(3)*, 495–512.

Yeager, R. J., Benson, P. L., Guerra, M. J., & Manno, B. V. (1985). *The Catholic high school: A national portrait.* Washington, DC: National Catholic Educational Association.

Youniss, J., McLellan, J. A., Su, Y., & Yates, M. (1999). The role of community service in identity development: Normative, unconventional, and deviant behavior. *Journal of Adolescent Research, 14*, 248–61.

Chapter Ten

Epilogue and Recommendations

Charles J. Russo and Gerald M. Cattaro

INTRODUCTION

Paul's first letter to the Corinthians recognized that in the Church, "God has given the first place to the apostles, the second to prophets, the third to teachers" (I Cor. 12:28, *New American Bible*). Taking Paul's words to heart, for the better part of a century before Pope Paul VI and the Fathers of the Second Vatican Council promulgated *Gravissimum Educationis* (*GE*) on October 28, 1965, the largely immigrant Roman Catholic elementary and secondary schools clearly played a decisive role in the developing the rich tapestry of American educational history. Of course, Catholic institutions of higher education have also made—and continue to make—significant contributions to the American intellectual way of life.

Beginning in the latter part of the 19th century, consistent with the dictates of the Third Plenary Council of Baltimore of 1884, leaders in the Roman Catholic Church opened elementary and secondary schools in many parishes. Even so, despite the exhortations of the Baltimore Council, Church leaders never achieved their goal of establishing a school in every Catholic parish in the United States. Still, these schools succeeded in providing quality faith-based education to untold millions of largely poor, immigrant Catholic children who were largely unwelcomed in American public schools due to the largely Protestant ethos.

In a major triumph, Catholic schools succeeded beyond the wildest dreams of the bishops. In fact, Catholic schools helped generations of their graduates to become successful adults who were well integrated in the wider society as they made significant contributions to the diverse mosaic that is the United States.

At the same time, as reflected by the issues addressed in this book, their proud and successful history notwithstanding, these same Catholic elementary and secondary schools, in particular, face an existential threat to their continuing viability even as Catholic institutions of higher education appear to be flowering. As documented in the chapters of this book, these threats largely loomed on the horizon as a result of demographic, personnel, and economic shifts that began to emerge as American Catholics entered the mainstream in the 1960s following the election of John F. Kennedy. Ironically, these threats were on the horizon prior to the promulgation of *GE* even as American Catholic schools were at their zenith in terms of enrollment.

Another contributing factor to the precipitous decline in Catholic elementary and secondary schools resulted, at least in part, by what can be described as an internal crisis of leadership (Greeley, 1992) accompanied by a loss of vision and identity. These shortcomings have wreaked havoc on an eminently successful system of loosely coupled schools as leaders failed to adapt to changing times both within and outside of the Church. Further, a related aspect precipitating this dramatic decline was the fact that American Catholic clergy at the national, diocesan, and, in particular, parish levels appear to have devalued their schools, failing to heed the message of *GE* by refusing to treat them as central in the lives of their communities.

THE NEED FOR CATHOLIC IDENTITY

Catholic identity is not an exterior varnish inherited from the past. It needs to receive life from the source of and from the Joy of the Gospel. Yet neither is Catholic identity a vision to be preserved. Rather, Catholic education is a vision to be transmitted. Thus the realities facing Church educational leaders as they seek to proclaim the Gospel of Joy in Catholic Schools necessitates a change in heart as American Catholics enter a high-tech, individualistic, and secularized society, one polarized by cultural and religious differences while so many seek material, rather than educational or spiritual, rewards.

It is important to take the words of Pope Francis to heart: "School can and must be a catalyst, it must be a place of encounter and convergence of the entire educating community, with the sole objective of training and helping to develop mature people who are simple, competent and honest, who know how to love with fidelity, who can live life as a response to God's call, and their future profession as a service to society" (2013).

The journey through the chapters of this book encountered the various benchmarks of *Gravissimum Educationis*. The authors of these chapters eloquently demonstrated the need to have a renewed passion for Catholic schools even amid the great challenges they face.

RECOMMENDATIONS

Against the backdrop of the material addressed in this book, and using many of the ideas generated by the chapter authors in this book as departure points, this epilogue offers the following overlapping modest proposals in an attempt to reinvigorate Catholic education at all levels. These ideas are offered in the spirit of Catholic charity in an attempt to help preserve a school system that has done, and still does, so much to advance the lives of individual Catholics, their faith communities, and the common good in American society in general.

First and foremost, insofar as the Roman Catholic Church is a large hierarchical organization, even if its school "system" can be more accurately described as a loosely coupled collection of largely independent parish and religious community elementary and secondary schools, leaders at the diocesan and national levels must make steps forward and make the reinvigoration of Catholic education a priority. To this end, the National Conference of Catholic Bishops in the United States needs to convene a new Baltimore-type Council. Rome must become involved in this process by highlighting the value of Catholic education and calling for its reinvigoration.

Second, as leaders gather, perhaps they could commission studies highlighting the great success of American Catholic education from elementary schools through graduate education. In this way, all interested in Catholic education would have updated data, rather than relying on studies that are a generation old. In this way, instead of hiding their accomplishment under bushel baskets, Catholic leaders can trumpet the success of their schools in the daylight so as to better serve the common good.

Third, amid the growing diversity of governance models and perspectives on leadership, whether in elementary and secondary schools or higher education, Church and educational leaders must strive to articulate a strong shared Catholic identity even as differences exist as to what this means. While it remains to be seen exactly what leadership models will prevail, it is important to begin discussions so as to better plan for the future of Catholic schools.

Fourth, in articulating a reinvigorated vision for Catholic education, leaders must truly make committed lay Catholic educators, parents, and students true partners in this renaissance. Such an approach must recognize that when a parish operates a school, as it is for the benefit of all (not just the children who attend and their parents), support must come from the broader Catholic community (Dolan, 2010). While recognizing the special role that ordained and consecrated religious continue to occupy, the hierarchy must look to the future in a conceptualized school system in which there is a strong working partnership involving shared ownership and leadership with the laity.

Fifth, in a closely related point, consistent with Greeley's almost quarter of a century old criticism (1992), Church leaders must call on men and women with vision and energy to reinvigorate Catholic schools. This means that bishops must be willing to turn to individuals who will "think outside of the box" and look for new models to once again make Catholic education a priority for parents.

Sixth, as Catholic schools struggle to survive, leaders should consider some forms of political action, using the legal system to access aid for students under the Child Benefit Test while preserving institutional autonomy. Even in conceding that parents freely choose to send their children to Catholic schools, bypassing the public sector, a sound legal argument can be made that they should not have to forfeit all forms of help for their children. If leaders believe in their schools, then they must fight for their fair share of support because Catholic schools clearly contribute to the common good in the United States while encouraging families to once again make Catholic education a priority.

Seventh, if Catholic schools are to survive in light of the economic realities of the present, it almost goes without saying that they will have a difficult time paying administrators, teachers, and other staff members what they might earn on the open marketplace. Catholic educational leaders can still attract the best and brightest to education as a profession by treating principals, teachers, and other educators with dignity and being open with them about such realities. While it is true that all educators, whether teachers or administrators, must pay their bills, too, by "opening the books" and sharing information with them in ways not often done in the past, leaders can build true school communities dedicated to educating children in the Catholic faith, doing so both by their words and actions.

Eighth, as they work to contribute to the common good, religious and educational leaders must help return Catholic schools to their roots by serving immigrants, the poor, and the disenfranchised. This outreach should also make every effort to be inclusive of the special needs of students and English language learners. In other words, amid growing demographic changes in the United States, Catholic schools must stand out as a kind of shining city on a hill, a model which practices what the Church preaches so eloquently in affording a preferential option for the poor if they are to survive, and even thrive, in the 21st century and beyond.

Ninth, in a related matter, leaders in Catholic schools must recognize the phenomena of multiculturalism, hybridization of cultures, and the movement of people in today's global society and use this to help reinvigorate their schools. Leaders can breathe new lives into their schools by providing curricula reflects the building blocks of Church social teachings. It is also incumbent for school leaders to create special atmospheres in educational communities animated by the Gospel in a spirit of freedom and charity (Congregation for Catholic Education, 2013).

Tenth, Church leaders must recognize that in the 21st century, mass media, the Internet, and social networks are essential to success not only for the current generation of students but also for schools. As such, educational leaders and teachers must be equipped to use these tools via professional development sessions. Such professional development sessions can help educators learn the benefits and challenges these technologies present as they employ them both to help spread the word about the value of Catholic education and to spread the virtues, values, and ethics demanded by the Gospel.

CONCLUSION

In light of all that has been covered in this volume, it is fitting to recall a key passage from *Gravissimum Educationis*:

> The influence of the Church in the field of education is shown in a special manner by the Catholic school. No less than other schools does the Catholic school pursue cultural goals and the human formation of youth. But its proper function is to create for the school community a special atmosphere animated by the Gospel spirit of freedom and charity, to help youth grow according to the new creatures they were made through baptism as they develop their own personalities, and finally to order the whole of human culture to the news of salvation so that the knowledge the students gradually acquire of the world, life and man is illumined by faith. So indeed the Catholic school, while it is open, as it must be, to the situation of the contemporary world, leads its students to promote efficaciously the good of the earthly city and also prepares them for service in the spread of the Kingdom of God, so that by leading an exemplary apostolic life they become, as it were, a saving leaven in the human community. (para. 8)

For all who are interested in, and support, Catholic education, let us hope that the schools can once again flower for the benefit of all not only in the United States but throughout the world as they promote the Joy of the Gospel.

REFERENCES

Congregation for Catholic Education (2013). *Educating to Intercultural Dialogue in Catholic Schools: Living in Harmony for a Civilization of Love.* Retrieved from http://www.vatican.va/roman_curia/congregations/ccatheduc/documents/rc_con_ccatheduc_doc_20131028_dialogo-interculturale_en.html Vatican City

Dolan, T.M. (2910). *The Catholic Schools We Need. America*, 203(6), 10–14.

Greeley, A.M. (1992). A modest proposal for the reform of Catholic schools. *America,*
    166(10), 234–38.
Paul VI. (1965, October 28). *Gravissimum Educationis.* Retrieved from http://www.vatican.va/
    archive/hist_councils/ii_vatican_council/documents/vatii_decl_19651028_gravissimum-ed-
    ucationis_en.html

About the Editors and Authors

EDITORS

Gerald M. Cattaro, Ed.D., is professor of education, executive director of the Center for Catholic School Leadership and Faith-Based Education, and former chair of the Division of Educational Leadership Administration and Policy in the Graduate School of Education at Fordham University in New York City. He is currently on the editorial board of the Education and Urban Society and the governing board of the *Journal of Catholic Education.* An administrator in Catholic schools in New York City for more than 20 years, he writes, speaks, and conducts research nationally and internationally on governance issues associated with non-public schools such as executive leadership, policy, and international issues. Dr. Cattaro earned his Ed.D. at Teachers' College of Columbia University.

Charles J. Russo, M.Div., J.D., Ed.D., is the Joseph Panzer Chair in Education in the School of Education and Health Services, director of its Ph.D. Program in Educational Leadership and former chair of the Department of Educational Administraion, and adjunct professor in the School of Law at the University of Dayton. The 1998–99 President of the Education Law Association, and 2002 recipient of its McGhehey (Achievement) Award as well as a similar award from the Australia New Zealand Education Association, he authored or coauthored more than 260 articles in peer-reviewed journals and authored, coauthored, edited, or coedited 56 books, as well as more than 950 publications. Dr. Russo has spoken extensively primarily on issues in Education Law in 34 states and 26 nations on all six inhabited continents.

AUTHORS

Bruce S. Cooper, Ph.D., is emeritus professor from Fordham University Graduate School of Education, with a long-term interest in American private and religious education. He is a former president of the Associates for Research in Private Education (ARPE), a special interest group of the American Education Research Association (AERA). He lives, writes, and publishes in New York City.

John J. Convey, Ph.D., the St. Elizabeth Ann Seton Professor of Education and former provost at The Catholic University of America, is the author or editor of eight books on Catholic education. Over the past 30 years, Dr. Convey has conducted strategic planning studies for Catholic schools in 20 dioceses. His awards include the Benemerenti Medal from Pope Benedict XVI and the Koob Award and President's Medal from the National Catholic Educational Association (NCEA). He has served as a consultant to the Committee on Catholic Education of the United States Conference of Catholic Bishops.

Sister John Mary Fleming, O.P., J.C.L., is the executive director for Secretariat of Catholic Education, at the United States Conference of Catholic Bishops. Sister John Mary is responsible for supporting and assisting the bishops with plans and policies for Catholic education including elementary and secondary schools, colleges and universities, campus ministry, and certification of ecclesial ministry. A Dominican Sister of St. Cecilia Congregation in Nashville, TN, she has served as a Catholic school teacher and administrator at the elementary and secondary levels, director of education for St. Cecilia Congregation, and as administrator for the Congregation in higher education.

Jordan Gadd is manager of communications and special projects for the Loyola Marymount University School of Education in Los Angeles. He leads the school's external and internal communications, including public relations, digital/web strategy, marketing, and media outreach, in addition to serving as chief of staff in the Office of the Dean. Gadd is the editor of *Edvision*, the school's digital magazine.

Michael J. Garanzini, S.J., S.T.M., Ph.D., was the president of Loyola University Chicago from 2001–2014 and is now chancellor. He is a seasoned university administrator, tenured professor, author, and scholar, and has spent the majority of his career working in higher education. Since 2011, he has concurrently served as the secretary for higher education for the Society of Jesus, coordinating and championing Jesuit higher-education issues around the world. Active in community service, Father Garanzini, known for his work on behalf of children and families, is a frequent speaker and has published many books and articles on issues such as child and family therapy, moral development, and Catholic education.

Regina M. Haney, Ed.D., is the executive director of the Department of Boards and Councils, a department of the NCEA. In this capacity, she shares her experience with school and diocesan boards across the country through workshops and publications. Regina has also served as assistant executive director of the Department of Chief Administrators of Catholic Education (CACE), another department of the NCEA, from 1997 to 2001. During the 1991–92 and 1996–97 school years, Regina served as acting director of CACE. Prior to joining NCEA in 1990, Regina served for nine years as the superintendent of schools for the Diocese of Raleigh, North Carolina.

Shane P. Martin, Ph.D., an educational anthropologist by training and expert in the areas of intercultural education; cultural diversity; and the spectrum of public, charter, and Catholic schools, was appointed dean of the Loyola Marymount University School of Education in 2005 and dean of graduate studies in 2012. He serves as a state commissioner to the California Commission on Teacher Credentialing and has authored three books and numerous articles and journal publications. Martin received the NCEA's Michael J. Guerra Leadership Award in 2005 and the Catherine T. McNamee, CSJ, Award in 2009, as well as the Loyola High School Alumni Association's Cahalan Award in 2008.

Dale McDonald, PBVM, Ph.D., is the director of Public Policy and Educational Research for the NCEA in Washington, DC. Prior to joining the NCEA, she was director of the Catholic School Leadership Program in the Boston College Graduate School of Education. She has been published in books and journals and has served on committees convened by the White House, U.S. Department of Education, U.S. Conference of Catholic Bishops, and other national associations in addition to having testified before congressional committees on education policy issues.

Karen M. Ristau, Ed.D., president of the NCEA from 2005 until 2013, was a teacher and administrator in Catholic schools and a faculty member at the University of St. Thomas in St. Paul, MN. She held administrative positions at colleges in Connecticut and Indiana. A published scholar and frequent speaker, she received the Neil D'Amour Award, the Murray Medallion from the University of St. Thomas, an outstanding service award from the University of San Francisco, a Centennial Medal from Mount St. Mary's, the Elizabeth Ann Seton President's award, and multiple honorary degrees. Dr. Ristau is currently working on a literacy project with the Library of Congress and other national boards.

Ming Zhu, an advanced doctoral student at Fordham University in the Contemporary Learning and Interdisciplinary Research Program, has an M.A. in philosophy and education from the Columbia University Teachers College. She has taught ESL courses and served as a college counselor at Reach Top International Education in Beijing, China.